THROUGH ADVERSITY TO GREAT HEIGHTS

HUCKS

THROUGH ADVERSITY TO GREAT HEIGHTS

MY AUTOBIOGRAPHY

WENSUM PUBLISHING

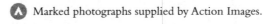 Marked photographs supplied by Action Images.

Typeset by Wensum Publishing, Norwich, Norfolk
Printed and bound by CPI Group (UK) Ltd, Croydon, CR0 4YY

Thanks to my mum and dad for your unwavering belief in my ability, without you I'd never have made it further than the park.

To my friends and family, your support from afar has always been appreciated.

To my beautiful wife Lyndsey and my two boys Thomas and Ben, your constant bickering and fighting still make me want to go to the gym — I've never felt fitter!

love you all.

CONTENTS

FOREWORD
by Dion Dublin

To this day, he calls me 'Partner', and I do exactly the same. To me, Hucks is simply 'Partner'. Believe me, there aren't too many people I'd call that, and he remains one of my closest friends in football.

I still remember the day that he first walked into our dressing room at Coventry City Gary McAllister, myself and the boys thinking what a confident young man he was. He was good-looking, incredibly fit, blisteringly quick, and he always had a prank up his sleeve. There was never a dull moment when Hucks was about.

It was a great dressing room to be part of – and, from day one, he fitted right in. We had people like, Gary Mac, Paul Williams, Richard Shaw, Paul Telfer and myself. The balance was just perfect, and they were really good days.

Somehow, you knew Hucks would do well. He had an incredible work ethic. He was so dedicated; he worked and worked and worked. In all my time in football, I've never seen anything like it – he was second to none on that front. I hesitate to say it; but his commitment to training gave him such an advantage that he seemed to defy logic when it came to fitness.

Thinking back to those games at Highfield Road, we played with real exuberance and belief. We genuinely went through matches with smiles on our faces. That's partly down to the way that Gordon Strachan managed and allowed us to play. It was simply because there was so much quality in the side.

HUCKS

That Coventry dressing room was probably the hardest, toughest school I had experienced. I'd come there from Manchester United, where it was a completely different set up. Coventry was the opposite, which suited me perfectly. From day one, I was just one of the lads, and that was the case for everyone. We all pulled in the same direction; you wouldn't last five minutes if you had an ego.

Hucks and I clicked as an attacking pair from the very first day, it was a natural partnership. I was always happy to lead from the front and left Hucks free to score and create goals.

There's a quote from Hucks I always remember reading. Someone asked him who his ideal strike partner would be – guess what his response was? He said: 'Well, if Dion Dublin was injured, I'd go for Gabriel Batistuta.' I'll never forget that line.

As well as being one of the most generous footballers I had ever worked with, he was also one of the liveliest. In the dressing room he'd cut your laces and cut your socks amongst other pranks, and no-one was safe. Everyone got done at some stage but the point was he could take it as well.

I think one of the reasons he and I bonded so well, is that we'd both taken the hard route to where we were. He'd come up through the YTS scheme at Lincoln; I'd come from Cambridge, having played non-league and had a job working in a factory making ice cream. We both knew what life was like for your average, lower-league footballer. Maybe we appreciated more than most that we were lucky to have the opportunities we did. It all made it that much sweeter to be playing in the Premier League. We never took anything for granted.

Hucks had changed by the time we hooked up again at Norwich. When he greeted me on my first day at Colney, he was much more self-assured and confident. At Coventry, he was still growing up; in Norfolk, he was King of the Hill. Everyone loved him. In fact, you'll struggle to find anyone in football who has a bad word to say about him.

FOREWORD

We didn't set out to do it consciously, but Hucks and I came to be in charge of that dressing room. The other players would respond to what we had to say, and respected what we brought to the table.

You always knew what you were going to get with him. He was never going to tackle; he was never going to head a ball; he was never going to track back. He was completely useless when it came to defending. But if I could have just one so-called 'luxury' player in the team, then I'd go for Hucks. You always knew that he would create you something going forward.

Has he been given the credit he deserves over the course of his career? Probably not. He has, after all, played with some world-class players, from Alan Shearer and David Ginola at Newcastle to Rio Ferdinand and Jonathan Woodgate at Leeds. Maybe he hasn't been given as much time in the spotlight as he deserves.

But, then again, not everyone knows the real Darren Huckerby. He is, at heart, quite a shy person but nobody knows him better than me.

Congratulations Hucks heres to the next chapter in your life!

1. LEARNING THE
   HARD WAY

Match: Shrewsbury Town vs Lincoln City
Venue: Gay Meadow
Competition: Football League, Division Three
Date: Tuesday, March 1, 1994
Result: Shrewsbury 1, Lincoln City 2
(Huckerby 86)

Shrewsbury Town: Edwards; Brown, Donaldson, Lynch, Patterson; Rutherford, Spink, Taylor, Walton, Williams, Withe
Subs: Summerfield

Lincoln City: Pollitt; Smith M, Smith P, Schofield, Ridings; Matthews, Johnson A, Hill, Johnson D; Brown, Baraclough
Subs: Campbell, Huckerby

Before I got given my big break by Lincoln City, I'd been rejected by eight or nine clubs. I'd started with Notts County; when I got to fourteen, the age when you had to sign schoolboy forms, Nottingham Forest and Sheffield United wanted to sign me. I decided to stay with County, largely because I'd come up with them from the age of nine.

No two clubs in England play closer to one another than Forest and County, so there's a fairly intense rivalry there. In Nottingham, there's definitely a sense that you're either a red or a black-and-white; however, it's not as if I was watching that much football back then. In those days, I was always playing. It's changed now, but when I was a kid you played on Saturday morning, Saturday afternoon, and Sunday morning. You were talking three games a weekend, so there wasn't the time to go and stand on the terraces.

Where I came from, you'd play for South Notts, then from there you'd go on to Nottingham Boys. They were my Saturday morning team, and I worked my way up from there. By the time I was sixteen, I was playing for Nottinghamshire. On Saturday afternoons, I'd play local football; from the age of nine to thirteen, I was at Clifton All-Whites, which is where I was spotted by County. They were a good side, and I met Tosh, one of best friends, while playing for their under-nines. After that, I went on to Pheasant Colts, where my Dad was manager. As you can imagine, it was pretty relentless – nowadays, the rules have changed, so youngsters enrolled at a professional club's academy are only allowed to play one game a weekend.

If someone had watched one of my teams from when I was fifteen, would they have singled me out as the one to keep an eye on? I'm not sure they would have done, to tell the truth. I was just this goal poacher. I mean, I was tidy and I could drift past people, but I wasn't especially quick. I played up front off a big man, just hunting around the box for opportunities. That was all I really did. It wasn't until I was in my late teens that I grew a bit and found some pace from somewhere, and then my game changed completely – I'd just try and destroy people every time I got the ball.

Strikers were the players I admired growing up. Having watched the Mexico '86 and Italia '90 World Cups on TV, my big heroes were England's front pair, Gary Lineker and Peter Beardsley. Lineker was the poacher, Beardsley was the provider, and they could rip teams to bits when they were on song, especially once they had Gazza behind them pulling the strings. On the rare occasions I did actually get to games, I enjoyed watching Nigel Clough at Forest and a guy called Tony Agana at County. They were different types of forward – Agana was quick and direct, while Clough usually dropped back into the hole to scheme – but forwards all the same.

As a kid, I didn't really play any sport other than football. We barely did anything else at my school – no rugby, not a lot by way of athletics. In the summer, there'd be a bit of tennis, which I wasn't bad at, and there was some table tennis from time to time. Football ruled though; everything else took a back seat. And it wasn't just at school – we took every opportunity to play.

The park was literally four yards from the back of our house. The garden joined right on to it and my younger brother Scott and I were out there all the time with all of the other local kids. We were always playing football; when it was time for tea, all my Mum had to do was scream over the back fence. I still remember it clearly. We were very lucky to have it there, even though it wasn't the best park in the world. It had a big bit of grass and the frames of some swings – the local scallies had nicked the swings, so they were easier to use as goalposts.

The great thing about football, and what probably makes it the most popular sport in the world, is that so little is required to play it. You need a patch of land, something you can use as a ball, and someone to play with. The first two were no problem and, with a kid brother just sixteen months younger than me, I was covered for the third as well. Obviously, Scott and I had plenty of battles and arguments while we were growing up, but he's a good lad and we've probably helped each other. He played in the lower leagues, having spells at Ilkeston and Telford, and he was at Lincoln for a short while.

Clifton, the area of Nottingham I come from, has a pretty good footballing pedigree. Viv Anderson, who won a couple of European Cups with Forest and went on to play for Manchester United, was born in Clifton; others who've made it in the professional game from there include Jermaine Jenas and Michael Johnson, who played for a number of clubs including County and Birmingham.

My Mum won't be too happy with me for saying this, but Clifton was quite a rough place to grow up. I had a good upbringing, and never wanted for anything as far as my family life was concerned, but it was pretty hard round there; at one point it was the biggest council estate in the world. There were loads of really good people there, but there was also a lack of expectations which affected the choices some people made. While my close mates never fell into the trap, I knew more than one or two people who found their way into drugs, and plenty of people would drink and smoke all the time. It was pretty tough. You could look around you at the opportunities to move on, but there weren't a great many options. The talent I had gave me a real chance, but if I hadn't had it I'd probably still be there with the rest of the lads. They've done okay, but the opportunities were limited – they're not brain surgeons, accountants, or lawyers.

Few people in Clifton were likely to get the openings you need to find a high-paid job of that nature. Without football, it's unlikely that I'd have done anything like that; I'd have had a normal job like everyone else. My mates were never jealous of me for having a talent, though. There's a group of six or seven of them who've never changed, a bunch who have been there for me all the way through, even when I was a car-less YTS at Lincoln and I had no way of getting back to see them. Even when I was away for eleven or twelve weeks, I could rely on them. Happily, we're still in touch. Tosh, Jazz, Cain, Nick, Johnny, Nursie — all used to come and see me play when they could. I've been lucky with them. None of them were ever about smoking or drugs, even though they liked a drink every now and again.

In a rough school, we helped keep each other on the straight and narrow. I was never tempted to experiment — even with smoking. It's just not for me. My Dad detests it, too, even though my Mum smoked for a long while. I guess knowing what I wanted to do helped, and being able to spot the outside influences that could get in my way and stop me being the best I could be. That considered, I've seen others doing it. I recall seeing David Ginola lighting up now and again, and he's one of the greatest players I've ever seen.

When I hit sixteen, County didn't want to know any more. There's a point at which clubs are supposed to let you know whether or not they're keeping you on; they usually inform you by mail. We'd got quite far past that deadline, but still they left me hanging on. Frustrated and unsure of what was happening, I was coming home from school at lunchtime and checking the post every day. After about a fortnight of this, I got fed up and rang the club, who told me they didn't want me. I left my Mum a dejected-sounding note and went back out for the afternoon's lessons, my prospects for a professional career looking slim. The letter turned up not long after.

They said I was too small, and that I wasn't strong enough. Everywhere I went for a trial, I heard the same thing. At five-foot eight or so, I wasn't exactly short, but I was frail; I couldn't impose myself. I was heading towards being a Michael Owen or a Jamie Cureton, a poacher. Slow I wasn't, but I wasn't blessed with blistering pace either.

I knew that I had ability. That was never really in doubt. But the club turning me down wasn't Man United or Chelsea, it was Notts County. When lower league teams are turning you down, there's not much further to go before you fall out of full-time football altogether and start having to think about balancing a day job with playing for a part-time club. Of course, some have done that and come back to have very successful careers, but the rejection from County did leave me feeling pretty bleak.

It can't be easy telling any sixteen year-old that they're not going to be offered a YTS contract. When a manager has to do that, they're making a decision with someone's whole life. That could have been it for me and football — if I hadn't got in at Lincoln, I've no idea what would have happened. I like to think that I'd have persisted and got someone to pick me up later down the line, but you never know. At the time, I was devastated, but I held on to an inner belief that I was good enough to play somewhere.

One thing I'd been smart enough to do was to start thinking about building myself up a bit. Even before my rejection by County, I'd begun going to a gym called Winners in Nottingham city centre. I used to take two buses to get there. That's what I would do after school and in the holidays, when everyone else was messing around. I knew I had to get stronger, and I knew that meant I had to knuckle down. I'd be in there with the local meatheads; perhaps they were the doormen from the local nightclubs. They were massive blokes, and there I was, this five-foot eight kid of fourteen knocking back the protein shakes to try and put some muscle on.

No-one likes rejection, and teenagers probably hate it more than most. I'd told myself over and over again that I could play, but it was always going to be important to have that confirmed to me by someone else. On my own, I couldn't be sure that I was going to make it. That period was a real test of my self-belief, of the will I could muster to keep on going and overcome the self-doubt. In the end, it made me much stronger and prepared me for the battles with confidence I was to face later in my career. I probably wouldn't be where I am now if things hadn't happened in the way that they did.

Still, that period – the three or four months I spent getting rejected – was really difficult. It was coming up to my GCSEs; I was meant to be concentrating on my school work, but my school wasn't exactly brilliant. I was struggling with what I was going to do if I couldn't make it as a professional footballer. My Dad was a plasterer and I could see how hard he worked – day in, day out. I didn't fancy that, to be honest. While I don't mind hard work, it just seemed to me that he was grafting hour after hour after hour. If I was going to put that amount of time into something, I wanted it to be something I loved.

Everything felt make or break. My exam results came through and they were, at best, okay. Decision time was looming; I was kind of in the last chance saloon. No way was I going to sit around the house all day doing nothing, which meant – if no club came through for me – returning to school for sixth form or getting myself a job. To be honest, the latter would have meant working with my Dad. Back then, that was what you tended to do. If you had no real skills, and your grades weren't good enough to set you on the path to university, you had to take what you could. For me, that would have been joining Dad as a plasterer.

All I knew was that I really, really wanted to be a footballer. At school, everybody could see that I could play a little bit, and assumed that it might be something I would do. But when you're getting turned down by Forest and County, and Grimsby and Rotherham, and all the other clubs in my neck of the woods – Mansfield said no, too – you begin to think that there's not much lower for you to go. Your mind gets taken over by the fact that you're struggling.

Then I got a trial with Lincoln – the late, great Keith Alexander, who was youth team coach there at the time, had played with my Dad for Clifton Town in the late seventies.

My Dad played for years, and is a huge football fan. He wasn't a Forest supporter or a County supporter as such, more a lover of the game in general. He played Nottingham non-league and, by all accounts, he was a decent player. People who knew him way back when still come up to me and tell me he was much better than me.

He was a completely different kind of player to me, though. I think he got the tackling genes; he was a midfield enforcer who could really put his foot in. He wasn't dirty, but he was tough as boots. While he wasn't the quickest, he got up and down like a box-to-box midfielder should. Off the pitch, he's kind-hearted and very laid-back, even if he gets angry when people speak out of turn. As a player, he wasn't mouthy, but he'd always have his say. I guess that's where I got it from.

My family have been very, very important all the way through, and they were particularly helpful then. You know how parents can put themselves out for you in order to help you along – for them, that involved driving me and my brother here, there, and everywhere to play matches. Every Saturday and every Sunday, they'd be jumping in the car to take us to a game. Later on, when I was an apprentice, they'd lend me money because they knew it was impossible to live on £27 a week. A CD cost £20 back then.

The problem was that I knew how well my Dad knew the game. He knew it backwards. I might say this, this, and this, but deep down he knew whether or not I was bullshitting. The majority of the time, he'd give me a bollocking and be absolutely right to do so, even though I didn't like to hear it. With his level of understanding, though, I just had to take it on the chin. I've had countless arguments with him, but he's right more often than not. Without a shadow of a doubt, he's been my biggest critic, yet his criticisms have usually rung true on some level. When I got to Coventry, there were times when I'd be playing against the best players in the country; I'd come off the pitch, shower, go into the players lounge and know he'd be there waiting to say something. I'd look at him and my Mrs and see that they'd had a bit of a ding-dong.

'What about this, then?' he'd say.

I'd reply: 'Dad, I'm not being funny, but I'm playing against the best players in the world here. At least give me ten minutes to come into the players lounge and have a drink!'

But he was always correct in what he said, and that was just his way. I wouldn't change him. Both he and my Uncle Ralph have come to watch a lot of my games, especially when I was playing at Coventry, which was relatively close to home, and they're similar in that they're fairly opinionated men. Even though it could sting a bit, they'd usually hit the nail on the head. I'm like the majority of us in that I don't take criticism well, and that was especially true when I was in my early twenties and trying to make a name for myself in the best league on the planet. Looking back, I'm able to see that it was all meant well, and that it helped me improve my game.

He didn't do it every game, and I think I could see where a lot of it stemmed from. I'm not sure he liked the way I played a lot of the time – he thought I should be more of a traditional centre-forward, and I didn't really want to play like that. Where I tried to develop my game so that I became better and better at beating people for pace and causing disarray in an opposition's defence, he would have liked to see me work on the skills an out-and-out striker needs.

He wasn't one of those full-on Dads who'd spend all his time out in the back garden with his kids training them up, but he did help me work on various things. On top of that, I used to watch him play; he was still turning out at a decent level. It was guidance, mostly – lots of my early learning just involved Scott and me kicking lumps out of each other in the garden. That was a reasonable enough education. The funny thing is that I look at myself now with my two boys, and think about all the travelling

I do to take them to their games, and it's exactly the same. I watch both of them and shout something and realise that I sound exactly like my Dad used to.

But then I like to think that I know the game a little bit, so I'm not just one of those that stands on the touchline yelling for the sake of it. Hopefully, when I do say something it's worth listening to. As far as I'm aware, I'm generally positive, but I also believe that when you've worked with kids and you know how they can play, and they get sloppy, then you've got to tell them. You can't keep on letting them make the same mistakes over and over again – you have to say something. I guess I like to win, and I find it hard not to take the game seriously. When you're like that, you come to expect the same from other people.

So, my Dad's had a huge influence on both my attitude to the game in general and the career I've carved out for myself within it. Of all the things he's done, though, having a word with Keith Alexander and getting him to offer me a trial was probably one of the most important. He could obviously see how tough the summer of 1992 had been for me, and he searched for an opening that I could make the most of.

Anything could have happened in that trial match; they'd probably already picked the majority of the players who were going to be in the youth team, and were scouting about for one or two more. To cut a long story short, I scored six goals – it was an occasion on which I really took my chances. Later on in my career, as you're probably aware, I became more of a provider than a finisher, but that day was all about showing what I was capable of in front of goal.

You like to think that you've done well and been noticed if you score six in a game, but you can never be sure. For a start, you've no real idea what it is they're looking for – they could have had all the forwards they needed already, and have been on the look out for defenders. Even after grabbing a double hat-trick, you still have to wait for the phone call. You still have to do time in limbo.

Luckily, the call came this time and they offered me a YTS contract. However, that meant moving away from home, something which isn't easy for a sixteen year-old. Fortunately for me, I've always been pretty comfortable living away, and I haven't spent that much time in Nottingham during the last eighteen years. So I moved to Lincoln, and straight into digs.

A couple called Gwen and Cliff looked after four or five of us in a little terraced house. Before I got there, someone told me there was a full-sized snooker table, which made me think that it was going to be amazing. It wasn't. The table was literally three feet by one foot. And it was in the garage. Aside from that, there was a room that was stacked so high with newspapers that you couldn't even get into it.

There was a kitchen, where seven or eight gerbils were kept, another little sitting room, and the bedrooms upstairs. That was it. We shared bedrooms; generally there were two of us to each, but there might be a third occupant if someone couldn't get back to their home on an evening. While it was pretty cramped, it was a good laugh, as it tends to be when you live with your mates at that age. Perhaps you have to get used to the real world quickly, because you don't have your Mum about doing everything for you, but living like that is good fun when you're sixteen.

There were no real ground staff at Lincoln. We didn't even have someone to look after the kit; there was no chef, no food. Nothing. Basically, we did everything. There was a manager, a geezer to cut the grass, and a youth team manager, Keith, who doubled up as a first team player. Anything else was down to us. We painted the goal posts, washed the kit, cleaned the stands, the changing rooms, and the boots. It was full-on. We could be there for half-eight in the morning and not get away until half-four or five in the evening. It's hard to explain how tough it was, especially in the first YTS year before the new lads came in to take over the chores that had been ours.

There was no training kit as such. What we had was the stuff the first team had used four or five years earlier. The socks didn't match, and the shirts were all ripped; in the winter, you were lucky if you got a jumper. The second years got the pick of all the best stuff, and whoever was in first got the few decent jumpers. Some days we didn't even train because Keith was off playing for the first team – on those occasions we'd come in, wash the kit, and work as ball boys for the senior players. I'm sure you can imagine what that was like in the winter, particularly for those who'd lost the race for the jumpers. When there was no-one to take us, we'd go into the gym and play two-man Wembley.

Keith was a top bloke. He was still playing; he was extremely fit, so we used to do a lot of running, and this helped us have a strong youth team. We finished third or fourth in our youth league, a competition which had the likes of Forest and Villa in it. That was something to be proud of, given that we were a Third Division side and we went everywhere in a clapped-out mini-bus.

It's hard not to look at the kids in football today and think that they have no idea how lucky they are. What you have to bear in mind is that the way we were treated back then was wrong. For me, there's a happy medium between being given lots of responsibilities and not having any at all, as is the case with young players now. I guess, in a way, that it's good that all they're asked to do now is concentrate on their football, but I'm firmly of the belief that a little bit of discipline doesn't hurt.

Some of the stuff we had to do would be unthinkable now. Because our digs were closest to the ground, we had to wash the kit. Then we had to dry in it in the dryers. We'd stick them on, go home, then one of us would have to go back about half-past nine with the keys, open up again and turn the dryers back on so that everything would be ready for the morning. That happened every single day. Just think – a sixteen year-old having to go into the ground all alone in the pitch black. Absolute madness. Nowadays, there are people paid to do those jobs, but we were asked to do it all, and it was worth a grand total of £27.50 a week.

If I'm honest, I look back on those days with fondness. I was playing against Forest and County and many of the other teams who had rejected me that summer, and it was great to show them how well I could do given the chance. But they were tough times. My weekly wages could get me a CD and a half, if I'm right in saying that the first one I bought after signing as a YTS cost £18. The digs were paid for, but the food wasn't great; it was meat and two veg on the menu every night at Gwen and Cliff's. Meat and two veg, meat and two veg, night after night after night. Eventually, one of us had to ask Gwen if it would be okay if we had pasta for a change, and she started crying. In fairness, she did relent in the end and cook it for us, and we started to get chicken burgers and fries on a Friday night before a game. She also used to make us a pack-up to take into training, but the sandwiches we got weren't exactly the best. If we forgot to chuck them at training, we'd throw them up onto the roof of the house, thinking she wouldn't notice. She didn't; or, at least, she didn't until one of the neighbours saw and told her what we'd been up to.

There were plenty of good times with the other YTS lads, and Lincoln itself was a lovely little city. Actually, it's not unlike Norwich – it's quiet, relaxed, and there's not traffic all over the place. It had a pretty, compact centre, and if you found the right places your £27.50 could go a long way. Tuesday night was student night at a place called Viennas, and it was only ten pence a pint, notwithstanding the fact that the pint was inevitably of the most watered-down awfulness you could ever hope to taste.

My room-mate, and big pal, was a guy called Kaseem. He came from Nigeria. There was no way he was ever sixteen – it was impossible that he and I were the same age – but he was a good little right-winger. Up front alongside me we had a big lad,

Steve Williams, who went on to play a few games as a pro. We had a competition between us to see who could score the most goals in a season for the youth team, and I was lucky enough to win both times we held it. Steve and I weren't a stereotypical big-man, little-man routine. He wasn't the bustling type; technically he was good, and he had a decent left foot on him. That suited Keith, who sent his teams out to play good football, unlike a few other managers at Lincoln – John Beck's name springs to mind – who just wanted to lump it. Keith wanted football to be played the right way.

I was only seventeen years old, and in the second year of my YTS, when I made my first-team debut. It was at Shrewsbury's old ground, Gay Meadow, and I really didn't think I was going to be involved at all. Usually, there would be two or three of us YTS lads who would travel with the first team just to make the drinks and that kind of thing. It was all a bit of a shock to find out that, with me being named on the bench, it would all begin there.

It's not a rude awakening, exactly, but the first time you go away to games like this it's a bit of an eye-opener. You get to eat with the senior players at a hotel, for example. The meal that day was a bonus, but, to tell the truth, it was enough simply to be going. Instead of cleaning boots and washing out changing rooms, I'd been invited to be with the first team. There I was, just seventeen, and picked as a substitute. Even so, there was no guarantee that I'd made it. After you'd made your debut, as I did that night, you still had no idea if you were going to be offered a contract.

I look back at that line-up now and there's Mike Pollitt in goal – he's still going strong. I can't say how many games he's played by now; perhaps not that many, given that he's been No. 2 for much of his career despite an outstanding spell at Rotherham. There's also Ian Baraclough, who went on to play for Scunthorpe and subsequently managed them until he was sacked earlier this year. At the time, though, my mates were in the youth team, and I'm still close friends with some of them. Dick — Ben Dixon, a year my senior — also became a first-team player, and I cleaned his boots. That never stopped us becoming really close, and nowadays we still go on holiday together every year.

It was all a bit last minute at Shrewsbury. As I say, I thought I was travelling to make the teas and stuff like that, but they told me at short notice that I was in. This was before anyone had a mobile phone, too, so I couldn't ring my Dad and Uncle Ralph and tell them to get in the car. That was a real pity, because they missed my first goal. With fifteen minutes to go, and the score at one-all, I was thrown on, and I got the winner. It was a decent strike, too. Someone played a through ball, I took it down first touch, went past the defender on the right and smacked it into the far corner. It was the first game Shrewsbury, who went on to win the league that year, had lost in seventeen. My granddad got it up on Ceefax — for those of you who remember it — and saw it — D Huckerby (86 minutes).

Happily enough for me, Keith was given the job of first-team manager at the start of my second year, becoming the first full-time black manager in the Football League in the process. Soon enough, I managed to get a decent contract — my first professional contract. It added up to all of £90 a week. I didn't feel like a millionaire, and it still wasn't a lot, but what can you do? I'm sure the average wage back then was higher than £90 a week, but I was being paid that to do something I really wanted to do.

I negotiated that deal myself, even if that basically meant me sitting there while I was told what I'd be getting. They couldn't really afford anything else, and it was typical for clubs that size to offer a kid the smallest contract they could. For a lot of the smaller teams, it's probably more or less the same now as it was then — it's only the Premier League and a small section of the Championship where there's any real money. Everyone else struggles. Whatever anyone says, though, being a footballer is a great life. Whether you're on £90 a week or £90,000, you're basically being paid to kick a ball around with your mates all week, every week.

Not that I was ever recognised as a footballer at that stage. Not in Lincoln. Not on ninety quid a week. I can't ever remember jumping to the front of a queue anywhere, and I'm pretty sure they'd have told me where to go if I'd tried it. I wouldn't do that in any case.

Then, of course, there was my first car. It was a Fiat Uno. I couldn't even afford that until just before I went to Newcastle when I was nineteen. It was old, and it cost me £850, but it's always nice to get your first set of wheels. The Uno got me from A to B, and it allowed me to go back home to Nottingham. Nowadays, there aren't a lot of kids turning up at training in a Fiat Uno, but the game has changed. Everything is a competition – everything is about keeping up with the Joneses, and I see a lot of players having that problem. Even if you haven't got the money, you're still expected to play that game. Everyone wants a Range Rover or a BMW. Or this. Or that. Or whatever. They want it even if they haven't got the money to pay for it. Perhaps that's an issue with society in general; we all want the next big thing, whether it's a car or something like an iPhone. That's just how it is, and I'm certainly not saying I haven't been like that at times.

We didn't mix with the older pros. As I've said, my mates were the other lads that had come out of the youth team and won contracts. When I went up to the first team, I knocked around with Dick and Matt Carbon; there was also a lad called Steve Parkinson. We all shared a house – and that got condemned.

It was a funny story, or at least it is when you look back on it. We all lived in this three-bedroomed house that we rented off the physio. Matt Carbon never used to like the cold, so every night he'd sit as close to the fire as he could. It was absolutely freezing in that place, a horrible little terraced thing. Carbs used to fall asleep on the floor all the time, and we'd presume that it was because we'd spent all day training. Then my Mum brought round one of those stickers that you use to check for carbon monoxide; if they turn black inside twenty-four hours, you know you've got a problem.

It turned black in about five minutes.

We rang the gas board, who came round and condemned the house instantly. I was, therefore, homeless. I had to move in with my Mrs' parents, and I stayed there until I moved to Newcastle.

Lyndsey and I met when I was an apprentice; she was a Lincoln girl. The one thing you can't say is that she ever married me for the money. When we met, she earned more than me by working one day a week in Tescos. Even when I turned pro, I didn't really have the finances to sort us out a place to live. So, having literally nowhere else to go, I moved in with the in-laws. By then I was on the fringes of the first team and the last thing I wanted to do was move back into some digs somewhere.

Even as a first-team player, we'd never go to places overnight and stay in a hotel. We'd always travel on the day and have a pre-match meal somewhere – and that would be omelette and beans. I can still remember we did Lincoln to Exeter in a single day – a seven-hour drive in either direction. We didn't have time to stop for something to eat on the way down, so all we had to eat were sarnies on the bus. On the way home, the chances are that the older pros would have had a crate of ale.

At seventeen or eighteen you wouldn't be invited down to the back of the bus; there'd be no summons to come and get involved with the card schools. I don't think they really liked the younger ones coming through – especially down in the lower leagues. We were a threat, because we were obviously looking to take their places in the team. It could be difficult, quite tense. At that level, football is a proper job, and being taken out of the team in favour of some up-and-coming youngster might mean the beginning of the end of a pro's career. Lose your first-team place at somewhere like Lincoln, and you might have been looking at a drop down into the part-time game, a move which would bring with it the anxiety of having to find a day job.

If you believe everything you read in the papers, football is non-stop money and glamour, but it's actually full of risk and disappointment. As a teenager, you didn't really take much notice of it, but a struggling Third Division side would have a number of players in it who were facing the uncertain future of a life outside the game. To them, we weren't just a threat to their place in the team, but question marks over their livelihoods. When you're eighteen or nineteen, you're trying to build a career, but your success always comes at the expense of someone else's.

I wasn't cocky, exactly, but I had a lot of self-belief. Senior players can take that as arrogance sometimes, and it can rub them up the wrong way. While they could have a pop at me about most things, though, they couldn't question my ability – I believed that I was, at that stage, already as good a player as any of them. I knew that I wasn't out of place, so I wouldn't let them abuse me for no reason. I wasn't there to be pushed around.

What was nice about nobody knowing my face was that I wasn't getting whacked in every game I played. Not back then. There wasn't the scouting that there is now, when the opposition know exactly who everyone on your team is and how they are likely to play. There was the odd one or two you knew about. For example, I remember we went away to Barnet who had Dougie Freedman, a Scottish Under-21 player who we knew would be decent. In general, though, you wouldn't know anyone.

Particularly when I broke properly into the team in my first season as a pro, I just don't think the opposition knew who I was or what was going on. I'd get it and run at them straight away and you'd see them wondering who this kid was who was coming at them. Clubs couldn't really afford to do that much scouting, so they'd have no idea who was good and who was bad, who was left-footed and who used their right, who had a good engine on them and who liked to pull tricks.

I'd got really, really quick, but my stamina was a joke. I'd go off on a run and then be knackered for about ten minutes. I had to adapt as I got older, learning how to make the most of the energy I did have. The downside to getting a run in the team was that I did start to get kicked, and there were some proper thugs down there in the lower leagues. They could really put their foot in, and in Division Three they've no time for people they think are trying to take the mick. I wouldn't say I goaded them, but I would purposely go out to try and make them look stupid. That's what it's all about. You've got to show people like that you're not intimidated by them, and that you're going to give it your best.

About a year after my debut, when I'd got a little bit bigger and a lot more athletic, I learned to run the channels properly and got really into taking people on. I never really liked playing up front after that; I liked to run at defenders, and expose them out wide. I realised both that I could run and that people really don't like being run at. Down at that level, some players make a living out of bullying you, smashing into you and the like. It struck me that I'd get whacked if I just stood around up front waiting for the ball, but going out wide and running at people gave me an opportunity. They couldn't just kick me then, and they ran the risk of a booking if they fouled me.

I knew that I could go past people pretty easily on both sides, and I thought that I'd rather do that out wide than stand up front and get booted and smashed into from behind all day long. Ever since then, I've hated having people ploughing through the back of me. That's why I don't go up for many headers; I remember one time that I did and getting elbowed straight in the head. I didn't have a clue what I was doing in the air, and it took me right out of my comfort zone.

Verbally, I was never going to get bullied. I might not have been big and strong physically – I'm not now, even – but I would always stick up for myself when people were having a go. Like my Dad, I've always had a bit to say for myself, within reason. Of course, things are said — what goes on in football is very similar to the sledging in cricket. You wind people up, especially if they've just left one on you — you tell them: 'I'm going to get the ball and I'm going to skin you...bring me down and you're going straight in the book!'

It's not malicious, you just want them to know you're not scared. You have to be like that with defenders in particular. It's their job to try and stop you, and they'll use any means available to them — booting you, marking you out of the game, or trying to get inside your head. All you can do is try to block them out. I remember how Martin Keown was always in your ear — he'd make silly noises, and pinch you. Players like him always want to try and get the upper hand. The thing is, though, I always had the same attitude. I always wanted them to know that I could knock the ball beyond them, do them for pace, and leave them in big trouble.

I could take a tackle. I was pretty robust — it wasn't often that I didn't get straight back up. Over the years, I got hit loads of times, but I'd always try to dish out revenge using my natural attributes rather than roll around on the floor. It had been the same since I was a kid — there were always the bigger lads at the park who played the game physically. You just had to weather it.

The game has changed a fair bit now, and I think forwards get more protection now than they did back in the day. Before my career started, it used to be a bit of a free-for-all, with people smacking each other all over the place. It's certainly changed for the better now, or at least I think it has. I guess I'm bound to say that as a forward; if I was a defender, I'd probably say that referees had started to interfere far too much. The thing is, though, that one bad tackle can literally finish someone's career.

I got a lot of attention once I really broke into the team. It was strange, though, because I went for a year where I pretty much didn't play at all. Keith went and Sam Ellis was the manager for a while; he saw a bit in me, but we were struggling and I don't think he could just throw me in. Keith was like that, too – when he was under real pressure, he couldn't just fill the team with unproven kids. Down there, you can't just gamble your career on youngsters coming good.

I was getting impatient. As I say, I believed in my ability, and felt that I was a better than a lot of the players in the first team. But I also knew that they had paid their dues, and that that's how it works down there. They'd worked hard for their entire careers and, in a sense, they deserved their places in the team because of that. There was always this hierarchy which, as a kid, you had to try and break down.

There were a fair few managerial changes as well. Sam was there for a year, then there was Steve Wicks – the ex-Chelsea player – for six weeks or so. And then in came John Beck. As soon as he arrived, I knew it was only a matter of time before I went. Upon his arrival at Lincoln, he started to do the same things that he'd been notorious for doing when he'd been the manager at Cambridge.

He painted the home changing rooms dark red and the away changing rooms dark brown. Crazy stuff. We started training on the pitch at Sincil Bank every day so that it would be all smashed up; I remember he fined the goalkeeper once for throwing it short rather than punting it. He was only allowed so many touches before he blasted it up front. Once, he threatened to take me off because I'd had a shot. I'd cut inside, beaten two men, and the keeper had saved my effort. He pulled me over and said: 'You do that again and I'll have you off! I want you to go down to the by-line to get a cross in or try and get a corner…'

He'd keep the grass on the wings longer so the ball would hold up and stay in play; he used to try and make us get in a cold shower before the game. At eighteen, I couldn't do it – there were older blokes just jumping into this freezing cold shower with ice buckets and stuff. I've talked to Dion, who played for Cambridge for a while, about Beck, and his angle is different. He got Dion's lot promoted and pushing on, and they were very close to making the Premier League under him. I guess it works for some people, but I knew that no-one was going to make me a better player by chucking an ice bucket over me. They'd just make me cold.

Beck put his stamp on the side straight away. He was going to play long ball, no two ways about it; he decided to play Matt Carbon, a centre-half, up front solely because he was big. People talk a lot about teams playing kick-and-run football, but this was the purest version of those tactics you could ever expect to see. It was all mathematical – Beck set out to play the percentages in a way that was pretty extreme.

At the same time, as far as I know, Steve Wicks was doing his utmost to bandy some of our names about. Steve really did believe in my ability – I once read that he'd said I was the best player he'd ever seen at that age, which was a massive thing – and, if word was to be believed, he'd managed to convince a few of the bigger clubs that I was worth the once-over. Rumours were going round that Manchester United and Newcastle were among those who were having me watched. However, although I was playing well I wasn't scoring as many goals as I possibly should have been. I was pacy, direct, and unpredictable, attributes which will always make people sit up and pay attention, but I wasn't hitting the net frequently enough. Goals tend to be the things that really get mouths watering at the big clubs.

All the same, I was the natural possessor of a way of playing that doesn't come easily to most. I just find it very easy to go past people. It's no good just being quick; I had a good turn of pace, and could go both sides, which not all wingers can. Generally, a wide player will either beat his man on the outside, going between the opponent and the touchline, or cut inside into the channel.

Particularly when I played on the left, I had it in me to take either route, which is what makes me difficult to defend against.

I had a good touch when I was fifteen or sixteen, but I hadn't acquired the pace which was to serve me so well later on. It wasn't until I got to Lincoln that I was able to go past people so effortlessly, and I'd like to think that the improvement came down to all those hours I spent in the gym. Every endless bus ride to Winners had been worth it; by putting the work in, I'd developed a kind of sprinter's physique.

I've never wanted anybody to be able to say that I wasn't fit enough. That would have been a rubbish excuse for failure – if you don't think you're big enough, you can always do the work to make yourself so. It's fair enough if someone says you don't have the ability; some people just can't do what's necessary with a football. But physique is always something that's yours to develop. The early rejections made me buck up my ideas, and helped me realise that nothing in life is easy – they set me on my path. It's hard to say what would have happened if I'd got in at County or somewhere; perhaps I'd have been less determined. I certainly wouldn't have met my wife in Lincoln, and I may well not have got the opportunity to go on to Newcastle.

We'd played Mansfield away and, afterwards, someone told me that Kevin Keegan had been watching from the stands. I hadn't a clue how true it was. I played one more home game, scoring against Hartlepool, and started to prepare for an Auto Windscreens Trophy game up at Darlington. Then Lincoln told me that I wouldn't play in that fixture; Keegan was coming to pick me up and I was to stay at his house ahead of negotiations for a move.

Steve Wicks had put me in touch with an agent, Phil Smith, who would go on to represent me throughout my career. The first time I ever met him, I drove down to Watford Gap services with Dick and my Dad. I'd never met an agent before, but he came across as alright – passionate, if a tad scruffy. I got used to Phil being like that over the years – it's just the way he is. He helped me do my negotiating for the move to Newcastle although, as we shall see, there really wasn't a lot of room for manoeuvre on that front.

The whole Lincoln experience was great for me as a player and as a person, particularly the first year of the YTS where we were really put through the mill. Proper work of the type we were asked to do really made us appreciate the step up into the first team; being an apprentice was so far away from that. Once I was playing in the senior side, my enjoyment was increased by the knowledge that only eighteen months previously I'd either have been clearing out drains with a bin-bag on my hand or standing on the terraces performing ball-boy duties while it hammered down with rain. I felt like I'd genuinely earned my place in the team.

The attendances at Lincoln were between two and three thousand, and I guess there are the same bunch of die-hards there now as back then. At Newcastle, you'd sometimes have the same amount just watching training, which absolutely staggered me at first. But the loyalty of the lower league fan is amazing, too, and it's a special part of the game. There'll always be a place in my heart for Sincil Bank, Lincoln's stadium – when I go to visit the in-laws, I often jog past it and on to the big common where Keith used to take us jogging every Monday. Not much seems to have changed. Dick still lives there, too, so I have a fair few opportunities to go back, but I've never played there again. I've never been drawn to play Lincoln in a cup game, or faced them in a friendly.

Keith went on to manage a few clubs. He was at Ilkeston for a bit, then he returned to Lincoln and led them to four successive play-off campaigns. He was at Peterborough for a little while, and was managing Macclesfield when he died of a brain haemorrhage on March 3, 2010. He was fifty-three; he died in hospital back home, in Lincoln. I went to his funeral with a lot of the players I played with there. He was a really top-class bloke. He never made a lot of the fact that he was English professional football's first black manager – he was just a good, honest guy. I'm sure he was proud of that achievement, but it wasn't something he'd talk about – football always came before questions of black or white for him. I used to see him occasionally in Portugal in later years, and, every time Dick and I spoke to him, he was still the same as he'd been when we were kids. He absolutely loved the game, and he'd always moan about how he hadn't got anything to spend on players.

Keith gave me a chance when no-one else did, so it was all down to him. I don't know where I'd have been without him, and I hope I've repaid his faith in me over the years.

2. WORKING IN A KEEGAN WONDERLAND

Match:	Newcastle United vs Chelsea
Venue:	St James' Park
Competition:	FA Cup, third round replay
Date:	Wednesday, January 17, 1996
Result:	Newcastle 2, Chelsea 2
	(Chelsea won 4-2 on pens, aet)
Attendance:	36,535

Newcastle United:	Srnicek; Barton, Albert, Peacock, Beresford, Watson; Beardsley, Clark, Ginola, Ferdinand (Huckerby, 64 mins), Kitson (Elliott, 87 mins)
Subs (not used):	Holland

Chelsea:	Hitchcock; Petrescu, Duberry, Lee, Myers (Clarke, 52 mins); Phelan, Wise, Gullit, Newton; Spencer (Peacock, 102 mins), Hughes
Subs (not used):	Furlong

And so I went up to Newcastle, a move which started a whole new chapter in my life. Looking back now, it's clear to me that Kevin Keegan has been one of the major influences on my career – even though he sold me on to other clubs both times I played for him. I've got nothing but good things to say about him. He builds exciting teams and signs players that the fans love to watch, and I've enjoyed his training immensely whenever I've worked with him.

That's not to say that we grew close personally as I did with Gordon Strachan, Nigel Worthington, or a couple of the other managers that I've come across. What makes Kevin stand out in my mind is that he's such a big name: it's hard not to be impressed by someone who's achieved what he has as a player and manager.

Wherever he goes, he makes things happen – especially, as we shall see, at Manchester City. His first real success as a manager, though, was taking over at Newcastle when they were down near the bottom of the old Division Two and turning them from a complete mess into a real powerhouse. They've always been a massive club in terms of support, but what he did there was staggering – taking a team who were on the brink of relegation to the Third Division and making them contenders for the Premier League title in just three or four years.

It's almost impossible to explain to people how mad they are about their football on Tyneside. Here in Norwich, people are passionate about the club and love going to the games, but it's literally life or death in Newcastle. Norwich are well-supported, but up there it's amazing how committed people are to the club. Maybe 'love' isn't a strong enough word for it.

When I signed, I stopped overnight at Kevin's house out on the estate of Newcastle's then owner, Sir John Hall. It was weird – overnight, I'd gone from being a kid in a Third Division side to staying at Kevin Keegan's place. I had one of those old mobiles, a proper brick, and I phoned Dick on it, trying to take everything in my stride. Then the next morning we met up with my Dad and my agent at a hotel in Gosforth Park, which is where we negotiated my side of the move.

To be honest, not that much negotiating happened.

They offered me £400 a week. I wasn't too happy with the terms, but they said that's that. So I spoke to my Dad and he simply said, 'You can't turn this chance down.'

When I think about it now, I realise that the players back at Lincoln that were earning three or four times as much as I was about to earn at Newcastle United were twenty-eight, twenty-nine, thirty plus years of age. They were coming to the ends of their careers – so they'd earned the right to earn that kind of money over the years. When you're a kid, though, you don't really take that into consideration. You just think, 'Whoa, surely I should be getting paid this?' It was a tough call. Even though there I was, joining Newcastle, what they were offering wouldn't make me much better off than I had been at Lincoln – particularly when you take into consideration that I had to rent a flat and pay for a car. As if that wasn't enough, £400 a week meant paying a higher tax rate.

Basically, I was going to come out with more or less the same as I was on at Lincoln. The experience, though? It was worth twenty times that. So I signed, on the 10th of November, 1995. Lincoln were paid almost £500,000, a record for them at the time. The talk in the press beforehand was that Manchester United were another of the clubs allegedly looking at me. But unless it's wholly concrete, you don't really know. I'd heard there were four or five teams watching me by then.

I didn't actually see Keegan in the stands at Mansfield that night, but the fact that I was told by people that he was there gets you thinking that they're obviously looking. It was a real gamble for them, though – spending the best part of half a million pounds on a nineteen-year-old from Lincoln City, who were then bottom of the old Third Division. Lincoln couldn't afford to turn that kind of offer down; it was a huge amount of money for a club like them. And it was one of those situations where a club had got a kid in and brought him up through the youth team, having cost them nothing in transfers and very little in wages. So £500,000, or thereabouts, was a lot of money for a club like Lincoln in 1995. Let's be fair, it would still be a lot of money today. Even now, what would it mean for a small club to sell a kid from the youth team for £500,000? It'd be happy days.

It was a progression, a big step for me. A real big step. I'd already left home, so I knew about living away, but the scale of things was completely different. Before I was in the youth team, I was in digs – well, until they got condemned – and went on to live with Lyndsey's Mum and Dad. But going from that to living completely on my own was a big step. And it wasn't just living forty-five minutes away from my parents in Nottingham – you're talking a three hour drive. It seemed like the other end of the world.

So, I got there, stayed in a little hotel for about three weeks and then took on a flat in Gosforth. Scott Sellars had just left, and he'd rented it too; it was a nice enough two-bedroom apartment. About a month later, Lyndsey moved up from Lincoln, which made things a lot easier, because I wasn't on my own all the time. We were paying £400 a month for the flat, which doesn't sound pricey in today's money, but was quite a lot for me at the time. It gave us a little base, though, and I guess it felt like this was our first house together.

There was a little press attention as the move went through, but, at the time, Newcastle were signing players for fees that were massive compared to the one they'd paid for me. Les Ferdinand had come in that summer from QPR for £6 million, and they'd also signed Warren Barton from Wimbledon for not much less. Then there was David Ginola, who'd come in for a few million from Paris Saint-Germain. In the grand scheme of things, I wasn't a huge signing for them. I was basically just a kid to whom they were giving a chance. My Grandad saved a few bits 'n bobs from the news, so it's not like they weren't interested at all, but it was obviously a much more important deal for me than it was for the papers.

The biggest thing at the time was the uncertainty. It wasn't like I was twenty and I was moving to somewhere where I knew that I was going to have a place in the side. It was really difficult to know whether I'd be anywhere near good enough, or even if my face would fit.

That was the problem I was facing. I knew that I wasn't going straight into the first team – I mean, Newcastle had paid a few million quid for Paul Kitson the year before, and he was only a squad player. It was clear that I was going to be in limbo for a while, and that waiting was going to be tough. Regardless of whether or not the club had taken a risk on me, in as much as they'd paid a fair bit of cash up-front, I knew that they'd want me to prove myself.

As I see it, what happened to me isn't so common these days. The big clubs are slower to take a gamble on young players coming out of the lower leagues – boards put so much pressure on managers to get results that they'd rather pay more money for a guaranteed quick-fix. That's what I had done, though. I'd gone from Lincoln – where there were some decent players, don't get me wrong – at the bottom of what was then the Third Division to a team battling it out with the best of the best at the top of the Premier League.

However low down the pecking order I was, they threw me straight in with the first team training-wise. Imagine it. For a lot of the time I was at Lincoln they were rebuilding the changing rooms, so we'd been changing in Portakabins and training here, there and everywhere. When I got to Newcastle, there were days when two or three thousand would turn up just to watch training. The pitches were immaculate. You were talking bowling green standard, every day; there was never a blade of grass out of place. And it's one of the only places I've been to where they had the pitches marked out for training. Little pitches were marked out every day to whatever size Kevin wanted them to be for our sessions. Everything was just spot on.

I'd gone from one extreme to the other – just like that. Did it take some getting used to? Yes and no. It wasn't that difficult because I was so well looked after, but I had to get my head around training with players that I'd only seen on TV. It was mind-blowing playing with Peter Beardsley, who'd been a real boyhood hero, but it was a bit of a shock to the system.

I'd effectively gone from being one of the better players at Lincoln to being a nobody, which was nice in its own way but meant having to prove myself all over again. I'd shown that I could make the jump from being a YTS lad to a pro, and now I had to take the massive step up into a group of players which at the time contained some of the best in England, if not the world.

For my friends back home in Nottingham it must have been strange. Even though I'd already been playing professional football, it had been with Lincoln – it wasn't as if I'd really made it. In a way, football at Lincoln's level was just another job; it wasn't as if they played in front of tens of thousands in the ground and a few million more on the television every week. Now I was at one of the biggest clubs in the country and, what's more, it was three hours away from home. But my mates were fine – pleased for me, in fact. When I did get to see them, it was like nothing much had changed – that's what it's like with good friends. You can go away for a while and come back and still get on in the same way, still find the same things funny, and so on. Anyway, none of them had too much time to worry about what everyone else was getting up to – they were all getting on with their own lives. And no-one was going to be too star-struck by a young forward who wasn't likely to be playing on TV for the first team any time soon.

Kevin never really described the role that he had in mind for me – whether he'd brought me in to play as a second striker, or a winger, or whatever, I didn't know. And I can't say this for sure, but you wonder whether they'd signed me just because they knew that others were looking at me – others who may well have included Manchester United, who were shaping up to be Newcastle's big rivals that season.

Obviously Newcastle must have seen something in me; they wouldn't have bought me if I was rubbish. But I do wonder about their motivation. There were definitely several teams lurking, and I was never going to go straight into their first team with Ferdinand, Beardsley, and all the rest of them. That meant that I was in the ressies with the likes of Jimmy Crawford, Chris Holland – who went on to play for Birmingham for a few seasons – and Aaron Hughes, who'd just come up through the youth team. There were also the lads who weren't getting first team games or were coming back from injury.

In one way, Newcastle's was an intimidating dressing room to walk into because you knew that some of the best players in the country would be there when you opened the door. I got changed with the younger pros, which made it a bit less daunting.

That said, I remember David Ginola would come round every morning, without fail, and shake everyone's hand. I thought that was a real class act. He'd go up to everyone from the Beardsleys and the Ferdinands right down to me and the other youngsters; the whole dressing room hierarchy, in fact. I've never seen anyone do anything like it since. Some might say that it was just show, but I don't think it was. It made you feel welcome straight away.

The standard of the players I was training with wasn't the only eye-opener in the first few months up there. Newcastle is no Lincoln – it's a big city. The MetroCentre, the shopping mall over the River Tyne in Gateshead, is probably bigger than Lincoln on its own. I got used to it, but it took a while. I started to get recognised a little bit, too. Geordies know their football and a lot of people would go to the reserve games as well – they can't get enough. Even with getting a bit of attention in the street, though, it was never as it was a little later on down the line when I was on Match of the Day most weeks. And Newcastle was a nice enough place. I was never one for being out every night anyway, so in some respects life there wasn't that much different from how it was in Lincoln.

As I settled in and started to play games for the ressies, I felt like I was doing OK. I was getting a few goals, and I was enjoying the training with the first team. You'd think, 'Wow, these people can play…' And it's not exactly like what you see on TV. You can see how good they really are in training, where there's less pressure.

I would often watch Peter Beardsley. Bear in mind that he was getting on a bit then – he must have been thirty-five or thirty-six, but he was absolutely brilliant in training every single day. The way that he kept the ball; the amount of work he put in. He just had this proper zest for training, for working hard. It was great to see that attitude in someone who was coming to the end of his career. Come to think of it, I can still remember – it must have been on my first or second day – we had a little five-a-side tournament. I was on Beardsley's team and he actually said to one of our team-mates, 'OK, this lad can play a little bit…'

For him, it was probably just an off-the-cuff remark; he probably thought nothing of it at the time. But for me, it was huge – I was telling everyone. My Mum and Dad, my Uncle Ralph, everyone. I'd been singled out for praise by the player I'd once watched leading the line for England with Gary Lineker.

Whatever was said about me, though, it was clear that I wasn't going to get anywhere near the first team for a while, which was frustrating. We had so many good players, and we were fighting Manchester United to win the league. Everyone remembers that season. Newcastle were twelve points clear and Manchester United caught up with them – and the pressure was massive on

Keegan. No-one will ever forget his outburst on Sky after Newcastle won at Leeds to take the title race down to the last day of the season: 'We're still fighting for this title and I tell you something, I'd love it if we'd beat them, love it...' That one.

And the pressure meant that he couldn't chuck kids in to play – realistically, I'd have had to have been unbelievably good for him to pick me. And honestly? I wasn't good enough that he was going to drop senior players to give me a chance.

That's just fact. I wasn't good enough. I wasn't mature enough. Newcastle were fighting to win the Premier League and they wouldn't just throw in a nineteen-year-old kid from Lincoln. It was never going to happen.

I did get a few run-outs for the first team that season, though, and my game had changed since I'd left Lincoln. It was all about taking people on; running past them. In my debut against Chelsea in that FA Cup replay, I came on and did that really well.

At that point in time, I was probably getting quicker. When I was at Lincoln I was quick, really quick – but my stamina wasn't what it should have been. I was a work in progress. However, I always went out to test the first defender, to see if I could put them on the back-foot straight away. 'Let's see what he's got,' I'd be thinking. As in a game of chess, you need to get that psychological advantage over your opponent, especially when you're out wide. It's a bit different when you're up front because there are other factors you need to think about. But usually, when you're out there on the left, it's one-on-one – to start off with. And then it's a case of letting the best man win.

It's not solely down to pace. If you push the ball beyond the defender, you have to hit it with the right weight, and that's not easy. That's why there aren't that many players that play that way these days – it's not easy, especially given how quick and strong players are now. But that – pushing the ball past my man and sprinting – was the one part of my game that I did pretty naturally. And, while a lot of people used to say that I played off the cuff, I knew what I was doing.

Maybe you'd go inside the first time, outside the second. Or you'd maybe go twice down the inside, then go on the outside and cut back to cross it. Whatever. You just had to put the defender on the back foot so he didn't know what was going on. It works both ways, though. I've played against people who, first time, will come and smash you and then back off the next time the ball comes to you. So you're expecting them to whack you, but they don't. It's a mind game. One thing you do know is that your pace terrifies them. Most of them, anyway. Because there's nothing they can do. There's nothing worse for a defender than if you knock it past them and then they're stranded – you've gone. Left them. It gives them nightmares.

Michael Duberry was playing for Chelsea the day I made my debut and, when we were at Leeds together, he always used to tell me that when I made my debut that day, I kept on knocking the ball past him; he said that he didn't know what was going on. I gave them a good run for their money, even though we eventually lost four-two on penalties.

So that was my debut. As was the case with my first game for Lincoln, I didn't know until an hour before kick-off that I'd be on the bench, and I don't know why I came on after 64 minutes – perhaps Ferdinand was carrying an injury or something. But I came on, did well, and almost scored a couple of times. Ruud Gullit scored a leveller in the eighty-ninth minute to take the game to extra time and a shoot-out we would lose. The atmosphere was amazing. This was before they put the new upper tiers on at St James', so it was all on the one level and it was fever pitch in there. It was crazy; a great stadium to play in.

The funny thing was, though, I should have made my debut in the League Cup in November, the month that I moved. We were away at Liverpool – my first game for Newcastle should have been at Anfield. Unfortunately, there had been an oversight…

So – I travel down there, Kevin names the team and the subs an hour before kick-off, and my name's down to be on the bench.

And I'm sat there thinking: 'Right, I'm going to make my debut here – at Anfield!'

But then I start thinking to myself: 'But I've already played in this competition this season. I'm sure I have…'

Then the penny dropped. Right back at the start of the season, Lincoln had played Notts County in the first round. We'd played County home and away, and I'd been in the team.

And so I'm debating with myself: 'Do I say anything? Have the rules changed? What do I do? Do I tell him?'

Bear in mind I'm nineteen and I've been at the club less than three weeks – this is a big moment, and I don't know what to do. In the end, I decide I'm going to have to tell him. So I say: 'Gaffer, I've already played in this competition this season, I don't think I can play…'

And he goes: 'What do you mean, you've already played in this?'

'I've played in this for Lincoln already!'

It wasn't the best way to go about making my name at Newcastle. Anyway, Kevin found another sub, and I had to wait for the third round of the FA Cup in January to get a game.

I have to say that, as a rule, I've always liked to be told whether or not I'm playing the day before a match. Even though I'd prepare the same whether or not I knew if I was in the team, I preferred to know so that I could get in the right frame of mind. I've played for managers who named the team an hour before kick-off, and I've played for managers who named the team the day before. There are different schools of thought. That said, I think most players have a fair idea if they're going to be in the team – even if they're not officially told till an hour or so before kick-off. Deep down, they're aware. Training gives them a clue, particularly Thursdays, which tend to be the technical day when you go through what the other team are expected to do.

Like I say, Keegan always named his line-up on the day of the game; Nigel used to do it the day before the game; Gordon would also do it on the Friday. Everyone is different. Certainly at Coventry, under Gordon, we used to work extensively on corners so you knew then whether you were in or out.

I used to get on well with Arthur Cox, who was Kevin's No.2 at the time. They didn't do the 'good cop, bad cop' routine particularly. He was a tough fella, but a nice one with it. You could talk to him and he'd be blatantly honest with you. Terry McDermott was there as well – I got on fine with them all, to be honest. As the season progressed, you couldn't particularly tell that the pressure was mounting. Kevin and Terry McDermott seemed relaxed, playing head tennis against everybody at training every day. And they were the best at it by miles; so they'd play everyone. Every day. Head tennis wasn't really one of my specialities. But we all had to pair up and give it a go. Kevin still had us doing that at Man City.

So there I was. I'd made my debut, played against Bolton and then, in that February, we signed Tino Asprilla from Parma for £6.7 million. He was a huge character. I don't think he knew what to expect, especially when he landed at the airport in the snow. You look at the news pictures from that day and he's wearing a huge fur jacket, seeming as if he's wondering if he's made a good decision. Coming in from Serie A, Tino was probably used to a slightly different style of play, and the team had to be shuffled to fit him in. Obviously, his arrival also left me even further from the team. In some respects, the signing was weird – it wasn't like the team were struggling for goals, but Kevin went and got a new striker.

The title fight developed and became more intense, but Kevin was still the same character in spite of the enormous amount of expectation. Because Newcastle hadn't won anything for ages, and they'd gone twelve points clear by playing the most exciting, attacking football in the Premier League, I think everybody wanted them to win that title that year. It wasn't like it is now where only Manchester United fans want Manchester United to win and only Chelsea fans care about Chelsea – this was a year when, apart from Man United fans, literally everyone wanted Newcastle to win the league. They were the neutrals choice, and everyone's second team.

One of the best atmospheres that season was when our title rivals came to Tyneside in the first week of March. I think that the championship swung on that game. We were much the better team – we absolutely battered them, but Peter Schmeichel was unbeatable. Then, early on in the second half, Eric Cantona scored a volley at the far post, and they held on for a one-nil win.

For me, that set the ball rolling in their favour. And then they did what they do every year – they just kept going. They just grind out results, like a machine. You have to say that's the beauty of Ferguson. Even though he changes three or four players every year, he still instils a win-at-all-costs mentality. Even now, no-one else can cope with that.

After the defeat against Manchester United came Newcastle's visit to Liverpool, a game which turned out four-three in favour of the hosts and is often said to be the greatest game in the history of the Premier League. I didn't travel with the squad, but we watched the match on Sky in our flat. Liverpool broke the deadlock early on before Ferdinand equalised, then Ginola scored a goal which showed just how deadly Keegan's team could be on the counter-attack. Liverpool levelled, but we regained the lead, Tino finding the net from outside the area after some amazing craftwork from Beardsley. It looked as if we might come right back into the title race, but then Liverpool equalised for the second time before our defence fell asleep and let in Stan Collymore for the winner. It was fantastic to watch, despite the outcome, and I still feel happy about having been on the fringes of a team who could entertain like that. I remember turning round and saying to Lyndsey that it was the best game I'd ever seen, and that I'd be going in the next day with all of those players.

There was entertainment off the pitch, too. I remember at the end of that season my mate Tosh was up for the weekend – it happened to be the Player of the Year dinner during his visit. We were all there at the Gosforth Park Hotel and everyone decided to go back to Tino's for a party. I wasn't at all sure about it – they were all a bit older than me.

Tosh was a little bolder than me about the plan. He was saying: 'We've got to go, got to go – when's this ever going to happen again?' So, perhaps against my better judgement, we went along with the others. There was a lot of beer and the Colombian rum was coming out, and Tosh was playing bongo drums at Tino's place with a band that he had there.

The night wore on, and took a funny turn. Tosh had been knocking back the drink, then made the fatal error of lighting up a cigar, which is never the best move for a non-smoker. Now, he's pretty pale anyway, but I looked at him and noticed he'd gone a greenish colour. So we had to go outside, where – guess what? – he was sick. Badly. And then he went missing – I couldn't find him. I'd no real idea of where we were or where Tino's house was, and Tosh had disappeared. Then I heard all this beeping outside the house and there he was – unconscious in the middle of the road. Outside Tino Asprilla's house. I think he's lived off that story for the last ten years. It's not the kind of thing you'd forget in a hurry.

But, yes, Tino was certainly known for his parties. And I only ever went to the one of them. That dressing room was full of characters, though. Lee Clark was a local lad who liked a laugh and a joke, Steve Watson was pretty funny too. It was a great time to be there. Look back and that's probably the best spell that they've had for the last twenty-five years – more probably.

WORKING IN A KEEGAN WONDERLAND

It was good to have been around all of that. In the end, though, it wasn't enough to be stuck on the periphery of it. That summer, Kevin signed Alan Shearer from Blackburn for £15 million – another striker, and the undisputed best in the country this time. It was a statement of intent which said that we were going to put the disappointment of Man United catching up to win the title behind us. It was also, from my perspective, a bit of business which set my first-team chances back still further.

Shearer was a goal machine and, for my money, the best English centre-forward that there's ever been. I would often watch him in training and, even years down the line, I still go on and on about it to people. He didn't mess about at all. You see some players trying to chip the keeper, do silly things, and generally mess around. Not Shearer. Even though he liked a laugh and a joke, when he was doing shooting, he just smashed everything. And nine times out of ten it would hit the target. I used to tell Dean Ashton about him – how serious he was about scoring goals.

His goal-ratio was ridiculously good, but he also survived some horrendous injuries. On top of that, he was one of those who managed to change his game as he got older. When he was younger he was quick and could get into the channels; later on, he adapted so he was holding the ball up more and bringing other players in.

Lastly, he was as strong as an ox. I remember when I was playing for Coventry a bit later on. We were playing Newcastle at our place; I was injured, and our two usual centre-halves – Richard Shaw and Paul Williams – were both on the bench. We had these two new lads who had come in; two foreign lads – Jean-Guy Wallemme was one – and they beat us five-one. Shearer scored twice that day – for his last goal there was a scramble in the box and the ball looped up; he trampled over one of his own

43

players and both our centre-halves and scored. Trampled over them all with his studs to get to the ball and score the goal. Whatever it took to score, he'd do it.

And I was in the stands and I can remember both Richard Shaw and Paul Williams looking round at me and you couldn't help laughing, and their heads were down laughing too. You knew what they were thinking: 'Jeez, that could have been me that Shearer's stamping all over...'

With us bringing in a player of that calibre, I desperately needed to get some game time from somewhere. Footballers should just want to play. And that's what I say to the kids now. If you've got a chance to be playing, go and get a loan deal so you can play – because there's nothing like being on the pitch in a competitive game. With that in my mind, I went off on loan to Millwall at the beginning of 1996-97. I played six games in a month, and scored three goals.

Kevin had disbanded the reserve team, so I wasn't getting games. Even though Millwall were in Division Two, going there meant that I was playing matches. I think I must have asked to go out on loan, because I had to do something. The lack of activity was sending me crazy.

I'd gone from Lincoln to Newcastle at the top of the Premier League, but I wasn't playing. I was just training, so the move to Millwall was yet another eye-opener. I went from training week in, week out and doing nothing at the weekend to actually playing on a Saturday. And wherever it is, that's the most important thing.

I went straight into their team. Jimmy Nichol was the manager and I scored on my debut. They were playing at the New Den, which had just been opened.

In a way, it was a bit like going back to Lincoln, where everything was geared towards Saturday. In the lower leagues, there's no other reason to train than to get ready for a Saturday – it's not about improving as a player, it's about results. I enjoyed it there, regardless. It reminded me that, wherever it would turn out to be, I had to go and play somewhere. And it was good playing down the Den, where the fans are as passionate as they come. As well as the goals I got, I created a couple and they obviously wanted to sign me on for longer. But the problem for Millwall was that other people had seen me go there and score – Newcastle didn't want me to stay for longer, and it was only a month in the end.

On my return from South London, I had to start thinking about the future. The lack of reserve team football at Newcastle was the final straw. I couldn't do it for another year, playing a game every four or five weeks as and when one was arranged. I couldn't do it. I had to do something.

The players at Newcastle were just ridiculous, even though the signings of Tino, Shearer, and David Batty weren't quite enough to give us the edge over Man United. That said, I can still remember the day when Newcastle beat United five–nil. It was October, just after I came back from Millwall and just before I left. Shearer scored, Ferdinand scored, and Phillippe Albert ran through and chipped the keeper. I've never seen anything like that; it was the kind of game when the hairs on the back of your neck are standing up.

At the start of the season Man United thumped us four–nil in the Charity Shield and this was the first time that we'd played them since.

And we beat them by five. That was one of the best atmospheres that I have ever felt. And I was only watching it; I wasn't involved in it. I was in the stands and it was unbelievable. They were the enemy from the season before; they'd come back from twelve points behind and won the title. It was a proper calling card as far as Newcastle were concerned – the victory was even sweeter given that Shearer had turned down Sir Alex that summer to come back to his hometown.

But I couldn't feel a proper part of it — as I've said, I was on the periphery.

What eventually happened was that I was told I was going out on trial. Obviously, this sounded strange at first, and it took me a little while to figure it out. It turned out that Coventry were off to Jersey on a training camp; they had a friendly lined up and they wanted to take a look at me. I went over and played in that game alongside Noel Whelan, and I scored three times. After my return to Newcastle, things moved swiftly. I got a phone call to say that Coventry had agreed a fee, and did I want to go and talk to them? I said yes; moving didn't bother me much, because I knew I had to do something.

The fact that Coventry wasn't too far from Nottingham possibly helped, but I'd have gone anywhere really. I just needed to be playing. In truth, I'd have signed for Millwall if they'd come in for me. One, I'd have been playing; two, a few of the Millwall players had told me how much they were earning, and all of them were on more than me. I'm not saying I was a Premier League player then, but I was at a Premier League club, and I was making less than everyone I spoke to at a Division Two club.

So, if I knew then what I know now, would I have moved to Newcastle? I'd have to say yes, but it was a tough time. There were periods there in which I did nothing but train. Obviously, there was a lot of soul-searching. I would be thinking: 'What's going on now? Am I going to end up going back to Lincoln? Am I going to end up back playing at that kind of level?' Without getting onto the pitch, I couldn't tell if I was a Premier League player; I worried that I was going to be one of those who spends their career flitting up and down the leagues. I needed to test myself at the top table before my confidence dipped too badly.

Shearer was always going to play. So was Ferdinand. And then there was Tino, Beardsley and the rest. At that age, I was always going to be sixth or whatever in the queue. But you knew there was a reason. It wasn't because you lacked ability. It was because the ones that were in front of you were better, at that time at least. Coming in from Lincoln, I had to know my place.

I think Newcastle understood my position. And, let's be honest, they made £500,000 in a year, doubling their money. I went to Coventry for £1 million. It wasn't bad, given that I'd played less than two games for the Geordies.

For me, it was — ultimately — a valuable learning experience. I trained with players who were amongst the best in the world, which helped my game no end in the long run and showed me the attitude you need to get on at the highest level. Wherever I've been, I've tried to learn, to take both the good bits and the bad bits in. Being around the likes of Shearer, Beardsley, Ginola, and Ferdinand is about as good an education as a young player can get.

I needed to put that education into practice, and to feel wanted. Millwall wanted me and, after the trial game, Coventry did too. I felt really lucky to get another crack at the Premier league straight away, but I didn't know what was around the corner. And I was going to Highfield Road as a million-pound player, which was strange as I felt I hadn't played enough games to justify the fee.

I'd come from Lincoln, made two appearances for Newcastle and six for Millwall, and become a million-pound player. At twenty years of age. All that put me under a little bit of pressure straight away. I'd proved nothing in the Premier League, so it was a massive, massive gamble for Coventry.

3. STRACH'S REVOLUTION

Match: Coventry City vs Newcastle United
Venue: Highfield Road
Competition: FA Premier League
Date: Tuesday, December 17, 1996
Result: Coventry City 2, Newcastle United 1
Attendance: 21,538

Coventry City: Ogrizovic (Burrows, 90 mins); Shaw, Williams, Daish, Telfer; McAllister, Richardson, Salako, Whelan (Jess, 77 mins); Dublin, Huckerby
Subs (not used): Genaux, Boland, Filan

Newcastle United: Srnicek; Peacock, Watson, Elliott, Albert; Lee, Beardsley, Ginola, Gillespie; Shearer, Ferdinand
Subs (not used): Kitson, Clark, Hislop, Brayson, Barton

STRACH'S REVOLUTION

I officially signed for Coventry City on November 23, 1996. Gordon Strachan had been appointed manager just three weeks earlier, succeeding Ron Atkinson who had been made Director of Football.

Noel Whelan had already been signed by Atkinson from Leeds by the time that we first played together in that trial match in the Channel Islands. I think Noel was actually bought on Gordon's recommendation after the two of them played together at Leeds; Strachs was just the first team coach at Coventry then, working under Ron.

It wasn't a proper serious game in Jersey, but you could still tell that some of these players had real ability. It was my first game with Dion Dublin, and there was Gary McAllister too, a superb player who pulled the strings in midfield. You just got the feeling that they all could play. The day that I turned up to play in that trial match was actually Gordon's first day as manager. I don't know whether they had been grooming him to take over the top job, but I was his first signing.

From the off, Strachs and I clicked. Kind of. It was always a love-hate thing. I think he saw potential in me and wanted to work on it – Gordon's biggest asset is probably that he always wants to make you into a better player. There's no doubt that, for a lot of managers that I've worked with, it was just about the performance they expected from you on a Saturday. Gordon actually wanted to improve my game, which was very important to me.

When we talked about the move I didn't insist that I had to play games, but I do remember that, when we were negotiating the contract, that I didn't let him push me around as much as Newcastle had, even though I was probably in a similar bargaining position. I made sure that I was paid fairly for what I was going to do. But, of course, I wanted to go there and play games. So while I didn't say: 'I'm coming here and I've got to play!' my message was very much: 'You give me the chance and, hopefully, I'll produce the goods for you...'

Money-wise I made a pretty big jump, going from £400 a week to £1,600, which was quite an increase for a twenty-year-old. Phil Smith, my agent, was there again, but this time I fought my corner a lot harder. Being a year older had given me the extra confidence to negotiate the terms more and stand up for myself.

It was a three-year deal and they were paying a million pounds for me – a lot of money for a club like Coventry. But when I first arrived, I don't think anyone there envisioned the impact I would have at the club. From that very first get-together in Jersey, it just felt right. I was pretty lucky in that some of the older lads took me under their wing straight away. I'm talking about Paul Williams, Richard Shaw, Paul Telfer and, of course, Noel Whelan, who everyone called Snowy because he settled easily.

We all bonded straight away, and then there were the likes of big Dion, Kevin Richardson and the skipper, Gary Mac, who were the older heads in the team.

I think both Richard Shaw and Paul Williams could see that I was lively and messed about quite a bit, so they both worked on helping me settle in as quickly as possible. I was a bit sparky; I did act the idiot. But that was bit of a ploy. Because it's hard going somewhere where you're not established, and you need to find a way of fitting in. In his book, Gordon wrote that I always acted the idiot, but deep down, when I was on my own, I was a little bit different. I think he saw that serious side when I was negotiating my contract at Coventry. It's just easier to blend in if you're making the jokes – or you're the butt of the jokes. And, especially in those early days, I needed to fit in.

When it came to the training ground, there was definitely a time to work and a time to play. And Strachs worked an awful lot with me – and a lot of that happened when everyone else had gone home. It might just be me, Dion, and the kids in the afternoon, working away on our partnership. No-one saw that.

All they ever saw was the work that we put in on a Saturday. But there we were, every single day, putting the time and effort in. I can only assume that Strachs brought me to Coventry specifically to play alongside Dion; I would assume that he went for the old 'big man, quick man' combo – and it worked, straight away.

My first appearance was as sub in the derby against Villa, but after that I think I started in the majority of the matches Coventry played while I was there. While we lost two-one, it took me very little time to make an impression; with almost my first touch, I took it past Steve Staunton and laid it back for Dion to score with a tap-in. I spent much of the remainder of the game terrorising Gareth Southgate, and I felt pretty pleased about my performance as I came off. Phil Smith also represented Mark Bosnich, Villa's keeper, and, because Bosnich was injured that day, the two were sitting together in the stands. Bosnich was apparently asking questions along the lines of 'Who's that kid?', and I got a similar response from Des Lynam on Match of the Day that night.

However, I wasn't allowed to feel pleased with my showing immediately. As I came off, I was told I'd been picked by the drug testers and I had to supply a sample. It was my first time, and I'll never forget it. As it always has done subsequently – you're extremely dehydrated after a game, and the tester watches you very carefully, which is off-putting – it took me some time to, well, produce the goods, and I had to drink loads of water to get my system going again. Obviously, this meant that I had to stop two or three times while I was driving to Nottingham that evening as nature took its course.

For whatever reason, I've been tested loads and loads of times in my career. I once got really frustrated with being asked to give a sample after Norwich had just lost four-nil to Palace; in fact, I kicked a wall in anger and got a warning from the FA regarding my future conduct. What's odd is that I haven't ever been aware of anyone using performance enhancing drugs, which I suspect aren't really a problem in football. In contrast, the vast majority take anti-inflammatories at some time or other, purely because the amount of wear and tear the game subjects you to means you're often in pain. Perhaps they should be regulated – when I went out to the States, the doctors were genuinely concerned at the amount of them I'd taken, and sent me to hospital to get my kidneys checked.

Looking at that Coventry line-up now, it's plain to see that there were a lot of solid players in there. I think Gordon would say that his team was built on really solid foundations. They were pretty much all hardened, established Premier League players. And Gordon went on to mould that team around me and Dion; the whole thing was set up to give us a platform to cause other teams problems. Dion and I clicked straight away – on the pitch, at least. It wasn't one of those situations where you're out drinking together all the time; it wasn't that kind of friendship. In fact I was a lot closer to him personally when he came back here to Norwich. When I was at Coventry I was one of the younger ones, and he was one of the older ones. Later, when we joined together again in Norfolk, I was one of the older ones – and he was one of the ancient ones.

I've got a lot of time for Dion. He's top, top bloke. And I appreciate everything that he did for me back then because I am one hundred per cent certain that if we hadn't had his presence up front at Coventry I would never have got the goals that I did. I suspect he will probably say the same thing – that I created a lot for him.

As the focal point of the team, he took so much pressure off me. That meant I could get on with my own stuff. Dion won all the headers. He roughed people up if they needed roughing up. And if someone was getting on my back, he would go and sort them out. That's what Dion did – he was a leader. Always has been.

I think that a good understanding underpins any great front pairing. And Dion and I had a great understanding. He wasn't just a big lump – he brought people in, was clever with the ball. He didn't just flick the ball on, he'd put it right into your path all the time. It makes your life so much easier when you've got someone alongside you who is really, really good.

Dion would be the one who would generally stay in the middle while I'd be the working the wings and running the channels – the way we understood our roles made us one of the best strike partnerships in the Premier League. Nowadays, teams like Coventry were then – the likes of Wolves and Bolton – don't end up with strikers that pair up that well. It just doesn't happen – bigger clubs would come in and break them up. So we were a one-off.

Dion leaving a few seasons later was the beginning of the end for what Strachs had built at Coventry. When I first joined, Gordon's project was just beginning. Of course, this was his first managerial job, and he was still playing too. That didn't make it easy for him, even though – at forty – he was still one of the best players at the club.

In training he never gave the ball away. In demos, he could hit the top corner with his right foot; he could hit the top corner with his left foot. You couldn't ask for much more. Being able to show that kind of ability obviously builds respect. We'd be doing shooting drill and he'd say, 'I want it like this!' then hit a sixty-yard ball wide with his left-foot and volley it into the top corner when the winger put it back in.

'That's how you do it!' he'd say. Great players can do that.

As I've said, the Strachan way of playing revolved around a solid base and Dion and I. I think he's even admitted that. Dion and I – and maybe Noel – were who he based his team on. Well, us and Gary McAllister's ability on the ball, his set pieces and his corners. We weren't a long-ball team, but we got it forward early and tried to cause other teams problems. You've got to play to your strengths, work with the players you've got. No-one could say a team with Kevin Richardson and Gary McAllister were a long-ball team, but we were direct and didn't just knock it around for the sake of it. We knew that Dion was great in the air; we knew that I was quick; we knew that teams didn't like getting turned round; we knew centre-halves don't like running. So we played to our strengths.

And we mixed it up well. When we wanted to keep the ball, we could do. Gary McAllister was technically one of the best footballers I've ever played with. But there was always that steel there; we knew that that if we knocked it up to Dion, he'd go and smash the centre-half if needs be.

Dion is a lovely, gentle fella off the park, and his demeanour and presence make the players around him better. I've no doubt he did that for me. Once he crosses that white line, though, he changes. He's an out-and-out winner, and there's a nasty side to him. You can't play at the level he did and get so many goals unless you're willing to do the dirty thing occasionally. I'm not saying that Dion would drop an elbow on someone for no reason – he's not that kind of dirty. But you have to be able to look after yourself.

There were big centre-halves out there trying to smash him – over his career he's broken his neck, broken his legs, had cuts here, there and everywhere. He's had all sorts of injuries. So you've got to be able to look after yourself when you're playing in a competition as tough as the Premier League

Some will probably think that I'd respond to someone smashing into me by waiting two minutes and saying, 'Meet my friend, Dion.' I guess that did happen occasionally, but that didn't make him a dirty player. Just a big, strong one who looked after himself and could sort someone out if he had to.

My own way of looking after myself was different. I didn't go in with flying tackles or big headers, I'd just try and expose the opposition in different ways. I'd drift out wide to cut back in. So we had a good balance, and a good understanding as a team. We were able to play the right way, while being able to put other teams under a lot of pressure. And everyone knew what they were doing; we were solid like that.

Look at some of the other names in that team – Kevin Richardson, for example. I used to batter him absolutely every day because he was so old. He was thirty-five, thirty-six. It wasn't until later that I realised that he'd won the old First Division title twice, first with Everton and then with Arsenal – and there I was calling him an old fogey, a pensioner and everything else. When you're young, you don't always recognise what great players you have around you.

That's the thing. Gary McAllister had won the title with Leeds; Richard Shaw and John Salako had both been in the Crystal Palace side which nearly won the FA Cup in 1990 and finished third in Divison One the season after. We had a bunch of good, solid pros. But then you look at that Newcastle team that we played that night, and see that, at £15 million Shearer probably cost more than our entire squad put together.

We had McAllister and Richardson in the middle; Sally was a very good left-winger; Snowy would play wide right. But you couldn't call Noel an out-and-out winger – he was one of those that could play anywhere along the front-line, out on the left, or in midfield. He was probably a year older than me and had come in from Leeds for £2 million, a fee which meant that there was pressure on him as well.

Pressure or no pressure, the banter was great – as it is in any good dressing room. The ringleaders were usually Richard Shaw, Paul Williams and Paul Telfer – to be honest, I just jumped on their bandwagon. They were good times. I've been at a lot of clubs, and that was one of the closest dressing rooms I've been in.

I wouldn't say we were punching above our weight exactly, but we were mixing it with the big guns a lot of the time. The fact that there were a good few times where we came out on top is a credit to those players, Gordon's organisation, and our ability to play in a certain way which caused problems for the other team.

And you can't forget Steve Ogrizovic – Oggy – in goal. He's larger-than-life, to say the least. When I joined he was nearly forty and coming up to the end of his career, but he was one of the hardest workers I have ever seen. First in, last out. He was also one of the bravest. I know he wasn't the best-looking man in the world, but he would put his head right in there if it stopped a goal. He would dive, head first, at a striker's feet time after time. And it takes a certain type of bravery to do that. I know I couldn't.

He was massively into his cricket and was, simply, a Coventry legend. Some will argue that he's Coventry's greatest-ever player, which would be some achievement. He'd have earned that accolade – he played six hundred-odd games over a twenty-three-year career, and played a huge part in them winning the FA Cup, one of the club's biggest achievements. I still see him from time-to-time and he's just the same decent bloke.

The two leaders, though, were Gary McAllister and Dion. None of the lads were shy in terms of chucking their views forward, but it was definitely Gary Mac and Dion that led.

I'd been there no more than a month before Newcastle arrived at Highfield Road on that Tuesday night – just a week before Christmas. And I was nervous, to be honest, playing them again so soon after the move. I was part of the squad, but not part of that Newcastle team, not part of the inner circle. There was obviously an incentive to show them what they'd missed out on.

So it was a big game. And it started off perfectly.

Remember, I still hadn't scored a goal for Coventry at this stage.

And I scored after six minutes. And, trust me, it doesn't get much better than that.

Kevin Richardson put the ball through and it was basically a race between me and Philippe Albert. No disrespect to him, but there was only going to be one winner. I got to it and finished it well; it was just an amazing start to a game that I desperately wanted to win. If I remember correctly, I just kept on running into the corner by way of celebration and then nearly slipped over on the side of the pitch.

As a striker, you've only really 'arrived' at a new club when you score your first goal. Once you've done that, the pressure lifts – for a little bit, anyway. And then you can enjoy the rest of the game, which is exactly what I did. I set up Gary McAllister's goal for the second; I ran down the line, put it across and he knocked it in from about ten yards. There were no digs from me towards the Newcastle lads once I'd scored. I'm not that type, and I had far too much respect for them as players. I knew how hard they worked, and how much ability they had – I just wouldn't have done that.

We certainly weren't expected to beat Newcastle that night. We were in a dog-fight at the bottom; a genuine relegation battle which would go on until the end of the season. And look at Newcastle's front four – Beardsley, Alan Shearer, Les Ferdinand, Ginola. Players right out of the top drawer.

With half an hour left on the clock, Shearer scored – and then it was game on. We fought and fought to cling on. When you're fighting for your lives down at the bottom of the table, you'll take any kind of win. But we deserved it when it came. We played well and caused them a lot of problems.

Of course, there were a few headlines in the papers – 'Hucks back to haunt Keegan!' and that kind of thing – which was nice. It kind of made me feel better, because I knew that he let me go. But, as I've said, fair play to him – I was never going to play there, so in the long run he was doing me a favour. Afterwards, I think he said, 'Well done!' Kevin's not one to hold grudges – he's a decent fella. And why would there be a grudge, anyway? Newcastle made a £500,000 profit, and Coventry, I'd like to think, got a good player who was learning the game and who went on to be a good servant.

You are aware of this '£1 million' price tag attached to your head, but you have no choice in the matter, and no say in how much your value is. Are you worth it? Well, you can never tell until the end of your contract. It's only then that people look back and say: 'Well? Did we get good value for money?'

I was lucky in that Coventry did get good value for money. Not only did I score a good few goals for them which helped keep them in the Premier League, but in the end, they sold me for five times what they paid for me. Not bad, all in all.

With Dion there, I would look to play on the shoulder of the last defender – and that's why, at Coventry in particular, I got caught offside so often. I think one season I had the record for the number of offside calls made against me.

But I always thought that if I got caught three or four times, there'd always be one or two times where I got in… that was the theory, anyway. My problem was that I was sometimes too quick for my own good, and always so eager to get in behind. So by the time that the linesman had looked up, I was already five yards past where the defender was. And we'd look back on the videos and see that I was clearly onside. Even so, I should have learned my lesson and tried to take my time a bit more.

There was many a time when I'd drive Strachs to distraction because I'd do my own thing. There were quite a few ding-dongs. I was reading an old newspaper report the other day which said the police had to separate us at Newcastle once.

I honestly can't remember it, but apparently he was trying to strangle me – and I was trying to get at him. But it was definitely love-hate. He used to be on my case all the time. Against Arsenal that season I didn't pass to him when he had a chance to score, and missed with my own shot; he subbed himself off because, as he put it, he'd have strangled me otherwise. Whenever he was having a go at me, though, it was always for my own good. I see that now, at least, but at the time I sometimes wondered if he was picking on me. I gave as good as I got, though.

But as a kid – before I really knew the game – I would try and do silly things. I'd try and beat five players instead of beating two and then laying it off, or try something else ridiculous. I was still young, and I didn't know the game like I do now. I'd played twenty or so games in Division Three, half a dozen with Millwall in Division Two, and made a couple of appearances in the Premier League with Newcastle.

So I was very raw. But I had very good natural attributes – I just didn't really know how to use them effectively. I'd compare it to a golfer and his decision making process – which club to select; which shot to make. 'Do I lay it up here? Or do I drive for the pin? Do I use a three-wood? Or a four iron?' Back then I could cause absolute chaos in the opposition half; they didn't know what to do. Sometimes, however, I wouldn't make the right decisions, which I know was really frustrating for my team-mates.

I'd go from the sublime to the ridiculous. I'd beat five men and try to bend one in the corner or I'd beat three men and try something even crazier. I played instinctively. Funnily enough, Brian Borrows took me for my Level Three coaching course recently and that's what he told me. He said that I was one of those players that you could only coach so much, because a lot of what I did I did naturally. So, looking back, I think Gordon was just trying to channel the natural, individual attributes that I had into a team game and a team environment.

Gary Mac and Dion, likewise, must have been frustrated at times; I'd try this and go and lose the ball for the third time on the trot or whatever. But I think Dion knew that – eventually – something would happen. It's not like I'd try something once and then I'd drift out of the game. I would keep trying. I wasn't one of these that would let my head drop and then disappear for the rest of the game. I would keep going and going and going, until something happened.

There had to be a mix. It couldn't always be encouragement; there were times when Dion or Gary Mac or someone would say: 'Come on, Hucks. That's the fourth time you've lost the ball trying to beat people...' So you sometimes need a bollocking. I had my fair share and, as I say, Gordon was on my case five days a week. But it was only to make me better, which he achieved. The work that I got through there and the work that I got through with Dion after everyone else had gone home helped me learn the game and made me a better player. By the time I played for Manchester City and Norwich, I was much, much more consistent.

There were a lot of big characters in the Coventry dressing room – Snowy was particularly memorable. Noel was one of those that just wanted to please people. He had a heart of gold, which probably got him into a lot of trouble, but he was a great lad. It's just that he wanted to be everybody's mate.

He was definitely one of the most talented players that I've ever played with. He was six-foot two, could run all day, had two great feet and unbelievable technique, and he could head it. While he wasn't rapid, he was quick enough. All in all, he offered the perfect template for any would-be attacking midfielder.

He had a bit of everything – that's what was so good about him. He was good on the ball, but he had a great engine as well. He could literally run up and down all day without getting tired. It's not often that you find a player with the mix of attributes that Snowy had.

Usually a player's either quick or they're strong. Or they're good on the ball. He had the whole package.

Where did it all go wrong for him? Well, he probably drank a little bit too much. And as I say, I think he just wanted to please people so much that he'd end up in situations when he probably should have been at home putting his feet up in front of the TV.

Some of the things that happened were crazy, and you wish you could have sat down with him and had a word. But we were all young lads at the time. I was with Lyndsey, so I'd only go out for a drink occasionally.

But Noel and Paul Telfer would spend a lot of time together. Telf could handle it; Snowy probably couldn't. Together, they were something of a double act. Both lived in Leamington, and I guess they went out a bit too much. Telf was one of those who could drink twenty pints or whatever the night before without letting it show in training, but Snowy couldn't do that. His inability to say 'no' was his downfall.

People would say, 'Snowy, you coming out?'

And he couldn't say, 'No, I'm not' – it was always a case of him saying, 'Yeah, why not? Just the one…'

I remember when I was getting my ankles strapped one morning and he came in limping. He said: 'Hucks, go and get the physio, but don't tell Gordon…'

'Why, what's happened?'

He sat on the physio's bed. Basically he had twenty-five stitches in his Achilles because the night before he'd tried to put his foot through a window and someone in A&E had had to sort him out. He'd been out with Telfs somewhere and he could literally have had his leg chopped off. That put him out for three or four months.

There are only so many times you can do that before something has to give. Gordon found out, of course, and I think he actually had him living with him for four or five weeks. Strachs made Noel move in with him. It was just mental, looking back now. He needed help, but whatever people tried, they didn't really get through to him. He's a completely different person now – recently, I played with him in the Leeds Masters team – and, as I say, he was still a great lad. He wasn't a horrible one, he was lovely – everyone liked him; everyone got on with him. He just wanted to please people too much.

So, was it tough to play Premiership football every week? Did it drain me – physically and mentally?

To be honest, I didn't find it that tough. I used to love Christmas when the games came thick and fast; when there was a game every two days. Of course now – when you get older – it's a lot harder. But at twenty? I was ready for game after game after game. It didn't really matter how often they came. I just wanted to play. Especially in those early days at Coventry. If we'd had to play a match every two days it wouldn't have mattered to me.

I still spent a lot of time in the gym, as I had done since the age of fourteen. Dion, though, didn't do any weights at all – seriously, he did none. It was funny. It was only when he came back to Norwich later on that he was in the gym every day. He told me that getting a bit older meant he had to get more physical to make up for not being as quick.

Looking back now you can see that we'd followed similar paths to get to Highfield Road. Mine went Lincoln, Newcastle, Coventry; he'd gone from Cambridge to Manchester United to Coventry. He'd gone from the lower leagues to the top and then had to re-evaluate where he was and where his career was going.

I think the difference with Dion was that he'd played a lot of games with Cambridge – over one hundred and fifty, in fact – whereas my story was more a case of 'Bang! Bang! Bang! You're there...' With Cantona at Manchester United, he had to go elsewhere to play football. He was far too good to sit on the bench.

But, like me, I definitely think he came in with a point to prove. Manchester United had paid £1 million for him and he'd moved on to Coventry for £2 million after a move to Everton had fallen through. There was pressure on him, like there was on Snowy and I. People would have thought of him as a lower league player; he'd only played a handful of games at United, so he had it all to prove again.

Injuries didn't help us that season. I can remember Liam Daish did his cruciate in training. I still remember crossing the ball, and he was suddenly on the floor in a heap. It's hard to forget that, because you could tell, straight away, that he'd done his knee.

We all know that it happens in football. But it's awful. It's the worst thing that you can see – especially on the training pitch. In a game – fair enough – things happen. But on the training pitch, where you're all basically mates? If someone goes down in training with a serious injury it means a lot more.

Perhaps it meant even more than usual for that group of lads. You have to remember that it was only the April before I'd arrived that David Busst had done his leg at Manchester United. People still call it the worst injury ever sustained in the Premier League – it was a compound fracture to both the fibula and tibula. The players at Coventry knew full well how fine the line was between playing and being absolutely finished.

Bussty was still there getting treatment when I arrived in the autumn. There was no way he was ever going to play again. His leg looked like it had been in a car crash.

Arguably Bussty's injury pulled that dressing room together; made that group of lads tighter than most. Everyone would have seen the incident; seen a mate's career finish in an instant – and not just seen his career finish, but seen his leg in a real mess. I'm sure it will have affected everyone on the pitch that day. They might not have thought so at the time, but I bet – even years down the line – they still have a thought for him.

That's the point. When supporters talk about how much footballers are paid, they don't remember that we have no idea how long our careers are going to last. I didn't play with David Busst, but I've played with others whose careers are cut short in their prime. It doesn't happen all the time, but you are only ever one bad tackle away from being finished. There's always a chance that it can happen.

And I was getting whacked constantly. Constantly. It got to the stage where Gordon was saying that the referees had to do something to protect me. Whacking someone is always an easy option; the best defenders are the ones that don't get the yellow cards, and defend properly.

But getting whacked is part and parcel of the game. What would I do if I was a defender and I couldn't run as fast as a forward like me? It's the easiest way to try and stop somebody, especially back then when the attacker wasn't so well-protected. Obviously it wasn't like the 60s and 70s when people were just taking lumps out of each other, but fifteen years ago there were still some hefty tackles going in. It is difficult for referees. I like to moan at refs like everyone else – actually, I definitely moan more than most. But I got kicked more than most, so it worked both ways. I think the best way to referee me would be to keep giving me free kicks all the time…

The best referees – and I think it's been said many times before – were the ones that would return your banter back. I can't be doing with the ones that don't want to know – whatever's happened. If you can't talk to them, then your frustration just builds up and builds up. I probably got twice as many cards for mouthing than I ever did for tackling. There are some who know how to speak to you, like Mark Clattenburg – I was playing for Newcastle Reserves in one of the first games he ever took, and he was really approachable. Some aren't though. And I saw the red mist loads of times – never in a malicious way, but if someone whacks you every time you get the ball what are you supposed to do?

Of course, as soon as you've got a defender booked then the tide turns; then they can't really touch you again – otherwise they'll be off.

There's loads of things that never really get seen. I remember Martin Keown, who'd be grunting, screaming down your neck, and pinching you every time the ball came near. That was an old pro doing what he did best. It's just part and parcel of the game and Martin Keown was one of the best defenders I ever played against. He was quick; he was strong; he was aggressive; he put his foot in. And I think that's all you can ever ask for from a top defender.

And if he didn't get you, then Steve Bould or Tony Adams would be waiting just behind him ready to snap you. Arsenal had two good full-backs in Lee Dixon and Nigel Winterburn – they were a tough nut to crack. I don't think I ever scored against them for Coventry, although I remember a game where we drew two-two and all four of those defenders were playing. It was quite funny, because Keown had to go off just before half-time because he'd pulled his hamstring – chasing me.

I was developing a good relationship with the fans, but I didn't see a lot of them away from Highfield Road. We'd found a house in Loughborough, which is basically halfway between Nottingham and Coventry. This meant that, for the majority of the time, I'd either be back in Nottingham or out in Loughborough. We didn't consciously avoid living in Coventry, but I wanted to be able to work there while being close to my family and friends in Nottingham.

At the time Gary McAllister lived nearby in Ashby-de-la-Zouch; he was five minutes from me and we used to drive in together every morning and go to the games together. And that was good too – in those car journeys I got to listen to the insights of one of the best midfielders in the Premier League.

Day in, day out I'd listen to him. Just hearing his thoughts about the game, about different players, he was a fountain of knowledge for any young player learning the game. We got pretty close. And then when he went on to play for Liverpool and I played for Manchester City, we again lived in the same area. So Lyndsey and I knew both Gary and his wife, Denise, very well.

Sadly, she was diagnosed with breast cancer in 2000 while seven months pregnant with their second son Oliver; this happened while Gary was at Liverpool. She would ultimately lose her fight against cancer in March, 2006. Awful. Just awful.

Gary is, quite simply, a top bloke, and he was a world class footballer. He maybe strikes people as a bit arrogant, if that's the right word, but to me he's just one of those people who is incredibly proud of everything that he's achieved. I'm privileged to have played with him.

And I'd like to think that the supporters at Coventry had a lot of time for the both of us. I was one of those that would always have a go. If things weren't working out then there was always a chance that I could do something out of the ordinary – something unexpected. I think that's true of wherever I've been. Even at Leeds, where I didn't really show them what I could do, I think they still appreciated the way that I tried to play.

We all know that going to watch football is not cheap these days, so people demand entertainment. Of course, on one level it's all about winning for the fans – but they also want players to get them out of their seats, get them involved in the game, give them something to shout about. Even if it's for the wrong reason, the supporters want to go home after the game having been brought to their feet by events on the pitch.

I wouldn't say that Gordon sent out his team to entertain – he sent it out to win. If he could have us entertain, though, he would.

What I would say is that he is probably one of the best coaches I've worked with. In fact, I saw him more as a coach than a manager. I know that sounds weird, but he was always at his happiest when he was out there on a training pitch working with people. I don't think he enjoyed the other side of the management 'game' – signing players, dealing with the Press, and everything else. I know one hundred percent that he was at his happiest making players better. He was far closer to the players than most managers are. Don't get me wrong, not everybody liked him. He had a certain way about him – he was short-tempered. Scottish. However, for all my fall-outs with him, I did get on really well with him.

He would hammer me all the time, and it's only these days that I realise that he was just trying to get the best out of me, and that I was lucky to have him. Especially at that time in my career – when I was just making a name for myself in the Premier League – it was great that he would take the time to work with me in the way that he did.

He didn't have to; a lot of managers wouldn't have done it. A lot of them don't care whether you get better as a player or not; they're only bothered about what you do for ninety minutes on a Saturday afternoon. I'll always be grateful to Gordon for being willing to help me down the line by helping bring my game on.

So Dion and I would come in again in the afternoon and work with the kids. All the rest of the lads would have gone home, but we'd be in again – just to work on our partnership. At the time I'd be thinking: 'Wait a minute, I'm playing in the Premier League at the weekend...' But it's now – fifteen years later – that I can see that he just wanted to make me a better player, and that if, in the fullness of time, I go into coaching I will definitely adopt that attitude. There's always enough time in the day to make yourself a better player. You can work on your finishing, your crossing, or your fitness, or do some weights. There's no excuse to slack off – you can always find the time.

It wasn't ever really a case of me going out there to prove Strachs wrong. I could play, and I could do stuff that other people couldn't do – and I know that he knew that. Still, it's hard getting dug out every day, especially when it happens in front of other people. In fairness, it's not as if I was the shrinking violet type. I gave as good as I got and, on occasion, I would purposefully set out to try and wind him up. He had a rule that said we weren't allowed to wear hats in the dining room – so I would wear a hat every day, and he'd have to tell me to take it off.

To be honest, I never wore a hat before that; I was just doing it to get on his nerves.

Strachs was big on time-keeping as well. I remember I arrived late for a game — a pre-season game, I hasten to add — once and he told me to go home. It didn't matter that it was a nothing match — he just said: 'No, not here on time. Just get in your car and go home.' And all that had happened was that I'd got caught in the traffic somewhere. Since that disagreement, I've always tried to be on time. I think it is very important.

It proved to be a relegation fight right till the end of the season that year, one of those ones that goes right down to the wire. Three were going down; Forest were long gone, but there were still spots to fill on the last weekend with a few teams in the mix. We knew that if Sunderland lost and we won we'd be safe — they were at Wimbledon, before they became MK Dons, and we were at Spurs.

We'd lost at home to Derby the week before. As we went down to White Hart Lane, we thought we could do it, but deep down we were all thinking that we were done for if Sunderland got a result. Had we gone down, the team would have been broken apart. Players like Gary Mac and Dion were way too good for the First Division, so it was hugely important that we stayed up.

We kicked off fifteen minutes late — there'd been traffic jams on the M1, I believe. On the final day of the season, everyone is meant to kick off at the same time, but we were delayed. Clearly, this didn't bother us, as Dion scored early from a Gary Mac cross. Gary then provided again, setting up Paul Williams to score from a corner. We were two-nil up.

And then, just before half-time, Paul McVeigh — of all people — got a goal back, scoring on his debut for Spurs. Just as in the Newcastle game earlier in the season we were hanging on and hanging on. The final whistle had gone at the other grounds before Oggy made a string of great saves – the first from Jason Dozzell, the second from Ruel Fox, then two in a minute from Dozzell and Neale Fenn. It was an onslaught.

We knew that Sunderland had lost; we just had to hang on for that last fifteen minutes. It was real backs-to-the-walls, it was just a matter of holding on. And we did. The sense of relief amongst us was amazing, and it meant so much to the fans. For teams like Coventry, relegation may well mean that you're never coming back – as has been proved since. Since they got relegated in 2001, they've never even looked like going back up.

I can tell you now that the atmosphere on a good night at Highfield Road was fifty-times as good as it ever gets at the Ricoh Arena – for me, moving has been one of the biggest downfalls of the club. The Ricoh is never full enough. At Highfield Road you might only have got 23,000-24,000, but when it was full it was rocking. Week in, week out. It was tight to the pitch, a great place to play. Plus, the playing surface wasn't always great and the big boys weren't very keen on that.

I think the celebrations that night were more about the pressure having come off us than anything. With about five to six games to go we were favourites to go down, then we managed to pull out some amazing results. We went to Liverpool and won two-one; we beat Chelsea three-one at home the following game. But it was still odds-on that we were going down. In our favour, we had togetherness, belief, and a good mix of old heads and youngsters.

For me, as one of those youngsters, it mattered a lot, but I knew that I'd still have years of my career left to make up for it. The likes of Oggy, Richard Shaw, and David Burrows all knew the severity of getting relegated; they knew that if the club goes down, everything changes.

As I look back now on those first seven months as a Coventry player, I realise that I must have taken some of it all on board learning-wise. But at the time, I was just enjoying it – even when things weren't going well, because I'd gone from not playing at all, really, at Newcastle to playing every week. Of course, it was a learning curve, but you rarely take notice of that at the time. While it was happening, I just thought of myself as going out to play football and enjoying it. I was playing in the Premier League against the best players in the world when, two seasons before, I was only just breaking into Lincoln's first team. I was playing at a club that was less than an hour away from Nottingham and my family were coming to every game. It was really important for my Mum and Dad to be able to come and see me at that stage.

I was proud to play there. Despite their recent struggles, Coventry are a fantastic club. But there was so little in it that season, just one point between being a Premier League club and being a Divison One outfit. One point.

The thing about football, though, is that every season is a fresh start. Everyone forgets about the season you've just had – it's all about the new season, the blank slate, and still being in that top league.

4. TOE TO TOE WITH THE BIG BOYS

Match: Coventry City vs Manchester United
Venue: Highfield Road
Competition: FA Premier League
Date: Sunday, December 28, 1997
Result: Coventry City 3, Manchester United 2
Attendance: 23,054

Coventry City: Hedman; Nilsson, Burrows, Shaw, Williams, Hall; Telfer, Boateng (Boland, 64 mins), Whelan (Soltvedt, 77 mins); Dublin, Huckerby
Subs (not used): Ogrizovic, Lightbourne, Shilton

Manchester United: Pilkington; G Neville, Johnsen (Curtis, 63 mins), Pallister, Berg; Beckham, Scholes, Giggs, Solskjaer (Butt, 71 mins); Sheringham, Cole
Subs (not used): Culkin, McClair, Mulryne

Strachs added some really good players during my first summer at Coventry. Roland Nilsson came in from Helsingborgs for £200,000 and was excellent. He was thirty-three at the time, a Swedish right-back with over one hundred caps for his country – he'd played in their World Cup semi-final against Brazil in '94. On and off the pitch, the bloke was real quality. He was a top class fella who made time for everybody, and he worked ridiculously hard on his fitness, getting straight into the gym after every training session. He was no spring chicken, but he oozed class.

Over the course of my career I've played with many Scandinavians, and I think that they're one of the few groups of foreigners who don't really represent a gamble for a manager. You know what you're going to get with them.

That's not always the case when players come in from abroad. For instance, some South Americans – Tino was a prime example – find it hard to settle. It may well be because the football is different for them, whereas the Scandinavian game is similar to the English one in that they're both pretty workmanlike, so the players who come over from Sweden, Norway, and Denmark don't have much adapting to do. They tend to gel pretty quickly. There's no real language barrier either – they seem to find English very easy to pick up. That helps a lot.

Trond Soldvedt, a Norwegian who also joined that summer, was exactly the same as Roland, hard-working and unafraid to get his foot in. Because they fitted in so easily, the new signings didn't disrupt our preparations for the new campaign at all. And preparation, as you've probably realised, is a massive thing for me.

I was always, always prepared for games. For me, I think that makes a big difference, particularly when it comes to avoiding injuries. If you prepare as well as you can and something happens – you do your cruciate, for example – you can't really help that. But you can avoid the little injuries if you prepare in the right way. I've never had a problem with little pulls or that kind of thing; there have only been a few over the years.

Luck comes into it, obviously, but if you're physically in the right shape before every game then it's more than likely that you're going to be OK.

Diet is another huge factor when it comes to getting yourself ready. I've always watched what I eat. For years and years, I had this routine where I ate the same thing week in, week out. If we had a Saturday game, it would always be light through the start of the week, Thursdays would be pasta, and Friday would be chicken and mash. On the day of the game I'd like to feel light, so I'd always try to eat really, really early – if we had a three o'clock kick-off, I'd look to eat my pre-match meal at eight in the morning. Then I'd go back to bed.

As you can probably imagine, I would be a nightmare on away trips. I would get up early on purpose to go and get my pre-match in before everyone else. And when the game was on Sky, meaning a twelve o'clock kick-off, it would completely mess me up. I'd be up at five o'clock in the morning…

It's strange how little things like that can become part of your routine. It was essential for me to do things my way, but I'd see other lads – like Malky Mackay at Norwich – have piles of food for their pre-match meals at lunchtime. I couldn't. I had to be light going into games. I'd be thinking how's he going to run.

Routine is very important to me – it's all preparation. And as long as I'd had a good week in training and I'd prepared the right way then, in my mind, everything was ready for the game.

By the same token, if something knocked me out of that routine then I wouldn't be happy. There were times when I'd have loved to have eaten what I wanted, but I just didn't feel that I could. This was my job. After games? That was different, obviously. You could go and have a drink – in moderation, of course – with the other lads.

In the four or five days leading up to games, though, I always ensured that I was doing the right things. That said, in the summer of 1997 I probably didn't take my fitness as seriously as I did a bit later on in my career. It was my first pre-season under Strachs and we worked really, really hard. I wasn't the fittest lad there, but the odds are that I was one of them.

I was always fit, but I hadn't yet taken it to the extremes I was to later on. We came back and on our first run Strachan took us round some course that he'd set up and I was looking to beat him. And the old git beat me...

I tried to break him, but he was pretty strong mentally and, even at forty, in good physical shape. As I've said, he was great at setting the standard for what he wanted us to achieve on the pitch.

Unsurprisingly, pre-season was always pretty tough at Coventry, which was a good thing because it gave the measure of the squad's attitude. I've been at places where, within two or three days, people are saying they've pulled this, done that, or don't fancy doing something or other. At Coventry, I just saw twenty lads working hard, and there was never any risk of any of them chucking it in. You can't overstate what a difference that kind of thing makes.

It makes it much easier for a manager, too. If he sets something up and he knows it's hard, and that it taxes your willpower – basically, a lot of these things are set up to test how mentally strong you are – then it shows him what he needs to know. It makes it clear to him who is psychologically up for what lies ahead.

We came out that season with guns blazing – we won three-two against Chelsea on the opening day and Dion scored a hat-trick. That was the first time we got to see Dion beating up Chelsea. For some reason, he just loved playing against Frank Leboeuf. Obviously Leboeuf was a wonderful player, but I just don't think he could cope with Dion, who'd leave one on him every time they went up in the air together. Whenever we pumped it up there, you could see Leboeuf looking around and thinking,

TOE TO TOE WITH THE BIG BOYS

'Where's Dion?' If we wanted to prove how much of a handful we could be, we went about it the right way from Day One.

Chelsea had some quality players. They were just starting to get a few of the well-known foreigners in; Gianfranco Zola played that day, and they had Gus Poyet and Tore Andre Flo as well.

I think getting off to a start as good as that is almost more important for the fans than for the players. That's the thing about football. Over the summer, the slate is wiped clean and the supporters all go into the next season thinking, 'This is going to be the one!' As you go into that opening game there's no bitchiness – there's no 'We haven't spent this, we haven't bought him...' It's all about everyone's expectations being sky-high. And on that day we matched the fans' expectations.

I wouldn't say we were super-confident; obviously, the year before we had only beaten the drop by one point – and on the very final day of the season, too. But we knew we had the makings of a team that could hurt other teams in that division. If you've got that, you've got a chance. If you tell yourself that you can cause problems for the other team, you'll always have a better chance of putting teams on the back foot.

Saying that, I think for the vast majority of Coventry fans, the ambition for that season was simple: survival. Staying up. For a club of Coventry's size to be in the Premier League was still a massive achievement.

They might have had certain expectations about the way that they wanted to see their team play, but, as I've said, our tactics weren't set in stone. We mixed it up. We weren't a long-ball team; we adapted to the players that we had on the pitch. If we had to go long, we went long; if we could keep the ball, we'd keep the ball. Strachs would always have instructions for us, but there were elements that were, in a way, beyond his control. Noel could be called unpredictable; I was definitely impulsive. So he couldn't always say, 'We'll do it this way', because one of us would get it and try to do something completely different.

There was a general way of setting up, and we knew that, with the right preparation, the players we had could adapt around it. It was just important that we'd prepared properly for set-pieces and things like that. We were a massive threat from corners. Dion's second goal against Chelsea that season was a four-yard, near-post header from a Gary Mac corner which showed just how religiously we practiced them under Gordon on a Friday. Seriously, our corner preparation was religious. Someone once told me that Gordon got that from playing under Howard Wilkinson at Leeds – I heard that they also used to practice and practice and practice corners. Whether or not that's true, I know we certainly put the hours in on them.

My role was simple. I had to stand out of the way, or else to stand on the goalkeeper and hope that something would drop down to me. I don't think I've ever attacked a ball with my head from a corner – ever. And no-one has ever used me in that role. I was told either to stand on the goalkeeper or on the edge of the box. I had no interest in trying to go in anywhere and head the ball.

We'd spend a good twenty to twenty-five minutes on corners every Friday, preparing for the forthcoming game. It wasn't all about Gary Mac to Dion. Paul Williams was pretty decent in the air; Noel could head it; Marcus Hall could, too. But we'd worked out a specific corner for Dion at the near post – just like the one he got against Chelsea that day. He must have scored some fifteen goals in his Coventry career just by doing that – off that same, well-rehearsed, corner routine.

Dion's really hard to mark. It helps, of course, that he's big and strong and got a leap on him – it was a bit different later when he was thirty-eight or thirty-nine at Norwich and his legs couldn't really get off the floor like he used to, but when he was in his late twenties he was a real handful.

However, we suffered a massive blow that season which meant that we couldn't rely too much on set-pieces.

Gary Mac injured his knee in December and went on to develop a serious cruciate ligament problem. With the World Cup coming up in France in the summer, he tried to go without an operation, but the ligament went again and he was forced to have the surgery.

He'd tried to build it up with weights, keeping it simple so that he could get through the World Cup with Scotland. I think he knew that something wasn't right, but he was desperate to go to France. The rigours of Premiership football took their toll, however, and that was that.

A damaged cruciate ligament is, as we all know, the kind of football injury that really makes the headlines. These days surgery has improved, so the outlook for someone who suffers one is a lot better than it used to be. Now you're looking at six or seven months, then you're back playing again. Back then you'd be facing at least a year out and, of course, all the doubts about whether you'd be able to play to the same level you were at before. Gary, of course, went on to win a Treble of sorts – the League Cup, the FA Cup, the UEFA Cup – with Liverpool, so the operation was obviously a massive success. There's some, though, who can't reach their old standards after they've done their cruciate.

What happened with Gary was an enormous setback given how influential he was for us, both on and off the pitch. So much of our passing went through him and, obviously, a lot of Dion's goals came from his corners. No-one delivered a ball better than Gary Mac, so we'd lost one of the key weapons in our arsenal. It really rocked us.

Skipper-wise, Dion was a ready-made replacement. Some people don't need the armband to lead, and Dion was one of those. He speaks his mind, so there was no-one better in the squad to pick up where Gary had left off.

We had the captaincy covered, then, but the midfield needed reinforcing. That's where George Boateng came in – he was just young at the time, and we paid Feyenoord £250,000 for him. He gave us a lot of energy in the centre, and Coventry was where it all started for him. Afterwards, he went on to have a really good career at Villa and Middlesbrough.

So, we went into that game against Man United just after Christmas with no Gary Mac. The autumn had been mixed for me – I'd been playing well, but I'd had sad news on the personal front. We'd played West Ham and drawn one-all, our goal coming from me. After the match, I was pulled into Strachs' office. My Dad was in there, which was unusual given that family members didn't usually show up in the manager's room. It turned out that my Grandad had died on the morning of the match, and that my family had collectively decided not to tell me until after I'd played.

I'd love for him to have been able to watch that United game. You look at their line-up that day and it's incredibly, incredibly strong. The only thing you could say against it was that Peter Schmeichel wasn't playing – he was injured and they had Kevin Pilkington in goal.

Otherwise, they had Gary Neville, Gary Pallister, David Beckham, Cole, Sheringham, Giggs, and Scholes. Pallister was the taller of the two centre-halves, so he, rather than Johnsen, would be the one tasked with marking Dion.

Gary Neville was one of those that played the game hard, but fair. Just a good player, and not one that was ever particularly dirty. He wasn't overly fast; he wasn't overly-aggressive. Just a really solid player. I'd see him in the same way as I would two players I played with at Norwich – Adam Drury and Marc Edworthy. Obviously they're not quite at Neville's standard – he won eight or nine Premier League titles. But they were similar players in that you knew what you were going to get from them, namely a mark of seven or eight in the sports pages every single week. They will, sometimes, come up against players who'll get the better of them. But you'll take that as a manager if you know that, for the other thirty-five or thirty-six games in a season, they're going to be as good as you're going to get.

As for Ryan Giggs? In my opinion, he's the greatest Manchester United player of all time. I know people usually give that accolade to George Best, but Best was finished by the time he was in his mid-twenties. Giggs is now in his late thirties and he's still pulling strings, having adapted himself from a flying winger to a midfield schemer. To do that at the very top level verges on the ridiculous.

He's a one-off, which begs a big question. How are United ever going to replace him? Who else are you going to get who can give you twenty-one years of top flight football? And I know he's been used sparingly at times – Manchester United can do that because they've got that many players – but for him to still be playing in a Champions League semi-final against Chelsea in 2011, and look the best player on the park, is unbelievable.

He's lucky in the sense that he's always been one of those that's never carried any weight; Paul Scholes is exactly the same. But they must have looked after themselves to be in a good enough shape to play the kind of football that they do. I can't remember either of them ever having had really bad injuries. I'm sure that neither of them have ever done their knees badly and that makes a big difference.

Some people are just born to play forever, but they're the exceptions to the rule. Usually when you get to thirty-four or thirty-five, it's realistically the time to try something else.

Sheringham probably played on for so long because he was one of the cleverest footballers around. He wasn't one of those that relied on taking people on or winning big headers like Dion did. But he was a clever player; he always got himself in the right holes. And he was never that quick anyway; it wasn't like he ever lost any real pace. He just adapted his game very well.

They just had some great players – especially that front four or five. Andy Cole, Teddy Sheringham, Giggs, Scholes and Solskjaer. It was hard to see us beating them.

Maybe Dion had a point to prove that day against his old employers. I think you always do when you come up against one of your old clubs. You always want to do well. You want to prove to them that they shouldn't have let you go. That said, I know Dion isn't the type to hold a grudge. Well, only against a couple of people...

We took the lead in that game after only twelve minutes – Snowy finished smartly from close range after I'd worked hard to retrieve the ball from the byline – and we were playing pretty well. Then Manchester United did what Manchester United always do and steamrollered back into it. Solskjaer made it one-one, knocking it past Magnus Hedman after a step-over to beat Roland Nilsson that I've not seen many people do. It was as if he went past him in slow motion. After that, Sheringham gave them the lead with a diving header at the back post which followed a mix-up in our defence. He was about six inches off the ground to meet a cross from Scholes.

So they went two-one up. It all looked inevitable – they'd gone about fifteen games unbeaten, and seemed as if they were cruising to yet another title. By contrast, we'd lost six of our previous seven games. Not only that, but they'd beaten us three-nil at Old Trafford in August. It must have appeared to be something of a banker for the Manchester United fans.

In that context, what happened next was unbelievable. It must have been in the eighty-fifth minute or so; I was tight on the far touch-line and I managed to squeeze my way through two of them and darted on into the penalty area where Henning Berg panicked and brought me down. Dion smacked in the penalty, and we were level.

And then I scored arguably my most famous goal – the one that most people remember, even to this day.

Soltvedt put the ball into me on the right. And I cut in and beat Nicky Butt – Gary Neville was next, and I think I did well to stay on my feet as he tried to bring me down. I cut inside Berg and squeezed it past Pilkington. There were eighty-eight minutes on the clock. Snowy helped me by getting in the way of one of the defenders, but he also almost blocked me on my way through to the goal.

I've seen it again hundreds and hundreds of times. I guess I must have been thirty or forty yards out, and it was that late in the game that I thought I just had to keep running. You beat one, beat two, beat three and then, all of a sudden, you're one-on-one with the goalkeeper. At which point you just slip it past him and hope for the best.

Instinct took over that time. I'm not saying I was one of the best finishers; I was adequate. The top strikers just know what they're going to do naturally. They've got the knack. I got into dangerous areas just because of my ability to beat people, but I never had that ability to be in the right place at the right time, which is what proper poachers have.

And only the best players find those spaces. I look at someone like Shaun Goater, who I played with at Manchester City. People might not say he was a great all-round player, but he was a great finisher.

I found that knack that day.

At two-two with eighty-eight minutes gone – against the champions and league leaders – would Strachs have expected me to play safe? No, he'd have known what I was going to do; he'd have known that I would try and create something because that's what I tried to do every time that I had the ball. It was a magical moment. We were two-one down against the league leaders with five minutes to go and the fans must have been thinking the game was up. And, somehow, we turned them over.

I'm not saying that it was this one game that cost them the title that year, but it did seem to turn their whole season on its head. For it was after this match that Arsenal caught them up and went on to win the league. They lost their momentum after we beat them.

Every Coventry fan I've ever spoken to says that that was the greatest game there's ever been at Highfield Road. I know a lot of people will have seen it on the TV, but for people who were actually there to see it, it was something special. Even now, fifteen years down the line, people still go on about it.

Afterwards, Sir Alex just said it was 'ridiculous defending' – which he would do. He obviously wasn't happy because he would have been expecting to beat Coventry, particularly by the time that United had taken the lead.

But we were – at this stage – starting to play like a really good team. Six days later, we went to Liverpool in the third round of the FA Cup and beat them three-one. At Anfield. You don't do that unless you are a decent team.

We were just getting to that point where we were very strong and there was no-one we were afraid of playing. We had a couple of dodgy spells at the beginning, but, at Anfield, we outplayed Liverpool. Not many teams could claim to do that, given that they had the likes of Fowler, McManaman, and Ince playing. We came out of there with a three-one win, and it could have been a lot more.

I have to say that I was lucky in that I was one of those players that never got nervous going to places like Anfield and Old Trafford. I just really relished the chance to go out there and play.

Obviously it's great when you're at Anfield and they sing 'You'll Never Walk Alone' – you think, 'Wow! This is a proper place!' At the end of the day, though, it's still Them vs Us. Of course, you've got to appreciate you're playing against good players. You don't go in there thinking it's going to be a walk in the park.

But you have to hang on to the experience, because most people never get to have it.

The noise is always there; you can't tune it out. But you can use it to your advantage; you can play to it. And playing in those kind of games is special – although it's probably only years later that you really come to acknowledge just how special those atmospheres and those matches were. At the time, you're caught up in the moment and you just get on with it.

You don't know what each game means. At the time, it's just another three points. It's only when you look back at the end of the season that you see, for example, what a massive blow that defeat at Highfield Road was for Man United, what with them being that close, just five minutes away, from another victory.

As big a blow as it was for us to lose Gary McAllister in December, Trond Soltvedt, Telfs and George Boateng allowed us to deal pretty well with his absence. Much of that was down to the fact that we were so industrious – everyone worked really hard.

I guess on the back of the results we were starting to get and goals like the one I scored against United that day, I was starting to make a little name for myself. But it was more a case of Dion and I doing well together. We were seen as a difficult partnership, so I guess there would have been speculation about this move or that. But speculation is all it ever is.

By this stage, Dion and I didn't exactly know each other's games inside out. But, as I say, we'd worked hard on it. It wasn't ever like we were just chucked on up-front and it just clicked. We put time and effort into making it work.

That, in turn, was down to Gordon's determination to make me a better player. I wouldn't say that Dion was carrying me in those early days, but he was certainly using all his experience to make it work, while I was using all my various, raw attributes. Gradually, Dion and I developed this really good understanding. As a strike partnership, it was head and shoulders the best I've ever had.

In Dion you couldn't ask for any more – especially for someone with my playing style. He won ninety percent of his headers; he brought people in; he was a leader. You really couldn't ask for anything more, and his aerial ability meant that he could get a goal out of nothing.

By way of return, having me alongside him meant that he could stay in the middle and wait for the ball. I did a lot of my work out wide, so that was perfect for him as a centre-forward who liked to get on the end of things. Dion didn't want to be running around in the corners. That wasn't his game. So it was ideal for the pair of us.

It was a team thing; it wasn't ever wholly down to just me and Dion. But we worked so well together. And I was just as proud as he was when he won the award that season for being the top scorer in the Premier League. That's something that no-one can ever take away from him – being the top goal-scorer in the top league in the country.

Don't get me wrong; scoring is something else. But I do like creating goals; beating three men and knocking it across for your team-mate to tap in can sometimes give you more pleasure.

In some ways that was one of the reasons why I didn't like playing up front so much – there the pressure is absolutely always on you. That particular season things were going great; come the next season, when Dion had left, the pressure on me to score was intense. And then it's classed as a bad game if you don't score. You could cause chaos in the opposing box and set four chances up – all people see, however, is another game without a goal. And that's a tough thing for all forwards.

Dion was top goal-scorer with eighteen Premier League goals – alongside Michael Owen at Liverpool and Chris Sutton at Blackburn. Andy Cole would only get sixteen at United. I finished that season with fourteen. So for a one-two that's pretty good – thirty-two between us. Sutton and Kevin Gallagher got thirty-four between them.

The funny thing is that I don't look back at that year as my best; I was a much, much better player when I was at Norwich than I was at Coventry. I knew so much more about the game.

But my natural attributes – my pace and power, in particular – were at their best at Coventry. It's just that my know-how wasn't.

I did too many erratic things. I shot when I should have passed it; I tried too often to take too many players on. But I was still only twenty-one years old. As you grow older and wiser, you weigh up the percentages that much better; your decision-making improves. Still, I don't think anyone who saw me play at Norwich would say that I was a run-of-the-mill player as such.

The older you get, the more you learn, and you know when to do things and when not to do things. And I'd still get it wrong when I was at Norwich. Probably more than occasionally, too. But the vast majority of times, you'd get it right. And I guess, therefore, I became more reliable.

Gordon was still always on my case. But it was always well-meant. Of course, Ron Atkinson hadn't left; he'd just gone upstairs in a Director of Football role, a post he stayed in for a while before moving on.

Ron was a character, too. I remember I came in one day and I'd just bought a new car – it was a BMW Convertible. Silver. It had cost me a few quid and I came in and parked it right outside. I looked at it; it was brand new; I'm thinking: 'That looks the dog's bollocks, that does…' Sunny day, roof down, shades on.

I walked in. All the lads were there; they'd noticed my new car.

And I can remember Ron Atkinson saying: 'Nice car that, Hucks. That's what I'd have got if I didn't have any money…'

He said it in front of everybody. And I suddenly felt about two inches tall and went and hid in the changing room.

Ron was only there for a bit of the time that I was, but everyone liked him. Later on all that stuff came out about him being racist, but you look back and he brought five or six black players to Coventry and they were all one hundred percent behind him. I think he just came from a different era; he wasn't a racist. The cigars, the champagne… that's just the way he was. He was just very comfortable with himself.

I can remember one of my first days training – and you've come from Newcastle under Keegan where everything is set out perfectly – and Ron would come out, point and say: 'Right, we're going to run around that tree, that tree and that tree. Come back and then we'll be ready to go…'

That's just the way he was.

At this stage, I was earning decent money – £1,600 a week, perhaps a bit more with bonuses. But after these games – the win over United and the cup game at Anfield – I was probably one of the most sought-after young players in the Premier League, so a new contract wasn't long in coming.

In fairness, I suspect that Coventry knew that I only had a year and a bit left on my existing contract and they were just covering themselves. I was never one for banging on doors and saying: 'I should be getting this, should be getting that…'

I signed a new contract on the same day that I watched Dion make his full international debut against Chile in the February of that season. There'd been an England 'B' international against the same side the night before at WBA – I played in it, then sorted out my new deal the morning after. I went from £1,600 a week to £10,000 a week in one hit.

At the age of twenty-one, it was very strange having that kind of money coming in, particularly bearing in mind that it was little more than a year since I was on £400 a week. It was a massive jump. I bought a house and then invested everything else; I've always tried to be careful with money. Get a nice house, a nice car, and that's about it. I was never into gambling – maybe a tenner on the first goal-scorer in a game now and again.

But I've been lucky over the years in that I've worked with good people and I am, by nature, pretty cautious. Obviously I've spent money on holidays and other bits and bobs, and looked after friends and family here and there. But it was all a bit weird. Now I was paying twice as much in tax alone as I was earning before.

That sort of money is part and parcel of the game these days. I think the trick is to be able to put it into perspective and not to get too silly. I've always had a decent car, but I've never been one of those that changes his car every other month. I'd get one and then change it four or five years later; I've known people to get a new one two or three times a year.

The only thing that I do buy, and even then only occasionally, is watches. And that was Gary McAllister's fault. He got me into that. He bought a few as an investment, and I tried to be a bit like him. And it's never been the really blinged-up numbers. Those that know watches never buy diamonds. As soon as I stopped earning money, it stopped as a hobby. They'll go to the kids one of these days.

By this stage I'd also played four or five games for the Under-21s alongside players like Frank Lampard and Jamie Carragher. Peter Taylor was the manager and I think Darren Eadie, who was at Norwich at the time, was also part of that set-up.

It was OK going away with the Under-21s. I wouldn't say it was a chore, but sometimes − especially when the season has finished and you wanted a bit of a break − getting a call-up to the Under-21s could be bit of a ball-ache.

I'm not saying that representing your country isn't great. It's just that when you've played a tough game at the weekend and then you've got to go away to play another one in mid-week − with your eye on another game on the Saturday after that − it can be tough. And it's even tougher now with the Champions League. These lads appear to be playing all the time. They don't really seem to get a break at all.

By the January, we were sixteenth or seventeenth in the table; we would finish in eleventh. By the end we were probably only four or five points off seventh spot and a place in Europe, which was a massive achievement for that group of players. Even though we had good players and a great team ethic, we were playing against teams that had real quality in them.

The other big game for me that season was the three-three draw at Elland Road in the April – a game that probably did as much as any to seal my eventual move to Leeds. That day I was virtually unplayable.

Particularly when you play out wide – as I did more and more later in my career – you can have days when things just don't go your way. You maybe don't see much of the ball as you want to, or you get shackled by a full-back. But I always believed that in each and every game that I played in, I would get a chance. I believed in my ability. Even if I was having a shocking day or I was up playing against someone who was unbelievable, I always believed that one time – at least – I would be able to get myself into a position where they wouldn't be able to stop me.

I've always believed that. All the way through. And on that day, as I say, I was just unstoppable.

It was just before Leeds really started to spend the money, but they still had some good players there under George Graham. They had Jimmy Floyd Hasselbaink, Harry Kewell, Ian Harte, Nigel Martyn and Gary Kelly, who would become one of my best mates at Leeds.

Hasselbaink put them one-up and then I equalised. They got Gary Kelly to man-mark me after that. And I terrorised him. Mind you, he always used to say: 'I got you that move. I let you run through every time...'

It was my first Premier League hat-trick and all three were good finishes – and you usually don't get that. Usually you get a skanky tap-in or a penalty, but these were three really good finishes. All right-footed. And one was a run right from my own half too, followed by a top-corner finish.

The shame was that they scored a goal right at the end to make

Above: Me and my brother Scott.

Left: Playing for Nottingham Boys. I played from the Under 11s to Under 16s. I'm the idiot in the middle.

Bottom: My beautiful wife Lyndsey, with my boys, Ben and Thomas.

Above: On holiday with my family.

Right: The in-laws, Bill and Margaret, with the kids.

Bottom Right: On holiday with our good friends Ben (Dick), Claire and the kids.

Above: Pictured with my Mum and Dad at my brother and Nicola's Wedding.

Below: All my Grandparents together.

NOTTS COUNTY FOOTBALL CLUB

Meadow Lane, Nottingham NG2 3HJ. Telephone: Nottingham (0602) 861155
Facsimile: Nottingham (0602) 866442

Founded in 1862

Our Ref RS/RMH

27 March 1992

Darren Huckerby
10 Scafell Way
Clifton
Nottingham

Dear Darren

With regard to our Y.T. Training Scheme, we regret to inform you
that all our vacancies have now been filled. It goes without
saying that this has been a very difficult decision and I hope
that your association with Notts County Football Club has been
enjoyable and beneficial.

I am in the process of sending circulars, enclosing all your
details, to numerous clubs that have shown interest in the
search for talented young players.

On behalf of the club I would like to wish you every success in
pursuing your footballing career.

Yours sincerely

Russell Slade
Youth Team Coach

Chairman: D.C. Pavis, Vice-Chairman: J. Mounteney
President: F. Sherwood, Directors: W. Hopcroft; P. Jackson; D. Ward
Chief Executive: Neal Hook, Manager: Neil Warnock
VAT No. 116 8675 48 Registered No. 32208C (England)

Above: My rejection letter from Notts County, March 1992.

SCHEDULE

(a) The Player's employment with the Club began on the ....1st July.... 19 94

(b) No employment with a previous employer shall count as part of the Player's continuous period of employment hereunder.

(c) The Player shall become or continue to be and during the continuance of his employment hereunder shall remain a member of the Football League Players' Benefit Scheme (and a member of the .... Pension Scheme) and as such (in the latter case shall be liable to make such contribution and in each case) shall be entitled to such benefits and subject to such conditions as are set out in the definitive Trust Deed or Rules of the Scheme.

(d) A contracting out certificate is not in force in respect of the Player's employment under this Agreement.

(e) Basic Wage.

£ ..90.00.............. per week from ..20/03/1995.......... to ..30/06/1995......

£ ..150.00.............. per week from ..01/07/1995.......... to ..30/06/1996......

£ ..190.00.............. per week from ..01/07/1996.......... to ..30/06/1997......

£ .... per week from .... to ....

(f) Any other provisions:–

1. The Player will receive £50 per match when playing in the first team including that of non playing substitutes (Endsleigh League, F.A. Cup, Coca-Cola Cup and Autowindscreen Shield only will apply).
2. The Player will reside within the Lincoln area on a permanent basis throughout the duration of this contract.
3. The Player will be eligible to participate in the agreed incentive bonus schedule throughout the duration of this contract.
4. The Player will receive an accommodation allowance of £40 per week throughout the period 20/03/95 to 30/06/95.
5. Please refer to the continuation schedule attached.

Signed by the said .... Darren Huckerby.

.... (Player)

and .... P M Hough

.... (Club Signatory)

in the presence of

(Signature)........... Clait

(Occupation).......... P.A.

.... Club Secretary

.... (Position)

(Address)........... 8 Archer Street

.... Lincoln

4

Above: Big Keith and the YTS squad – Dick is next to Keith.

Right: Playing for Lincoln after breaking into the first team.

Below: The late, great Keith Alexander. RIP 1958 - 2010

Above: Playing for Millwall against Stockport while on loan from Newcastle. [02/10/96]

Left: Playing for Newcastle United at St James' Park. [1996]

Below: Kevin Keegan, during the famous 4-3 defeat against Liverpool. [03/04/96]

Above: Signing autographs after training at Newcastle next to one of my all time heros, Peter Beardsley. [1996]

Right: Lining up for the England Under 21s game against Switzerland. [01/04/97]

Below: Leaping over the tackle from Luis Fuentes in the England B international friendly against Chile B. [10/02/98]

it three-three. Hasselbaink scored the first two, but didn't get the third, so at least I got the match ball that day. It's still in a cabinet here at home with the others. They all lose air, so you have to keep pumping them up.

All the Coventry boys signed the ball. They're all signed by the Coventry boys; you would never go into the opposition dressing room straight after scoring a hat-trick against them and say: 'Excuse me boys, can you just sign my ball…'

We finished in eleventh place, a fantastic achievement. Before that we had the PFA's end of season awards for 1997-98. Dion got nominated for the Player of the Year award and I got nominated for Young Player of the Year. On top of that, Oggy was up for the Lifetime Achievement award. As you'd expect, Gordon was there, along with all the lads. There were six nominees for the main award and six for the young player of the year. We had one player in each of those and, as I say, Oggy was up for sure for his Lifetime Achievement award. As is usual with these events, they ran a series of video clips containing the highlights of the season at the start. And they didn't show us once. They didn't show Coventry a single time.

Strachs wanted to leave. He stood up and said: 'Come on, we're going! This lot are taking the piss!' We were in for three awards and they didn't show one highlight of Coventry – Coventry, who had beaten Chelsea and Man United at home, Liverpool away in the cup, and drawn with Arsenal. Obviously, when it came to the individual awards, there were short clips of everyone that was nominated. But in the highlights of the season? Nothing.

We only stayed because Oggy had still to go up on the stage, sweat for England, and pick up his award. But it was a kick in the teeth. We'd been playing against some of the best teams in England and we'd been fighting for our lives every week. You would have thought that they might have shown us a little bit more respect.

In the end, Dennis Bergkamp won the big prize, while Michael

Owen won the award for Young Player of the Year. I wasn't in bad company – I think John Hartson, Nicky Butt, Paul Scholes, Kevin Davies, and Rio Ferdinand were also nominated for Young Player. My Dad's still got it on video somewhere.

I'm not sure that Dion ever really got the credit he deserved. But if you don't play for the top clubs week in, week out then you're probably lucky to get so much as a nomination. Should he have gone on to get more than the four caps that he did? It's difficult to say when you look at the likes of Shearer, Owen, Fowler and Sheringham, all of whom were ahead of him in the queue. I guess no-one can take what he does have away from him, and he should be proud of those caps – he deserved each and every one.

The final real drama that season came in the FA Cup. Having beaten Liverpool, at Anfield, in the third round of the FA Cup, we made it through to the last eight of the competition – we made it to the quarter finals. Neil Warnock and Sheffield United were waiting for us there, and we ended up losing on penalties.

To this day, I believe that Gordon got the team wrong for that tie.

Half-way through that season, Strachs brought in another centre- forward, a Romanian lad called Viorel Moldovan. He came in for £3.5 million from Grasshoppers, the Swiss side. If you ask me, he played games when he shouldn't have done, and, to accommodate him, Dion had to play at the back.

Dion was banging them in, but, to make room for Moldovan, he ended up getting stuck for five or six games at centre-half. This spell included both the FA Cup quarter-final games against Sheffield United – the one-one draw at Highfield Road and the replay at Bramall Lane ten days later, which also ended one-apiece. Now I'm not saying Moldovan wasn't a good player, but he was more of a goal-poacher. And he wasn't a big lad. He was smaller than me.

So, in spite of the fact that everything had been going so well as it was, I'd been stuck up front with a poacher.

Strachs would name the team and I'd have to ask Dion what was going on. I don't think he knew, either. It was frustrating – I knew how much of a handful we were. For him to be told to go back and defend was confusing, and I just couldn't get my head round it. At twenty-one, it didn't feel like my place to ask the manager what was going on – not when Strachs had been so good to me anyway.

But United were in the Championship then; we were in the Premier League; we were drawn at home. We were thinking: 'The quarter-final of the FA Cup... We've already knocked Liverpool out...'

I don't know whether the chairman brought him in or if they knew that Dion was going to leave – I really, really don't know. Maybe there were things going on off the pitch that we weren't allowed to know about. But it just seemed absolutely ridiculous. If someone gets injured then, fair enough, you bring a replacement in. Here, though, no-one was injured and we had a front two that was firing on all cylinders.

Moldovan and I just didn't click, not least because – if I'm going to be honest – I didn't really want to play with him. He'd scored lots of goals internationally and for clubs on the continent, but when you've spent the best part of a year getting used to playing with someone and you've worked hard together, it's hard to see the logic in disrupting a good thing. It wasn't just odd, it was mental and there was no need for it. If it ain't broke, don't fix it, as they say.

In fairness, Moldovan scored a couple of goals, but – in my opinion – Dion was much better used up front. If we'd not tinkered with the forward line, I truly believe that we would have got to the final that year.

We drew one-one at our place – and we should have won, although Dion was stuck away at the back. We should have won comfortably, in fact. Even when we went to Bramall Lane for the replay, we were by far the better team. But they got an equaliser in the last minute of normal time, snuck the draw, and then beat us on penalties.

To this day, I think that was a chance missed, and I never got anywhere near the FA Cup final again. At the time, when you're 21, you think that you'll get another crack of the whip, but it wasn't to be. I haven't had a sniff of it – and I am 100% certain that if Dion and I had been allowed to start up front together, we'd have won that game.

As for Warnock, I have to say that, over the years, I have grown to like him. That was just one of many battles we've had – but it was more banter than anything, and when I left Norwich, he wanted me to come and join him at Palace. Much of what he says and does is just front; he just does it to wind people up. I know many people who have played for him and they all say he knows his stuff. It's just that he's one of those blokes who thrives on the thought of people not liking him.

So, Warnock's Sheffield United side went on to the semi-final, losing to my old club Newcastle at Old Trafford. I'm sure we could have given Shearer and the rest a good game – for me, that year's FA Cup was a huge missed opportunity. Me and Dion up front? I don't think Sheffield United would have coped with us. We could have got at anybody that season and given them a really good game.

5. DON'T KNOW WHAT YOU'VE GOT TILL IT'S GONE

Match: Coventry City vs Chelsea
Venue: Highfield Road
Competition: FA Premier League
Date: Saturday, August 15, 1998
Result: Coventry City 2, Chelsea 1
Attendance: 23,042

Coventry City: Hedman; Nilsson, Burrows, Shaw, Williams; Whelan (M Hall, 70 mins), Boateng (P Hall, 88 mins), Telfer, Soltvedt; Dublin, Huckerby
Subs (not used): Ogrizovic, Haworth, Wallemme

Chelsea: de Goey; Babayaro, Leboeuf, Desailly, Le Saux; Ferrer, Poyet, Wise, Di Matteo (Zola, 76 mins); Vialli (Flo, 69 mins), Casiraghi
Subs (not used): Hitchcock, Duberry, Newton

The summer of 1998, of course, brought the World Cup and a slightly longer break than usual. But after our successes the previous year – the decent finish, the cup run, and the PFA nominations – we came back looking to push ourselves further. We believed we could get a top-half finish, a place in Europe, and even, perhaps, one of the cups.

We wanted to build on the squad we already had, a squad which, after all, had beaten both Manchester United and Chelsea at Highfield Road and Liverpool at Anfield. Obviously, we weren't complacent, but we knew that we could afford to start aiming higher based on what we'd achieved. Europe had to be the target; as players, we felt that the momentum was there. Back then, as Norwich had proved a few years earlier, the door was open for smaller clubs to get into those positions – it was a much more open Premier League than the one we have now. There was every chance that we could be there or thereabouts, and we also knew that we'd been but a penalty kick away from the semi-final of the FA Cup, which we'd really fancied our chances in.

I'm not sure if money was tight at the club. Once again, we played Chelsea on the opening day of the season, but Gordon hadn't really strengthened the team. Yes, we had Nilsson, Shaw, Williams, Snowy, Telfs, me, and Dion – but that should have been a platform to develop on. The only real change was Oggy dropping to the bench for Magnus Hedman, and that only came about because Oggy was about to turn forty-one and Mother Nature was taking her toll. He'd been a great, great keeper, but he knew that it would be difficult to keep on playing at the highest level.

Magnus, I think, was Sweden's second-choice keeper at the time, so he was obviously of a high calibre. He didn't weaken the side, but he was a different kind of keeper. More agile than Oggy, I'd say, but probably not as brave. We were obviously going to have to adapt a bit in terms of how we defended.

The biggest chink in our armour, though, was the lack of strength in depth. It wasn't even the case that we lacked strength beyond the first fifteen or sixteen lads, because we didn't even get to that. We couldn't afford to lose anybody at all; any serious injury would be a massive dent in our chances.

Gary Mac was a case in point. He was still with us, but he was coming back from his cruciate. That summer he was still a good three or four months away from playing; maybe two to three months away from normal training, even. We had to get through the first few months of the season without his enormous presence in central midfield, a presence he provided us, due to his experience, his know-how, and – obviously – his ability.

We'd been to Scotland for our pre-season tour – it was always Scotland with Strachs – and it was hard, hard work. I know that supporters tend to think that pre-season trips are always something of a jolly for the boys, but it's usually the complete opposite of that. They nearly always take place in the middle of nowhere where there's nothing to do, and the only things to look forward to are the couple of matches that may or may not get thrown in over the course of the week. Believe me, it's boring. You might get one night out, and that's if you're lucky.

It's set up so you can't do anything, to tell the truth. The whole point is that you get to know any new team-mates, and you work on your fitness. They're very, very tough, especially when you have a manager as committed to having his players in shape as Gordon was. Of course, we had to be fit, because so much of our game was about work-rate and preventing the other team from playing. Knowing this didn't make it any more fun, though. I've never been one for pre-season tours, and they were particularly bad in the age before iPods and iPads and all the rest of it. We probably got a TV with five channels, and Scottish ones at that.

I shared a hotel room with Noel Whelan for a while, before Strachs broke up that particular partnership. I snore, which didn't help matters, but the final straw came on an occasion when we had an evening game and we were 'relaxing' in the hotel beforehand. Snowy and I were on the PlayStation, teaming up against the computer, and we were going mental. Predictably, there was a knock on the door, and – equally predictably – it was Gordon. 'Everyone else is trying to sleep,' he yelled. 'Can you two just shut up?' Of course, we'd been jumping around like idiots. That was it for Snowy and I rooming together.

Obviously not everyone gets on with everyone else all the time, and there are occasional falling outs. But we did have a close-knit group at Coventry, especially on Friday nights before away games. We'd all go to a hotel together, have a meal, sit down and just chat amongst ourselves for an hour or so afterwards. They were all good lads.

If you're allowed one, the night out on the pre-season tour is important, especially if there are a few new lads. You get to know people that much better over a few pints than you do in training. If it's just training, you're usually straight back to your hotel room to sit in it and do nothing for the next six or seven hours. When you go out, though, you get to talk to each other properly, something I can really see the benefits of in terms of camaraderie. Way back when, when players would always be out drinking together, you could see how they grew close and developed a good team spirit, how they'd get to the stage where they would run through brick walls for each other. That's very significant. When there's such a fine line between winning and losing, you've got to know who's on your side and that you're all in it together. Twenty-odd footballers out on the town together can be a bit of a sight, but when it was Coventry City visiting Scotland, I'm not sure that anyone knew or cared who we were. The press certainly didn't.

Amongst the supporters, expectations were pretty high going into the first game. But it was going to be a battle. Chelsea were starting to look much as they do now, their side full of expensive foreign players. In fact, if you look at that team there's only one proper English player in there – Dennis Wise. Le Saux's from Jersey, he doesn't count. Of course, Leboeuf and Desailly had just won the World Cup with France, and all the cameras were there to see how Desailly, who'd just signed, would cope in the English Premier League.

In that particular game, Chelsea as a team didn't cope very well. It was a red-hot day, and we went in feeling confident and prepared. The changing rooms at Highfield Road were next door to each other and I remember the Chelsea boys coming in wearing sunglasses and strutting around the pitch beforehand. It was a bit like waving a red rag to a bull – we were all thinking: 'Come on then – this lot have come up here thinking they're the dog's bollocks.'

Perhaps they were. In the event, though, it couldn't really have gone any better for us. We were two up inside the first twenty minutes, and we bullied them a little bit. Leboeuf, as I've said, hated playing against Dion – there was a lot of manhandling going on – and it was all new for Desailly. They just couldn't get their heads around the kind of football we played.

Dion and I knew each other's game inside out by this point. Our first came when Dion flicked on a long goal kick from Magnus, causing a race between Desailly and me. I got there first and chipped it over de Goey. Then we got another, after Dion had won a free kick from Leboeuf smashing into his back. Snowy swung the ball to the far post and Dion muscled in between Poyet and Desailly to head home.

We went into that fixture knowing our game plan backwards, and we knew that it was going to be Chelsea's job to stop us. It was obvious to us that they'd try and pass it around and that their movement would be good. We were ready for them, though, and our tactics were spot-on. Dion, Snowy, and I did the creative bit, and the rest of the boys worked themselves into the ground. That's exactly how it was. Telfs and the others wouldn't give them a moment's peace.

So there we were. We had a squad that had been built up slowly, and looked like it had every chance of achieving something that season. On top of that, we'd gone into the first game of the season and beaten Chelsea with both Dion and I scoring in the first twenty minutes, giving every impression that we could better our tally from the year before. What could possibly go wrong?

Well, Dion leaving, for a start.

After that Chelsea game, he played eleven more games for Coventry – his last appearance for us was away at Southampton at the end of October. And then he was gone. He'd only just signed a new contract, too, at the end of the previous season. Having been joint top scorer in the Premier League, he'd have been on good money. That can't have been the reason he left.

To this day, I don't know whether or not Coventry realised that they couldn't afford to pay one player those wages. All I know is that he signed that deal then, four months later, was on his way to Villa for £5.75 million. It was a strange one, to say the least.

I didn't have a clue that he was leaving, or even that the idea had been mentioned. Until he was sold, I didn't see it coming at all. And it really, really set me back.

All of our play was built around Dion and me, but particularly around Dion as the focal point of the team. We'd worked for a year and a half getting it just how we liked it, and then it was gone – just like that. It made no sense to me. Also, with Gary Mac injured, Dion was the leader in the dressing room, so we were short of a captain again.

I don't recall actually banging on Gordon's door to ask him what was happening, but I do remember that I wasn't happy in the least. I must have said something or other to Strachs, though – it seemed to me that everything we had been working on had been taken away in thirty-six hours. It was that simple. We saw him in training, and he told us that it had been agreed that he

98

would join Villa. That's one of the hardest things about football, though. You build up partnerships, and friendships, and then they're gone, completely unexpectedly.

In fairness, it was good money for a club of Coventry's size back then. They were what's known as a 'selling club', after all, and perhaps they wanted Dion's wages off their hands. Given what we'd done over the previous year, though, it was a huge risk to take. I can't remember exactly how the fans reacted at the time, but there's no way that they could have taken it very well. He'd joined Villa, the team who were basically the enemy. I could never have done that – I couldn't have moved from Man City to Man United, or from Norwich to Ipswich. Maybe it wasn't that hard for Dion. He lived in Stratford, so at least he didn't have to move house.

Afterwards, I heard from a couple of decent sources that Villa might have been looking to take the both of us as a job lot. I'm not sure, though. They had some good players there in the John Gregory era, quick lads like Stan Collymore and Julian Joachim who might have been able to forge the same kind of partnership with Dion that I had. It's irrelevant, though. I'd never have gone there anyway, because you can't play for one club then pull on the shirt of their biggest rivals. I guess everyone's different.

Moldovan wasn't to be Dion's replacement – he'd been sold to Fenerbahce in the summer, having only stayed the six months. We had a couple of new forwards – Simon Haworth had come in from Cardiff, and we'd signed John Aloisi from Portsmouth. But they were completely different types of player to Dion. They were decent enough, but they were never going to do the job that he had. Okay, we had money in the bank, but money in the bank doesn't score you goals, does it?

It really messed my game up. There were spells that season in which I'd score goals, but it was difficult without Dion's presence and flick-ons. Snowy got pushed up front, and he's not a centre forward, let alone a target man. He's much more comfortable running from midfield and joining in. While he was gifted enough to play as a striker, holding the ball up with his back to goal, we were depriving the midfield of his energy and work-rate by playing him there.

It was devastating – that's the only word I can think of which sums up my mood at that time. I just couldn't see how we were going to keep on playing the way we had done and still be effective without Dion.

Funnily enough when we played Villa that season – right at the back end of February – we beat them four-one away from home, and I think it was the first time that we'd ever won against them at Villa Park. It broke a sixty-three year jinx. Dion scored from the penalty spot for them; Aloisi and Boateng got two apiece for us.

Even so, I think the Coventry supporters did hold the move against Dion for a while. As the years go by, though, they've probably had to question whether the transfer was down to Dion or to the club, and I'm certain they look back at the spell he had with them as their best excluding the FA Cup win in 1987. Maybe they also recognise now that, at the time, Villa would have been perceived as a much bigger club than Coventry, and one who were spending a lot on players like Collymore and Paul Merson.

Whether or not that is the case now, every game we played without him was tough. Maybe Gordon thought that we had the players in the squad that could adapt to new roles and we could get around it, but it just wasn't the same. We did okay, but only okay and, sure enough, we didn't finish the season as high as we had in 1997-98.

And I was frustrated – to be honest, I felt like I'd been let down. All the times that we'd come in to work in the afternoons; the time we'd spent working on our partnership; the fact that we'd both been nominated in the PFA Awards the previous season. All of that had just gone in an instant.

My game suffered. I finished with just twelve goals that season, only nine of which were in the league. After Christmas, I went on a run of not scoring for fifteen games. I felt the pressure more, and I wasn't getting the chances I had when I'd been playing off a big man who made openings for me. I'd got stuck in a rut, and suffered a crisis of confidence which led to a barren spell. While I was working hard and making chances for others, my finishing just wasn't up to scratch.

The funny thing was that just before that spell, I scored seven goals in three games – a hat-trick against Macclesfield in the FA Cup, a hat-trick against Nottingham Forest in the Premier League three days later and one against Chelsea at Stamford Bridge.

If truth be known, I also hurt my shoulder – it was my own fault.

I was doing a promotional thing for Puma, the day after we'd lost two-one to Everton in the FA Cup. They were doing weight-lifting competitions and, being the idiot, I thought I'd be the big man and try and lift something that I was absolutely nowhere near strong enough to. Predictably enough, with me trying to be Billy Big-Time, I felt something in my shoulder go as I lifted the weight. It wasn't the worst, but I couldn't lift any weights after that for about three months, a period which coincided with me not scoring a goal for those fifteen games.

It was a mental thing. I couldn't do my normal preparations, and my routine got knocked out of shape. Of course, I couldn't bring myself to tell the physio and Gordon about it, because it had happened while I'd been doing something I shouldn't have. So I had to get by as I was. While it wasn't the main reason I wasn't scoring, it's funny how little things like that can mess up your whole rhythm.

Is working on your upper body strength that important? I guess it depends on what kind of player you are. Nowadays, they are much stricter than they ever used to be in terms of training regimes and individual programmes, which is only right – not everyone wants to lift massive weights. For me, however, it mattered, as did my weight. I always knew what my best weight was, and I was a touch heavy at Coventry, probably weighing in at, say, just under eighty kilos. I was a super-middleweight.

When I left Highfield Road, I probably got a little bit lighter and started to do more cardio stuff in training. But while a lot of my game was about having explosive sprinting power, I also needed to be big and strong enough to hold people off the ball while I was running with it. It's no good just being quick — that way you'll end up falling over every time someone touches you. You need to mix pace with power, and it's a real balancing act because being too big means you can't run.

For the rest of that season, Noel and I didn't do too badly. He finished up with one goal more than me, scoring thirteen; ten of them were in the Premier League. Even so, we were obviously lacking a focal point to put the ball up to. Every team needs to have someone up front to make it tick, as you can see with Grant Holt at Norwich these days. Yes, there are variations on that theme, and an out-and-out target man isn't every manager's cup of tea, but we'd come to rely on having Dion there at Coventry.

My heart was still in it even after Dion got sold, but there were nagging doubts in my head. It felt as if I'd wound up at a selling club, and that any decent player we unearthed would get moved on once a decent bid came in. What kind of launchpad for success is an attitude like that? Of course, they ended up selling me too, which kind of proved me right to have those concerns.

Don't get me wrong — John Aloisi was a good player, left-footed and strong, but not a like-for-like replacement for what we'd lost. We'd have had to pay ridiculous money to get that. In regards to Aloisi, it's hard to come to a club and start firing straight away, but Dion was proving his quality by doing just that at Villa. Two on his debut at home to Spurs, a hat-trick in a four-one win at Southampton, two more at home to Liverpool. All in a fortnight, or something daft like that. It really underlined the fact that our loss was irreplaceable, but the fact is that clubs like Coventry and Norwich don't sell star players and then reinvest all the money they've received in new ones. Obviously, they're selling to make a profit.

That's understandable, but it doesn't help the team or the manager. It's hard to believe that any boss – and I'm not just talking about Strachs here – would happily agree to sell a player if he was aware that he wasn't going to be able to get someone just as good in.

If I've talked about losing Dion a lot here, it's because it was the defining moment of that season. We went in fancying our chances of a European place, lost our pivotal player, and didn't do much else thereafter. I wouldn't say that we were lucky to stay up as such, but we ended the season in fifteenth place. In truth, we'd found ourselves fighting relegation again, which meant that there were no question that we'd gone backwards.

There were some good moments amidst the loss of momentum. There were a few spells in which I think I played really well, and I bagged a hat-trick against Nottingham Forest, my hometown club, in the January. Having stormed Division One to return to the Premier League, Forest were once again in the relegation mix, so a good result against another team down at the bottom was vital for us. We won four-nil, and the hat-trick was probably my favourite amongst the ones I've scored in my career. The one against Leeds was good but failed to win us the game; this one put three points on the board.

I can still remember each of the goals clearly. Even before I got off the mark, I'd run the length of the pitch and slammed one against the foot of the post, so you could tell that I was in the mood. It wasn't until the stroke of half-time that I got my first, though, a smart first-time finish after the ball had come over from the left. The second, I'll admit, had an element of luck – I'd taken it down the wing and tried to cross it, but everyone missed it and it went in off the inside of the far post. You've got to take what you can get, though.

The third was an unmistakably good goal, and I think it's one of those that people tend to remember. The ball came to me around the halfway line, and I did what I often did, setting off on a run and beating three or four opponents. As I went through on goal, their keeper Dave Beasant came out to meet me and I slipped it under him. Me at my very best.

It didn't happen that day, but it always helps a striker if they can get a goal early – it lifts the pressure off them. Does it mean that they'll then try and do more risky things than they would have had they not already found the net? Well, I can't speak for others, but I knew that it didn't make that much difference to me – I'd do those things anyway. As I've said, though, it's never just been about scoring goals for me, and I can honestly say that I'd rather not score and win the game one-nil than hit the net and lose two-one.

I think of Earnie – Robert Earnshaw, who I played with at Norwich – in relation to this. He's one of the best finishers I've ever seen, but scoring was the only thing that mattered to him. I'd do a run, beat three men, cross it for him to tap in – and then he'd run over to the corner flag and do a somersault. I'd think: 'Hold on, I've just done everything to put that on a plate for you – and now you're off to do acrobatics for the crowd'. But that's how natural goalscorers are. They're just desperate to put the ball away, and it's all they're paid to do. It's surprising how rarely you find good team players who also score lots of goals – goalscorers are what you bolt on to a team that's already good.

There are exceptions, of course. Dion, Dean Ashton, and Grant Holt all score goals while making the players around them better. Mostly, though, the top scorers charts are full of players who have that selfish streak I think I lack.

Gordon tried to make Noel and I into a partnership by keeping us back after training in the same way he had with me and Dion, but we could never make it gel in the same way. Also, with John Aloisi coming in and other bits and bobs going on, we were never absolutely certain as to who was going to play up front. Usually it was me with someone else, with Noel fitting in wherever.

That uncertainty didn't help my preparation at all. I liked to have a good idea of who I'd be playing with, but I had to accept that that was how it was. Also, teams near the bottom that are struggling for wins tend to be changed around quite a lot as the manager seeks a winning formula. What had been simple – me and Dion, one working the channels while the other acted as a target man – became complicated, and adjustments had to be made. Without a shadow of a doubt, we became a much easier side to play against. We still had class, we still worked extremely hard, but the game plan wasn't as well-defined. Where once we'd known that the ball went up to Dion so he could hold it up and get it into the channels for me, we'd found ourselves unclear about tactics.

Finishing in fifteenth place reflected the fact that we were no longer guaranteed to cause our opponents trouble; it was a huge disappointment. Personally, I felt that I hadn't scored enough goals, and I was determined to set that straight as I started to think about the following season. As it turned out, I was soon to be on the move again.

The move to Leeds United – the next chapter in my footballing life – came that August. I did pre-season with Coventry, and played in their opening game – a one-nil home defeat against Southampton – but I was off soon after. I got the phone call while I was in a courtroom, of all places. One of my mates had been an innocent bystander to some event or other, and I'd gone along to Nottingham Crown Court with three or four others for the trial. Phil Smith called me while I was there, saying that Coventry had agreed a fee with Leeds.

There I was, thinking, 'Wait a minute.' I honestly didn't know the first thing about it – I'd heard nothing about Leeds watching, or me being for sale. Nothing. So I came back into the court room and mentioned to the lads that a price for me had been agreed on, and that I was possibly on my way. After that, I had no idea what to do. Was I meant to go into training? To go up to Leeds to talk to them? In the end, I think I phoned Coventry up in the morning and they asked me to come into training.

It was all a bit of a mix up as Phil wanted me to go straight to Leeds, but I ended up at the training ground. By then, everyone knew that I was off. I went for a walk with Gordon and we sat on a pitch away from everyone else and I told him that I didn't want to go. But the profit they were making – Leeds were offering the best part of five times what Coventry had paid Newcastle for me – meant that the deal was great business for the club, not least because it allowed them to get Robbie Keane in.

Gordon obviously knew Leeds well from his own time there, and he pointed out that this was a big opportunity for me. But I stuck to my guns, saying that I was happy where I was. I didn't want to go – I liked all my team mates, and I enjoyed playing for Coventry.

Whether there'd been much talk of me moving on that summer, I don't know. Basically, when it got to summer I'd just shut down and concentrate on preparing for the coming season. I wasn't in the business of reading all the papers every day to see where I may or may not have been going. Basically, it was all a bit of a shock.

So, I played in that Southampton game and that was it. I was gone. Coventry had brought in some good players that summer too, particularly the two Moroccan lads, Mustapha Hadji and Youssef Chippo. I felt fit, and my levels were very good in testing – it's hard not to wonder what might have been if I'd stayed.

In his book, Gordon admits that he might have got it wrong. Later on I was starting to play more and more on the left, either on the left-wing or on the left of a front three, and he felt that I could have done more of a job for him there. By the time he left in 2001, Coventry had been relegated – I wonder if he saw a way that I could have linked up with Robbie Keane to stop that from happening. But in fairness, I don't think I was ever going to be the 20 goal striker Strach wanted, he described me as a scorer of great goals not a great goalscorer, that probably summed me up.

Coventry were perhaps going downhill, and Leeds were starting to put together a good young team that were clearly going places. But it wasn't the fact that it was Leeds who were in for me – it might as well have been anybody. It wouldn't have mattered. I was happy where I was. There was also the small matter of Lyndsey, who was seven months pregnant with Tom, our eldest, when the deal happened.

Moving wasn't necessarily the problem, but we'd made good friends at Coventry and I'd like to think that I was a big part of everything that happened down there. At the end of the day, I wasn't forced out, but I got a gentle push – and it certainly wasn't the case that I'd banged on the managers door and demanded a move.

You've got to look at the positives. If I hadn't gone to Yorkshire then there's no chance that I would have stayed at Norwich for as long as I did; financially, I wouldn't have been able to take their offer when there were other teams looking at me. Maybe, then, all these things happen for a reason. But the closeness that developed between Strachs and I, for all our fallings out and ding-dongs over the years, made it really difficult. I'd count him, probably, as the biggest influence on my career bar my Mum and Dad.

I still have a lot of respect for him. I liked his funny antics, his banter, and his sense of humour, and I know that he liked me too. In his book, I'm described as his 'greatest ever' signing, which is quite something coming from someone who has managed for fifteen years. Whenever I see him on TV now, it reminds me of those days – he hasn't changed a bit. There's that dry wit, there's the mickey-taking. He's a funny bloke, and a kind one too. After I signed for Leeds, he drove up with a present for the baby. He didn't have to do that, but he and his wife came up to see us. You remember little things like that.

In theory, everyone should have been happy about the transfer. However, it's hard making the transition when the move isn't really your choice, even if you're going into a great club. And, make no mistake, Leeds are a great club. The team I was going to play in was packed with talented youngsters – Michael Bridges, Harry Kewell, Alan Smith, and several others. In Jonathan Woodgate – when fit – they had one of the best centre-halves I've ever seen; Nigel Martyn an unbelievable goalkeeper. On top of that, there was European football and the stadium was packed every week.

But, somehow, when I moved to Elland Road that summer, I didn't feel how I expected to feel.

When it comes to saying goodbye, well, that's one of the worst things about football.

You are there – and then you're gone. That's how it is, it all happens in a flash. And this happened before email and texting became as massive as it is now. You'd come in, pack your kit bag and go. The chances are you'd lose contact with your best mates. That's what they are – as a professional footballer, you spend every single day with them for nine months a year. It can be tough.

And it wasn't just the lads. It was the kit man, big Andy Harvey, the kitchen ladies, and the people in the office. You go from seeing these people every day for nine months a year to, basically, never seeing them again, unless you make the effort to go back again – which I have done a few times over the years.

Typically, within that first month at Leeds I was back – we played Coventry at Highfield Road in one of my first games. We won four-three and I scored, too. I think, for a little while after, the Coventry fans didn't like me very much, and they thought that I'd forced the move because I'd been looking to get away. I guess they'd have had cause to if all they'd had to go on were newspaper headlines saying things like 'Huckerby Goes to Leeds!'

Supporters often don't know the ins and outs, though. I could have come out at the time and said that I never wanted to go, but it would have reflected badly on everyone. So I just had to put up with the perception that I'd wanted to leave Highfield Road, and face up to the booing that started when my name was announced. That hurt a little bit, and I have to admit that I reacted by celebrating when I scored.

We've spoken at times about having a reunion dinner for that group of players. Richard Shaw is a coach at Millwall now, Paul Williams is an agent, and I expect Telfs is off playing golf somewhere or other. Snowy's had his issues, but I think he's getting on top of them these days. Of course, big Dion will be a friend for life.

There should be a get-together, though. It's not until it's gone, not until you look back, that you truly appreciate the times you had. There were five-a-sides on a Friday when Richard Shaw would be marking me and both of us would be trying to avoid touching the ball for as long as possible until Strachs realised what we were doing. Then there was David Burrows, who we'd be on at all the time for coming from Tipton and being a proper Black Country lad. He used to think that he was a connoisseur of fine wines. Where is he now? He's got a chateau in France. He's probably sitting in it somewhere sipping Chateau de Burrows.

Hopefully, Coventry will be back in the Premier League one day, but I'd like to think that when that happens their fans will still look back and say that that was one of the finest Sky Blues sides of all time. As a player, you can't ask for much more than that.

That said, I would still put all the great games and the good goals to one side. For the fact of the matter remains that Gordon Strachan made me a far, far better player. There's no doubt in my mind about it, and what really impresses me is that he didn't have to do it. Not everyone would have. Strachs, though, went out of his way to try and nurture the raw ability that I had, and for that I will always be grateful.

6. SUB STORIES

Match:	Galatasaray vs Leeds United
Venue:	Ali Sami Yen Stadium
Competition:	UEFA Cup, semi-final (first-leg)
Date:	Thursday, April 8, 2000
Result:	Galatasaray 2, Leeds 0
Attendance:	18,000

Galatasaray:	Taffarel, Korkmaz, Popescu, Capone, Ergun Penbe, Buruk (Unsal, 63 mins), Suat Usta, Emre, Hagi (Yildirim, 89 mins), Erdem (Hasan Sas, 79 mins), Hakan Sukur
Subs (not used):	Emrah, Santos, Bolukbasi, Akyel
Leeds United:	Martyn, Kelly, Woodgate, Radebe, Harte, Bowyer, Jones (Wilcox, 65 mins), McPhail, Bakke, Bridges (Huckerby, 74 mins), Kewell
Subs (not used):	Smith, Duberry, Mills, Haaland, Robinson

I remember my first meeting with David O'Leary very well. He was very upbeat, very positive, and he said that Leeds were trying to build a very young squad centred on English-born players.

It wasn't so much his enthusiasm that struck me as his ambition to try and get as many young lads as possible and encourage them to grow together, to gel gradually over a two or three-year period. Well, I think that that was the initial plan. After that, I reckon it all snowballed into something else entirely.

On paper, there was a fantastic mix of young talent and seasoned ability. There was Kewell, Smith, Bridges and Woodgate. Lee Bowyer and Michael Duberry were at the club too, and Danny Mills. Jason Wilcox was about to come in, and Ian Harte and Gary Kelly were in the full-back spots. The older heads were Lucas Radebe and Nigel Martyn; David Batty was there as well, before he had to pack up through injury. It was a young, fresh, and highly attacking line-up, and we took the league by storm that season. We were to let ourselves down in our performances against the bigger teams, but we had so much going for us.

Of course, my achievements with Coventry meant that there was no way I was going to go into that dressing room lacking confidence – I knew that I was a good player. But after starting the first couple of games, it seemed to me that my role changed, and I became a so-called 'impact player'. That might sound good, but it's really just another way of saying 'substitute'.

Joining Leeds marked the beginning of what was probably the hardest part of my career. No matter how the game was going, I'd start my warm up and come on at exactly the same time. Every match, they were just giving me the last thirty minutes.

When I signed, there was no indication that my role was going to be that of a player who'd be brought off the bench in the final third of a match to test the opposition's tired legs. That wasn't the brief. O'Leary's selling pitch was that I'd be joining a group of young lads that was being assembled to have a real crack at winning the Premier League title.

The tactics at Elland Road were different to what I'd got used to under Strachs. There wasn't the traditional target man, as such. A lot of the time Bridgey – Michael Bridges – would be stuck up top on his own, then people would just bomb on past him. Kewell was nominally on the left, but he had a free role which let him go and join the front men. Lee Bowyer would be pushing on from midfield.

To my mind, my best position is in a 4-3-3, with me playing on the left of the front three. That's my ideal scenario. But at this point in time, Kewell was playing out of his skin in that position and Bridgey was in the best form of his career – he would score over twenty league goals that season. Unsurprisingly, it was difficult to break in, and tough also in the sense that a lot of the time I would feel that I hadn't contributed.

It is always hard to come on as a sub. Often, you'll take ten minutes just to pick up the rhythm of the game – especially as a forward, because sometimes you don't get to touch the ball that much. So, it can take you fifteen-twenty minutes to get into the game and then, all of a sudden, the referee's blowing for time. It was so, so frustrating. I knew by heart the time I would warm up, and the time I would come on. For twenty-five games in a row it was the same, no matter what was taking place on the pitch.

I used to get to the end of games and have done thirty minutes work – I'd have to go to the gym once I got home just so I could feel like I'd done something. It got to that stage. Even if we'd won, I didn't feel a part of the team in the way I always did at Coventry. Only ever getting twenty-five or thirty minutes on the pitch made me feel as if I was cheating everybody.

From the manager's point of view, it was fine – he had a decent player to bring on. But, for me, the game was never set up right to show what I could do. I had no problems with O'Leary. He was good, and indeed everything behind the scenes was good. Eddie Gray was his assistant, and I had a lot of time for him.

Regardless of those facts, I can't think how any player can possibly be happy sitting on the bench every single week.

Of course, I went and saw the manager a number of times. In his defence, he pointed out that I wasn't being as creative as I was capable of being – a judgement I agree with, at least now. My confidence was lower than it normally is, and I was second-guessing myself. Normally I'd get the ball and take it past someone no problem, but I'd started to think about it too much. You don't play, you lose confidence, then you don't get back in the team because you've lost confidence.

It's the definition of a vicious circle. You think constantly about the fact that you're not starting, so you end up putting in performances which are well below par, which in turn becomes a reason that you're not playing. When you get on, there's ridiculous pressure on you to score. And while the team might be winning and you might be contributing in other ways, it still nags at you that you haven't scored. It preoccupies you going into the next game, so the whole thing continues, a cycle it's incredibly tough to break.

After losing at home to Liverpool towards the end of that August, we embarked on a thirteen game unbeaten run. I was coming on and I was setting up chances, but I wasn't getting them myself and the pressure built and built. Back then I was still widely regarded as a centre forward, mainly due to what I'd done at Coventry, so it was expected that I'd score. For me, however much I enjoy scoring goals, my game was about much more than that.

To add to it all, I was on good money. Not the silly money that became common a bit later on, but I was on the same as a lot of the others there at the time. And given the amount I was on, I was always going to be expected to score goals.

The dressing room was good, filled with a great bunch of lads who were nearly all of a similar age to me. They were good times, and we enjoyed a night out. But we trained hard, too, and the training was very well-structured. Tuesdays, for example, was always the running day, so we'd have running coaches come in and not touch a football all day.

Compared to Strachs, I think O'Leary trusted a bit more in the individual ability of his players. The tactics were less regimented, at least when looked at side by side with Coventry's system, which was based entirely on reliable players working the ball forward to Dion and I who could then think about creating things and scoring goals. At Elland Road, the overall standard was better. We had Bowyer's tenacity, which allowed him to zip up and down, and to create and score goals. Kewell, like me, was unpredictable, and Smith and Bridges were very talented. O'Leary tended to look towards those individuals performing rather than to dictate a particular way in which the team were meant to play.

As well as those I've mentioned, Ian Harte loved bombing forward from left-back and was a class free-kick taker, and Gary Kelly – Harty's uncle, believe it or not – was always charging up from right-back. Both had great technique, although they were very different types of players. Kells was a runner, Harty was a dead-ball merchant with one of the best left feet I've ever seen.

Those two and Stephen McPhail would come out before training and they'd be smashing the balls around all over the place without stretching or anything. And I'd be watching them and thinking: 'One of them is going to ping their hamstring in a minute...' But they'd all be at it – smashing balls all over the shop before they had even warmed up.

Put that lot into a team together and it was, inevitably, very attack-minded. Was it too attack-minded? Too loose at the back? I don't think so. The only games that we didn't come big in were those against Manchester United, Arsenal and Liverpool. Had we won just a couple of those games, we could have finished second and perhaps even have won the title. Ultimately, I think it just came down to know-how. We would give them as good as we got, but they all knew exactly how to grind out the important results when it mattered. They knew when to attack and when to sit back, when to invite pressure and when not to.

We got beaten by Arsenal twice. We got beaten by Manchester United twice. We got beaten by Liverpool twice. If we'd taken three points away from any two of those games, we would have been right up there. Was it the naivety of youth that cost us? Perhaps. We couldn't do what Manchester United or Arsenal could do. They'd just get into a rhythm where they'd beat anyone, even if they really ground the win out.

You'd like to think that if you'd been able to work on that Leeds team – added just a couple more names to the young squad that we had then – you might have been able to push on and to have got them gelling in the way that Manchester United and Liverpool always seem able to with their own up-and-coming players. They keep a core together – look at Neville, Scholes, and Giggs for United or Carragher and Gerrard for Liverpool. Then there's players like Dirk Kuyt, who's been at Anfield for five years now. Those players have learned the Liverpool way or the Manchester United way over a period of time.

We, on the other hand, tried to do things too quickly, and our inability to come up with the goods against the big guns was a huge problem. It was great to be around 'The Young Guns', as the press dubbed us, but it was a huge pity that that squad never won anything.

The away trips were decent. We had our own massive plane, which only had forty seats on it. It had a lounge and everything. The camaraderie was brilliant, but not everyone loved the flying – the story was that a couple of seasons earlier they had an accident flying home from Stansted after a midweek game against West Ham. One of the engines caught fire on take-off and the plane literally crashed at the end of the runway. The air stewardess was telling the boys to be calm and stay seated, but they looked out of the window and saw the pilot pegging it across the field as fuel poured from the wing…

That's what I was told, anyway. After that, Harty, Kells, and Stephen McPhail all hated flying. So I'd be there slapping them on the head, shaking their seats, blowing up the sick bags and popping them behind their heads. They were all absolutely petrified, their hands white from gripping onto the armrests. A plane's no place to be when you're with fifteen other lads who have absolutely no sympathy and are quite happy to fly. In fact, I think Kells has now retired back to Ireland and refuses to get on a plane.

It was a good craic – young lads enjoying it and, in general, getting good results.

I didn't room with anyone. Since Coventry and Snowy I've always roomed by myself, which suits me. You can go to other lads' rooms and doss about – and go back to yours when it suits. Again, everyone is different on those nights in a hotel before a game. Some lads do go to sleep really early, while others are up half the night playing video games.

And, okay, these days it's improved a bit. You can be in your room playing one of the lads on a video game in another, but it is still boring. People have this idea that it must be amazing flying all round the world playing in different places, but basically you're in a hotel room. You go to training. You go back to the hotel room. You go to tea. You go back to the hotel room. And that's what it's like for four days. You might get to have a walk for an hour or so on one of the days. And that's it.

It's the lads that make it interesting. You can have little card schools; play little games.

I remember Gary Kelly once tried to take loads of sleeping tablets and then see how long he could stay awake for. It was just for fun. Watching him stumbling around the room trying to stay awake was pretty funny – that's what Kells was like, though. You need characters like that to provide some relief from the boredom.

You say that you've been to Rome, or that you've been to Barcelona. But you don't see any of them. You see a hotel room. Well, you see the stadiums, and, obviously, they're great. But the hotel room? You could be anywhere. A Holiday Inn in Leicester or Reading. All hotel rooms are exactly the same.

It was a good thing, then, that I got on well with everyone. The young lads tended to stick together – Harty, Kells, McPhail. Michael Duberry – Dubes – was a really funny lad and one of the nicest of fellas, I still speak to him quite a bit now. Danny Mills was there, but he tended to hang around with the older players like Nigel Martyn.

Nigel had a great sense of humour, and we needed that older head about the place. He was the Head Boy charged with keeping a class of rowdy thirteen-year-olds in check; he was also one hell of a goalkeeper. People underestimated how good he was, especially that season. He was brilliant that year.

Then there was Lucas Radebe, known to us as The Chief. He was quiet, but a real nice bloke. His job was defending, and just got on with that really well by being solid and having a bit of pace. At the time, he was starting to get on a bit, so he was helping Woody – Jonathan Woodgate – to learn the game.

The season after, of course, Rio Ferdinand would come to Elland Road. For me, though, Woody was the better defender at the time. Obviously, Rio has gone on to be one of the best English defenders of the last 40 years, but if Woodgate had kept fit – a big 'if', I know – I imagine that he'd have won as many honours as Ferdinand. He was just class, a Rolls-Royce of a centre back. He was big enough, he was quick enough, he was good on the ball, he was calm and cultured. He could do it all. He was brave, and he could tackle. He just couldn't stay fit.

It just seemed that he was always on the verge of breaking down. Some people just can't take the rigours of the professional game; their bodies are simply not made to train and play as hard as they need to. Over the years, I've seen loads who have struggled with injuries. Kieron Dyer would be another one of that generation – his body just doesn't want to play ball.

Woody was daft as a brush, but he was a class act on the pitch. When he was playing, he was way ahead of his time in the way that he read the game and got himself into the right positions. It was a tragedy that he couldn't stay fit, because he was virtually the perfect defender. As good as Rio turned out to be, he made plenty of mistakes early in his career. Not Woody. He didn't make mistakes – that's how good he was.

And then there was Lee. Lee Bowyer had one of the best engines that I've ever seen. He could run all day, and at a good pace as well. He specialised in arriving in the box at exactly the right time. In terms of box-to-box midfielders, he was one of the best in the league on his day.

Has he got a certain streak to him? Yes. He's a real lovely lad, nice as pie. But he's one of those with a bit of an anger problem and, as a tenacious midfielder, he's often put in positions where he can lose his temper. It's probably hurt his career on a couple of occasions, but for the vast majority of that time he's been an outstanding player. There's a few out there who aren't nice lads, and I've met more than one of them. Lee is not in that group – you have to get close to him first, but he's a good 'un. The trouble is that fans often make a judgement based on what they see in ninety minutes of football, whereas there's the whole rest of the week that they don't get to see.

The other person who was right on top of his game that season was Harry Kewell. Again, he was another one who was perceived as being a bit aloof by those who didn't know him. Fans seemed to think of him as arrogant – maybe it was that bit of swagger he, like most Australians, has. A lovely guy, though. He married the Emmerdale actress Sheree Murphy, and Lyndsey and I used to go out for dinner with them along with Harty and his missus. We all got on really well.

We bought a house in Harrogate and we actually lived on the

same road as David O'Leary. Of all places…fortunately, I was at the bottom of the road and he was at the top, but there can't have been much more than eight hundred yards between our two homes. Harrogate was a beautiful place, though, and Lyndsey loved living up there.

On a personal level, then, they were good times. Everything was good – apart from the football. It was that personal problem that I'd first had at Newcastle all over again where I just didn't feel as if I was contributing. If I wasn't producing on the pitch, then everything else became irrelevant. That was the problem.

My first introduction to European football, mind – now that was great. I was on the bench, but not used, in the three-one away win at Partizan Belgrade, but then played the full ninety in the one-nil win in the home leg. And I scored. On my first full European start, which was nice. They were difficult games in Europe, and no-one can ever take a goal scored in them away from you.

Of course I enjoyed it. European nights are unbelievable – they just have a special buzz to them. The league is always important, but European nights are special. And the further we got in the UEFA Cup that year, the more confident we became that we'd be going to Copenhagen for the final. We were flying in all competitions, but by the time we got to the semi-final that spring, we genuinely fancied ourselves for a European prize.

We drew Galatasaray, which was never going to be an easy tie. We were due to go away in the first leg, to play in their old Ali Sami Yen Stadium, a ground regarded back then as probably the most intimidating in Europe. The locals in Istanbul all called the ground 'Hell', and we were soon to know why.

We were due to play on the Thursday evening; tragically, the night before two Leeds fans – Christopher Loftus and Kevin Speight – were stabbed and killed in the city centre. It changed everything. We went for a walk on the morning ahead of the game and, to a man, none of the lads wanted to play.

A lot of the boys had family coming out to watch the match and word was going round that the Leeds fans were planning to retaliate. Suddenly it wasn't about a game of football any more. We arrived a few days before, as soon as we'd got there and walked through the doors of the airport there were riot police everywhere and people chucking stuff at us. We got on the bus and the security police, equipped with riot shields, were running alongside as we moved off through the crowds – it wasn't great. Add on phone calls made to the players' rooms in the early hours, and you already had a situation in which concentrating on football was pretty hard work. And that was all before the murders. Istanbul looked a lovely place, but to lose two lives over a football match was utterly ridiculous and heart-breaking for everyone involved, particularly the families. The game should have been rearranged, no doubt about it.

It's easy to say it now because we lost on the night, but no-one was in any frame of mind to play in that game. It just didn't feel as if it mattered whether we won or lost, because people had lost their lives out there. On the morning of the match, all the lads could think about was whether they should let their families fly out, given the possibility of it all kicking off.

I don't recall how they actually managed to make us play that game, but most of the lads just wanted to go home. We just didn't think it was safe. I was on the bench and came on, but we lost two–nil. For some of us, that was going to be the biggest club game we ever played in, but it was wholly marred by what had happened on the streets of Istanbul the night before.

There was, of course, still the second-leg to come back at Elland Road, where – despite it being a big ask – we still fancied ourselves to turn it round. The game would end two-two meaning that we lost four-two on aggregate. Away goals counted double, but the damage had been done in the first leg. .

There's always an edge to Elland Road, but on this night the atmosphere was something different entirely. You literally had no idea about what was going to happen – whether there would be fights, riots, whatever. All I know is that it ruined the whole experience of playing in a European semi-final, a semi-final which might well have led to a trophy in different circumstances. We had a real chance that year.

I'm not saying that we would have beaten them had none of the trouble occurred, but I firmly believe we would have given a better account of ourselves in Istanbul. That was the big game. If we'd got an away goal out there and then anything could have happened – and we were more than capable of getting an away goal.

I look back at that FA Cup run with Coventry and the UEFA Cup run at Leeds, and it is a very fine line between success and failure. I'm lucky in that I've got two Championship titles to my name – first with Manchester City and then, of course, Norwich – but it would be horrible to go through your whole career and not win anything. These days, that's highly possible, because if you're not playing for one of the top four or five teams in the Premiership, then you're not winning anything. Whether it's the league title, the FA Cup, or the Carling Cup, one of the big five will almost certainly win it.

So, we ended up trophyless that season, despite having given it our best shot on all fronts. The summer came and while, initially, there hadn't been too many players coming in, by the time I left that following Christmas, it was getting ridiculous.

Jason Wilcox had come in just after I did, but there was more to follow. Rio Ferdinand, Mark Viduka…it was, near enough, a revolving door, and the board kept on adding and adding and adding. I got to the stage where I was starting to wonder what the point was. How can a club be successful if it changes seven or eight players every six months?

I don't think any of the lads ever asked themselves where all the money was coming from. You don't do things like that as an employee. As a club, Leeds only started to think about what was going on too late. For a good period of time, they were just revelling in it.

That attitude rubbed off on the players. I remember being in Milan, where we'd been allowed out shopping before going home. Harry bought this lovely coat for Sheree from the Prada shop; while we were looking at it – it was white leather – I was checking out the receipt.

I said to him: 'You do know how much this cost, don't you?'

'Yeh, about £1,500,' he replied.

It was, actually, nearer £40,000, or something daft like that, and he'd paid for it without asking any questions. In the end, he decided that he would take it back. But we did have a lot of lads earning a lot of money and not really knowing what to do with it.

Crazy things would happen. It was the end-of-year awards do and I'd just bought this smart Prada dinner jacket, brand new. It must have cost me £1,000, which is a lot of money for a dinner jacket. But I figured they last – usually – for ten years. I'd get some good wear out of it.

We had a great night. As we were leaving, I went to give Kells a big hug – and he just ripped the front pocket off completely. Ripped it off in one go, all the way down, leaving it beyond repair. Knowing Kells, he would have treated a fifty quid jacket in exactly the same way. Everyone had more money than sense, basically.

As far as I was ever aware, there was never a huge gambling culture amongst the lads at Leeds. I can definitely see how it happens, though, and it's through boredom more than anything. Add that to the fact that some people – and they can come from any walk of life – have addictive personalities, and you've got a dangerous mix. Young professional footballers have money to spend, and time to spend it in.

Of course, I was bored for different reasons. I was making all kinds of work for myself to make up for the lack of time on the pitch. It got to the stage where I went to the gym for a session before one of those big European games, which was ridiculous, but an inevitable response to the frustration I was feeling. Then, however, Bridgey got injured early on and I had to replace him. By the end of the game I was shattered; my legs had gone completely. I'd put forty-five minutes in on the bike in the same day.

I had, if truth be known, lost my way. I couldn't get rid of the idea that I wasn't giving anything to the team, and I always felt that I had a lot to contribute.

Again, if I'd only played for thirty minutes in a league game on a Saturday, then I'd get home that night and go into the gym that I'd set up in the house in Harrogate do an hour there before I went out for a bite to eat with the lads or the wife.

It just felt, to me, like I was cheating everybody. I was getting paid this much, but I wasn't contributing. I wasn't earning the money I was being paid. Wherever I've been, I've always tried to give good value. Even in places where I was being paid good money, I wanted to make sure that people could look back and say that I earned that money as much as the next man. But, at Leeds, I don't feel I achieved that ambition. I didn't do myself justice.

When the likes of Viduka arrived that summer, making the squad even more congested, it wasn't like when I was a kid at Newcastle and just wanted to get out and play games. I was still desperate to prove myself at Leeds. I wanted to show everyone that I could play. However, the set-up that O'Leary had advertised to me when I'd joined was starting to get out of control; as I said, it snowballed. Looking back, it's obvious that the club were heading for a massive fall, although the players were blind to it at the time. We weren't sure – but we should have been. Clubs can't just keep on buying, buying, buying.

One thing that the club never seemed to account for when they bought a new player in was that the men who'd be asked to make way were earning much more than they would have been elsewhere. This meant that there was no incentive to leave – if Leeds wanted to get them off the wage bill, they'd have to pay their contracts up.

Even after I left, they kept on piling up players and multiplying the wage bill. Robbie Keane and Robbie Fowler both signed in 2001, as did Seth Johnson. Amongst the endless stories that do the rounds about Leeds back then, the one about Johnson's signing is most notorious. Apparently, he arrived with his agent hoping for something like £13,000 and got offered around £30,000. That was the level they'd reached – the board showed no patience in their attempts to grow the club.

It was that little taste of the Champions League that ruined them. They wanted it every year and, what's worse, started to budget as if they were going to qualify for it every season. It was a dangerous game: when they failed to qualify, they missed out on the revenue they were expecting to cover the bills.

The trouble is, of course, that many football clubs are still run like that. I think we're still only seeing the tip of the iceberg when it comes to bad debt coming back to haunt everybody.

When the big collapse came at Elland Road, I was long gone. I left at Christmas in 2000, less than eighteen months after I'd signed. Once again, I got a phone call from Phil Smith. "Man City are interested in you," he said. "They're Premier League, but in a lot of trouble. Do you want to go?"

Joe Royle was still the manager at that time and I was thinking: 'Can I still play Premier League? It's a big club, too...'

And Manchester City are a big club – that was the case long before the oil money came in and they started flinging the cash about. The offer came in at the right time for me, because I couldn't see how my prospects at Leeds were going to improve. With Viduka in, it was getting to the stage where it was hit or miss as to whether I was even on the bench half the time.

I can't say this enough — as a player, you've got to play. You're only in the game for a short amount of time and the last thing you want to do is look back on your career and realise you've spent four years somewhere you weren't playing. While you might be getting paid all that time, you're not leaving a legacy. People won't remember you for anything apart from picking up a wage cheque.

Leeds United was the only club that I went to where I didn't show my best and, if I'm being honest, didn't even offer anyone a glimpse of it. Whether it was down to a loss of confidence, O'Leary's unwillingness to give me starts, or a simple lack of form, I didn't give a good account of myself. In the end, I think I didn't start more than a dozen games and I didn't take my chances when they came. Less than a dozen games in a year and a half — that's nothing like the run I had a Coventry.

Don't get me wrong. It wasn't down to the club — it was down to me not producing on the day.

We had some great times, I met some great lads, and I played for a great club. At the end of the day, I scored in the UEFA Cup and I scored in the Champions League, which isn't at all bad for a lad who started his career at Lincoln.

In fact that's probably one of my biggest claims to fame — I have scored in every existing English and European club competition. I can't think of anyone else who has scored in all four divisions, the FA Cup, the League Cup, the Champions League, the UEFA Cup, and the AutoWindscreens Trophy. That makes me a half-decent pub quiz question, and I like to think that I must have been at least a half-decent player to have that record.

So, I can't complain. As I say, though, it remains the only place which I left feeling that I'd let the supporters down a little bit.

7. FEED THE GOAT

Match: Manchester City v Barnsley
Venue: Maine Road
Competition: Football League Championship
Date: Saturday, April 6, 2002
Result: Manchester City 5, Barnsley 1
Attendance: 33,628

Manchester City: Nash, Dunne, Howey (Wiekens, 66 mins), Pearce (Mettomo, 68 mins), Wright-Phillips, Benarbia, Horlock, Tiatto (Jihai, 76 mins), Jensen, Macken, Huckerby
Subs (not used): Royce, Killen

Barnsley: Marriott, Mulligan (Sheron, 59 mins), Morgan, Flynn, Chettle, Gibbs, Neil (Gorre, 59 mins), Jones, Lumsdon, Betsy, Dyer (Naylor, 74 mins)
Subs (not used): Barker, Miller

Joe Royle is one of football's real characters. Before I signed for City, I went for a meeting with him and he was, as the saying goes, larger than life. A great bloke. Apart from his charisma, it was nice that he told me that he had tried to sign me before when he'd been somewhere else. It gave me the reassurance that he really did fancy me as a player. All he said was that he just wanted to add extra pace to the squad he had there already.

While going from one massive club to another was good, I was bugged by the thought that I'd failed a bit. In joining City, though, I was being given another chance to prove myself, to show what I could do. They were struggling at the bottom of the table, so the challenge was to go into a team that wasn't doing so well and make an impression.

To be honest, I wasn't quite ready for what awaited me there. It can be difficult if you go into a side that's got problems and you don't make an impression immediately. To be honest, there's usually a good reason that teams are in danger, and that's definitely the case if they're at the wrong end of the table come December. The Premier League takes no prisoners, and a lack of confidence can cut straight through a squad. When you find yourself on the kind of slide that City were on when I joined, it can be very hard to turn around. At the top level, the teams you're playing against are so good that they'll take advantage of any lapses in self-confidence they notice.

Joe was doing his best, but it's difficult to keep morale up when you're getting turned over week after week. A loss in confidence becomes a cycle that's hard to break, and then you can find yourself on a horrible losing streak. A few years back, Derby went near-on a full season without winning; Sunderland have done that, too. The defeats get on top of you.

I wouldn't go so far as to say that players start to hide, but some maybe don't look to get on the ball as much as they might if things were going well. It's just so hard to get out of those runs. Look at what happened to Blackpool in the season that's just finished – they started amazingly, but then they hit a patch where they won something like one in fifteen.

I've certainly never been one to hide. Even when I was having my leanest spell at Leeds, that was never the case. I always wanted to play, to get on the ball and make things happen. Okay, my decisions weren't always the best, but I never hid.

Losing is a habit, but so is winning. Look at the way we played at Coventry when we were flying. There was an exuberance and openness about the way we played that only comes with confidence. Get to the top of the tree and you see how teams like Manchester United have a mentality which allows them to make things go their own way. Bolt that mental strength onto the ability of the world class players clubs like that have and they almost can't help winning. It must be a joy to play in one of those teams.

When Kevin Keegan came in at City, we developed a set way of playing like we'd had at Coventry. At Highfield Road, we looked to get the ball forward as quickly as possible; with Kevin, we played balls to feet, something we could afford to do with players like Ali Benarbia and Eyal Berkovic making things tick in the middle.

While Joe was still in charge, that's probably what we missed – a playmaker who could set the tone and the pace of our play. If we'd had Berkovic, who could really pull the strings and make things happen, back then we might not have been in such a mess. Players like that cost money, though, and I suspect cash was easier to find once Kevin came in, because he's the sort of manager people at board level back to the hilt.

Obviously, it's also difficult to attract players when you're on a bad run, even if there's a ready supply of money. I wasn't put off, though. My aim was simply to play again, and re-establish myself as the player who was so feared by defenders when he was playing every week at Coventry. That was the principal motivation behind the move.

Off the pitch, another shock awaited. Leeds hadn't only spent money on players, they'd invested heavily in the training facilities at Thorp Arch. By contrast, City had just vacated their old facility at Platt Lane and taken over an old school in Carrington, right next door to Manchester United's training ground and academy. The school was absolutely shambolic. There was no real gym, the changing rooms were awful, and we couldn't rely on there being hot water when we wanted it. Instead of central heating, there were these big hot-air blowers stuck in the corners in an attempt to warm things up. It was, shall we say, a rude awakening.

On top of it all, it was the middle of winter so the pitches were a state. In fact, they were pure mudbaths. What we'd had at Leeds was state-of-the-art, so I'd pretty much gone from one extreme to the other.

Later on, under Kevin, going to training was a joy. That winter, though, it was a complete chore. A training ground needs to be a winning environment, something this wasn't by any stretch of the imagination. The place wasn't right, particularly for players who were losing every week.

The lads themselves were great. When I got there, City had Shaun Goater, Paulo Wanchope and Paul Dickov to choose from up front, plus Steve Howey and Richard Dunne in defence. Along with Nicky Weaver in goal, it was a good crop of players, but they were finding it very difficult.

It wasn't as if they were short of characters. Richard Dunne was one. Over his career, he's pulled off one of the biggest turnarounds that I've seen in my life. While we were team-mates, he was just a little bit lacklustre, on and off the pitch. He took things dead easy; he just wanted to get by in life.

The weird thing was that he was, for a lad weighing in at nearly sixteen stone, really quick. He was usually in the top three for sprints. Behind me and little Shaun Wright-Phillips he was the third quickest, and he could properly move.

He was still a kid, to be fair to him, but he was just so laid-back, a nice Irish lad who liked a beer or two. When I arrived, he needed to get into shape because he simply wasn't looking after himself. As ever, I'd go into the gym after training and put in forty minutes on a bike or something like that. Joe would tell me to take Dunny in there with me, but he only came a couple of times. It wasn't really his thing.

After that, though, he harnessed his ability to go on and become City's best player for perhaps four or five seasons in a row. From 2005 to 2008 he won their Player of the Year award every season, which is some going. All credit to him, too. He turned it around all on his own. Yes, everyone wanted him to do well, wanted the best for him, but he realised that the responsibility ultimately lay at his own feet and changed his attitude. He probably realised that he was drinking too much and decided that he didn't want to blow it.

The little things made you laugh with Dunny. He had this lovely brand-new Jaguar, but he had the spare, space saver wheel on it for four or five months. All it needed was for him to go and get the wheel changed, but he just couldn't be bothered. He was all about getting by. I lived round the corner from him, and I realised that he'd go for weeks and weeks without opening his mail.

Why City were in the position they were in when I arrived is hard to say. Paulo Wanchope was a menace on his day, and Goats was always going to score goals. As I've said, they lacked a bit of quality in midfield, but there were hard workers in there like Danny Tiatto and Ian Bishop, who was a good player despite being close to the end of his career. Kevin Horlock was a real grafter too. They just missed a bit of guile, and I think they'd have benefited from a Gary Mac. No-one was running the show, no-one was making them click.

At least there were always kids coming through. Wright-Phillips would play a few times towards the end of that season, and went on to blossom under Kevin. Dickson Etuhu, who I really got to know at Norwich, was another to watch.

It started well enough for me personally – I came on and scored on my debut at home to Charlton. I got brought down, won a penalty, and converted it. However, we lost the game four-one. When you're losing by that kind of margin at home to Charlton, you know you're in trouble.

I scored again in the FA Cup win over Birmingham two games later, and it was a really good goal. It was, sadly, to be my last of the campaign. After that, I just drifted in and out of the side. Moreover, I'd picked up a slight knee problem – three weeks after the move, it had started to ache a bit. Me being me, I ignored it and told myself that, like most aches and pain, it would go away.

This one, though, got worse and worse. It got to a point where I could barely bend my knee properly. I was still playing, but it eventually transpired that I had a little tear in my cartilage. Apparently, not being able to bend the knee properly is the classic sign of a cartilage tear. I remember that we'd done the so-called 'bleep test' in the morning with the shuttle runs being timed, and I'd come in first. In the afternoon, I went to hospital and was told that I'd torn my cartilage.

We got it sorted out straight away. It was my first operation for an injury, and my last until I had hip surgery while I was in the States with San Jose some nine or ten years down the line. Given all the tackles that I've been hit with over the years, I have to say that I've been pretty lucky.

Not being able to do anything in the immediate aftermath of the operation drove me mad, even though I was looking forward to marrying Lyndsey at the end of the season. I missed the last few games, so I wasn't around for the relegation itself, but the writing was on the wall by then.

The supporters could see it coming, I think. Joe had been on a great run and got City back-to-back promotions which, as everyone now knows in Norfolk, is no small feat – even for a big club. That season, though, the magic just wasn't there. So, my first few months at my new club saw my first operation and my first relegation. It was all quite difficult to take.

Looking back now at how that spring developed, with the results consistently failing to come, I have to be honest and say that, as a group, we just weren't good enough. There were times when we played okay, but we simply couldn't get it together to reach the standard we needed to stay in the Premier League.

Relegation is awful. It is absolutely awful. You feel for the fans, you feel for the club, and you're nagged all the time by the sense that you've let people down. I knew that Joe had bought me to do a job, and I hadn't done it. It didn't seem fair on him.

I played up front – sometimes with Goats, sometimes with Paulo Wanchope. And then, later, we'd try three up front when they brought Andrei Kanchelskis in on loan for ten games. He'd play on the right; I'd play down the left. We didn't do badly, but we weren't good enough to stay in the league.

Paulo would disappear to play for Costa Rica, and he had a persistent knee injury. At the end of the day, though, you can look for all sorts of excuses. None of them mask the fact that we weren't up to it. In the end, Joe took the flak for our inability to produce the goods, and it ultimately cost him his job.

In any dressing room, there are only ever eleven lads who are truly happy with the manager. You can guess who they are – the ones who play week in, week out. Maybe there's a few who are happy to sit on the bench, but they're few and far between. Keeping players who aren't in the team happy is an art form – one of the hardest things for managers of clubs like Manchester United and Chelsea, who run squads of up to forty, is keeping everyone focused on doing a good job. That's a real skill. Joe's personality put him up there with the best of them on that count. Other circumstances didn't help his cause so much.

I always had a lot of respect for his Number Two, Willie Donachie. Willie was a total workaholic and one of the fittest men I've ever known. I always liked the fact that the first team coach looked after himself, because it meant he was showing everyone else the right example.

Joe and Willie, then, had plenty going for them, but sometimes you just run out of time. Places need freshening up; it happens. The squad becomes too set in its ways and it's in the interest of the club to make a change. But getting a new manager in is always a gamble. I've seen first hand that changing things doesn't always work, and that it can get you into even deeper trouble.

City made the right call. I remember we were back in the flat in Harrogate for a weekend and I got a call. The phone rang, I picked it up. The voice on the other end said, 'This is Kevin Keegan…'

I thought it was a crank call. 'Yeh, good one,' I said, and was on the verge of putting the receiver down.

'No, it is – I'm the new manager of Manchester City…'

Of course, he'd sold me as manager of Newcastle, but he said in that first call that we all needed to push on together, and from that moment – the very moment that Kevin took over at Manchester City – everything changed for that football club. As he did with Newcastle, he set City well on the way to the success they're enjoying at the moment. There's no doubt in my mind that he's one of the main reasons for what's happened there since.

Everything changed immediately. You could see it when we returned from our summer break. It started with the facilities – you would not believe the amount of work that went in at Carrington in the two months from when they first started to when we came back for pre-season. The pitches and changing rooms were better, and a gym had been sorted out. It had gone from an old, run-down school to a place that at least had the makings of a decent training ground, and all within the space of six weeks.

Not many individuals have that effect on people, but Kevin does. He has the pull to make boards spend money on getting everything exactly right. It was amazing, but he has the power to make things happen in a way unlike anyone else. It's sheer force of personality, mostly, but what also impressed me was his ability to understand exactly the problems we were facing. He could see that Carrington was no environment to work and learn in; it was as obvious to him as it was to us that no player would improve there. It was the set-up of a struggling club. The minute he walked through the door, he must have said that he wasn't going to work under those circumstances, and that his players weren't going to either.

He's a born winner. Twice European Footballer of the Year, he's won European Cups, and played in World Cups. You could tell all that, as I've said, from the way he played head tennis. There was nothing he didn't want to win at. That attitude rubs off on those around him – his training sessions were, by miles, the best I've come across. He makes it enjoyable, which means that everything is a lot easier. With that kind of atmosphere, good facilities, and a decent first team coach, training is never a chore.

In the little five-a-sides we'd have, Kevin would now and again take the opportunity to show us he could still play. I've always thought that it is important for players to be able to see that the manager can do it. It doesn't mean that they all have to be world-beaters, but it does help if they have been there, seen it, and done it. When that's the case, you know that there are good reasons behind the things they tell you to do.

So if Kevin Keegan was to tell you, 'That's the way that you finish it!' and you were to turn around and say, 'No, it isn't!' then you'd be a mug, because he's delivered the goods on some of the biggest stages in the world. Not all managers have to have been great players, but I think it means that you can connect with them more easily if they were.

As Keegan was appointed in the summer, none of us had had the chance to speak much about our expectations of the new manager. After you've been with your team-mates day in, day out for nine months, they may well be the last people you want to see once the season is over. Of course, sometimes the team will go away together for four or five days, but they then won't see each other for six weeks. That summer, I definitely didn't see any of the City boys. Along with our families and best friends, Lyndsey and I went away on holiday – and got married.

My first thought on getting back was having my knee, which was still hurting me, sorted out. Pre-season wasn't too good, but a painkilling injection did the trick. Kevin, meanwhile, was busy addressing the squad's weaknesses. To rectify the lack of guile in midfield, he got Berkovic in from Celtic, and he also added Stuart Pearce. Even going on forty, Pearce still had this incredible aura around him, and he was fit and a good organiser. His presence helped Steve Howey and Dunny no end. Like Kevin, Pearce is a winner, although he arrived at City with only two League Cup medals to his name. It's hard to believe that, up to that point, they were all he'd won in his career – after all, he'd played seventy-odd times for England.

He was no longer the kind of left-back who would bomb on, though – not in the way that he had earlier in his career, or like Ian Harte did at Leeds. A lot of the time we'd play three at the back, so he would be the third centre-half. There, he could exert a calming influence in defence.

Alongside Berkovic and Pearce, Kevin went on to buy Ali Benarbia, who was just out of this world. He really was. He was thirty-two when he pitched up at City; I'd love to have seen him when he was twenty-eight.

We stuttered at the beginning of that season, and my knee meant that I didn't really feature much for the first ten or eleven games. We'd pick up a decent result, then be a bit ropey for the next couple of weeks. Of course, the problem was that everyone expected us to win every game. Our bench was as strong as most other teams' starting line-ups, and perhaps we felt a bit like we just had to turn up to take the points.

Above: Staying up in our last game vs. Spurs. The emotion on my face says it all. [11/05/97]

Right: Working on the training ground with Strachs. [09/05/97]

Below: The Coventry boys on a night out – one of the best dressing rooms I've been in.

Above: Celebrating with Gary Mac after my goal against Crystal Palace.

Above: With Willo
and Dion doing
his trademark
celebration.
[08/11/97]

Right: Leaving Gary
Neville on the deck,
scoring probably my
most famous goal
against Man Utd.
[28/12/97]

Above: Never an easy game against Keown and co. [17/01/98]

Right: Celebrating with Noel Whelan. He had it all, what a great player. [15/11/98]

Below: Scoring against Chelsea in the opening day 2-0 win. [09/08/98]

Above: Playing for Leeds United after a big money move away from Coventry City. Shame the goals were few and far between. [2000]

Left: Walking off the pitch with Jason Wilcox under police protection after playing against Galatasaray in the UEFA Cup Semi Final 1st Leg. [06/04/00]

Above: In discussion with the little magician Ali Benarbia. [10/10/01]

Bottom Left: Man City Champions. [06/04/02]

Right: Celebrating after scoring a hatrick for Man City. [30/03/02]

Above: With Shaun Goater, holding the Division One championship trophy. [21/04/02]

Above: Playing for Forest while on loan from Man City, against Ipswich Town. [05/04/03]

Bottom left: With my boys and the Nottingham Forest lads in the changing room before our home playoff game vs. Sheffield Utd. [10/05/03]

Bottom Right: In action for Forest, on the way to the Play offs. [10/03/03]

That was when we got Benarbia in from Paris Saint-Germain, and he galvanised the whole team. He was of that calibre. I remember his first training session; the story was that he had an unsuccessful trial at Sunderland and was on his way back to France when Kevin offered him a second chance. It was a Friday in the middle of September, and we were due to play Birmingham the following day.

He was a little bloke; not ripped and muscular, a bit heavy-set. All the boys were looking at him and thinking, 'Okay, who's this guy here?' In that first training session he wasn't bad, but when he played against Birmingham he was something else. His touch, his vision, his ability to bring people into the game. He saw things before the match even started – he was staggeringly good.

On top of that, he was a lovely, gentle lad. There was a fiery side to him, but it rarely came out. He really, really wanted to win, and he was perfect for a Keegan team whose philosophy was to outscore the opposition. There's a very good chance that he'd be in a Darren Huckerby XI, at least if it had to be composed of people I've actually played with.

Benarbia came in, I managed to get back in the team, and as a team we never really looked back – we won the league at a canter, ten points clear of West Bromwich Albion. We scored one hundred and eight times in the league, and finished on ninety-nine points with a plus fifty-six goal difference. Benarbia and Berkovic were unplayable, and it was a pleasure to watch them every week.

It was as attacking a formation as you can get these days. There were three in the back, five in midfield if you count the wing-backs pushing on, and two up front. One of Kevin Horlock, Dickson Etuhu, or Danny Tiatto would hold, but the system was otherwise incredibly flexible. It was like the Red Arrows when everyone was running forward, be it Berkovic, Wright-Phillips, Tiatto, or me.

We went to Ipswich in the FA Cup on a Sunday evening at the back end of January. They were in the Premier League then, and I remember Kevin told us before the game that this was a chance to set down a marker and show everyone what we were about. We went out and won four-one.

We had The Goat up front. Shaun Goater, MBE, was one of the most natural goalscorers I've ever seen. He wasn't quick, or strong, or particularly aggressive, but he just knew exactly where the goal was and where he had to be. His ability to be in the right place at the right time was uncanny. It would hit him on the head and go in. It would hit him on the shoulder and go in. He was born to score.

The Goat was another lovely bloke. He was a pleasure to work with, always happy and with a smile on his face. Whatever happened, he'd never be grumpy when he came in; he just took everything in his stride. Between him and me we got almost sixty goals – I got twenty-six in all competitions, including four against Birmingham in a League Cup game, and Goats got thirty-two. Paulo spent a bit of time in and out of the side due to his responsibilities with Costa Rica and an injury, but I think he still added thirteen goals.

I was happy with my tally – particularly given that I didn't start too many times in the early part of the season. But anyone would have scored with Benarbia and Berkovic making the openings and the likes of Shaun Wright-Phillips bombing on and causing chaos. It was a different set-up to Coventry, in as much as I wasn't feeding off the knock-downs and flick-ons of a big man. Goats was the poacher, but my chances were being made by an intelligent midfield.

At times, I used to ask Eyal if it would have made him happier to be scoring goals, but – honest to God – he wasn't that bothered. He'd be quite happy laying them on for other people.

I also created my fair share just by running at people and unnerving the opposition's back four.

Everything was just right. As is always the case with Kevin, the training was top-notch. The shooting sessions, in particular, still stand out as the best that I've ever been involved with. They were amazing. The trick, as a professional, is to find a happy medium between hard work and enjoyment. There really has to be a bit of both, because, if it's all work, then everyone eventually gets bored. Kevin knew how to make it both functional and enjoyable and, in doing so, got the best out of everyone.

Put simply, he's a legend of the game. People point to the fact that he's never won a major trophy as a manager, but at Newcastle, Fulham, and Manchester City alike he took a club and totally turned its fortunes around.

Today, of course, City have wealth that ninety-nine percent of clubs can only begin to dream about. Back then, they were seen as the poor relation to United, and as one of the sides fighting for the scraps left over by the big teams. Kevin coming in and delivering the Division One title that season, and delivering it in the fashion he did, was definitely the beginning of the change. It set them up nicely for leaving Maine Road and going over to the City of Manchester Stadium – if we hadn't won promotion at the first attempt, there would have been a good chance that City would start in their new ground as a second-tier side. It would have been full, but I can't see there being the same vibe for the visit of a Doncaster or a Scunthorpe as for a clash with United or Liverpool.

I also think that the supporters always appreciated the way that team played – and my role within it. All in all, 2001–2002 has to go down as a special season. It didn't start off too well on a personal note, but everything flew once I got into the team. It clicked, and we enjoyed ourselves on the field. When I speak to

City fans nowadays, they always say that it was one of their favourite seasons.

Obviously, one of the reasons it meant so much to me was that it was such a contrast to the time I'd had at Leeds. We were getting three points nearly every Saturday, but this time I was definitely contributing to the success. It was great for me, and it proved one of the great things about football, namely that the slate is wiped clean at the end of every season. A new campaign is a fresh chance, and you go into it full of hope and optimism.

If I had to pick one match out from that year, it would be the penultimate home game. I'd scored a hat-trick against Forest in the game before that – it's odd how I've managed to get so many against them – and then I hit another three against Barnsley, the victory which gave us the Division One title. The big one hundred came up in that match, too, meaning that we'd hit three figures goal-wise, and my three put me on nineteen in the league, a personal best-ever.

Games like the one against Barnsley show how silly it was getting towards the end of that season. It must have been a joy to watch, unless you supported the opposition – we were ripping teams to bits, and they just didn't know what to do. This was especially true when Benarbia was on song; he really was a little genius. The downside for him, and for us, was that he was going to be thirty-four as we went back into the Premier League and he didn't really have the legs to be a proper force at that level. To this day, I believe that, had he been four or five years younger, he would have taken the top flight by storm. In Division One, he had it in him to get away from people, but, playing at a higher level a year down the line, time had taken its toll and he didn't quite have the same impact.

It was virtually impossible for teams to stop us. We had runners like me and Wright-Phillips, Goats, who'd score nearly every time he got a touch, and the creativity of Benarbia and Berkovic. Winning became a habit for us, just as losing had been the year before. The mentality was exactly right, and we played to the Keegan philosophy of always believing that we could score. Some might argue that Kevin's teams are too open, too attacking, but football is an entertainment business. I like to win, whether it's one-nil or five-four, and I've been in teams – such as Nigel Worthington's at Norwich, that have been built around the defence. But this was different.

It takes all sorts. Jose Mourinho hasn't fared too badly by building teams that will look to strangle you and then nick something, but the fans nearly all prefer sides like those Kevin put together. That's what marked that season out. People don't pay their hard-earned wages to go and see nil-nil draws and be bored out of their brains; they want to see the game played the right way.

There's clearly a balance to be struck between winning football and attacking football. You can't just throw five forwards on and hope for the best – there has to be a structure to it. While some sides get on by playing the percentages, Keegan managed to put a smile on the fans' faces by mixing a good system with real flair and imagination.

So I have great, great memories of my time at City. And, until this summer and their FA Cup success, that was the only thing that they had won for ages. They had won the Play-Off final a couple of years before, but I was part of something special at that time. Manchester was a great place to live, the fans are amazing, and it was a pleasure to feature in a side with the likes of Berkovic, Benarbia, and Wright-Phillips. I always enjoyed working with Kevin and, in the end, he helped me come to Norwich – there were certain sacrifices made at the Manchester City end that made that move financially possible.

Obviously, I made sacrifices to make that transfer happen, but it was ultimately reliant on his input. He really helped me out and, for that alone, I owe him.

8. LOAN RANGER

Match: Sheffield United vs Nottingham Forest
Venue: Bramall Lane
Competition: Football League Championship,
Play-Off semi-final, second-leg
Date: Thursday, May 15, 2003
Result: Sheffield United 4, Nottingham Forest 3
Attendance: 30,212

Sheffield United: Kenny, Curtis, Kozluk, Page,
Brown, Jagielka, Rankine,
Ndlovu (Allison, 105 mins), Tonge,
Asaba (Peschisolido, 105 mins),
Windass (Kabba, 45 mins)
Subs (not used): McCall, Montgomery

Nottingham Forest: Ward, Louis-Jean, Brennan,
Scimeca, Thompson, Walker,
Williams (Hjelde, 114 mins),
Harewood (Lester, 61 mins),
Huckerby, Johnson, Reid
Subs (not used): Roche, Jess, Bopp

LOAN RANGER

After the season we'd just had – winning the Division One title with such ease – our expectations were pretty high going back into the Premier League for the 2002-2003 season. We made some big signings, too. Peter Schmeichel came in, along with Marc Vivien-Foe, Nicolas Anelka, and Sylvain Distin. We had all the makings of a side who were going to able to compete at the top level.

Schmeichel was immense. He was getting towards the end of his career at this stage, so he obviously wasn't as agile as he used to be, but he was still an unbelievable keeper. Presence is the word that everyone uses to talk about players like him, and you could only imagine how good he was when he was twenty-eight or twenty-nine. He must have been frightening.

Most keepers I've come across are slightly weird – maybe even all of them, in fact. I know it sounds like a cliché, but it's true. There are different degrees, however. Robert Green at Norwich was just a bit introverted, but some of Schmeichel's quirks were really bizarre. He had this superstition where he didn't like the balls being in his goal during training. Usually, you wind up with a net full of balls in the goal you're practising in, but he always wanted it to be empty. Typically for me, I'd throw balls in there when he wasn't looking to wind him up; he'd get proper angry about it. So angry, in fact, that he'd want to strangle me. He'd chase me, but he was so old and big that he had no chance of catching me. I'm glad he couldn't – if he had done, I'd have been bear-hugged to death.

He trained as he played – and nothing was going in that goal. Nothing. Let's face it, though, keepers have to be a bit unhinged to do what they do, diving around at peoples' feet and getting booted in the head for a living.

Regardless of his occasional strange antics, Schmeichel would definitely make the Huckerby XI. Nigel Martyn and Robert Green were both top-class keepers, but Schmeichel was in a league of his own, a living legend even at forty. He just filled that goal; if you've never seen him in the flesh, it's hard to visualise his size and presence. He's probably the best keeper in the history of the Premier League and, for me, one of the best the world has ever seen. That anger he had when he conceded a goal, even in training, just showed what a winner he was.

There was disappointment for me, though. Kevin broke up the partnership I had with Goats, even though we'd scored something in the region of sixty goals in the course of winning Division One. Once Anelka came in, we never started a game together again. Don't get me wrong – clubs always move on. They have to. But it was hard not to feel a little bit cheated.

I played the last half-hour of the first game of the new season – we lost three-nil at Leeds – and then started against Newcastle at home the following weekend and scored the only goal of the match. I played a few more times and then drifted out and never really started many more. Shaun played a couple more, and did okay. He scored a brace against Manchester United. We could see, however, that the writing was on the wall for us both.

It was hard to tell what Anelka was like. People have always talked about how moody he can be, but I don't really think of him in that way. He was just quiet; he kept himself to himself. There's nothing wrong with that, and he was always friendly enough. One downside was his abysmal timekeeping – we would start training at half past ten and he would turn up at twenty-five past. There would only be five minutes between his arrival and the point at which he'd begin training. Most importantly, though, he was a quality player, and he had the best change of direction I've ever seen.

You don't mind when your club brings in quality players, which he was. There were no two ways about it. Yet it rankles when, in spite of knowing how much work you'd put in the season before, you don't end up playing. I'm not saying I had some divine right to be in the team, but it's only human for me to look back at the achievements of Goats and I in 2001-2002 and be a bit frustrated that our partnership didn't get kept together.

Marc Vivien-Foe was another class player. A big lad, strong as an ox and a real presence in midfield. He'd played in the Premier League before for West Ham, but he'd spent a couple of years in France with Lyon before coming to City. It was a loan signing, but we'd had to pay a bit of money even to borrow him. It was worth it to have that kind of experience; Marc had played in two World Cups, one that summer and the other in 1994, when he'd only just turned nineteen.

Alongside the new signings, Wrighty – Shaun Wright-Phillips – was really beginning to make a name for himself after some brilliant performances in Division One. He's a lovely, hard-working lad, and a really good player. I used to call him The Elastic Band because he'd always bounce straight back up and keep going if you tackled him.

Ricky Hatton would sometimes come in and see us at Carrington. I'm a big fan of the fight game and this was the period when Hatton, who would go on to be a world champion, was starting to get noticed. Alongside the Gallagher brothers from Oasis, Ricky was one of the club's most prominent celebrity fans, and he was City through and through.

I guess the boxing thing all started as a kid watching Mike Tyson. I'd go through the records and the fights of all the old heavyweight champions, and loved watching Ali's bouts and stuff from the golden seventies period of Sugar Ray Leonard and Marvellous Marvin Hagler. The noble art is my great sporting passion after football – I was there in Vegas when Tyson bit Evander Holyfield's ear off, a crazy night with guns going off in the casinos. I've seen Roy Jones there, too. Whenever there's a big fight on, you'll find me watching it, even if it's on at four or five o'clock in the morning our time.

I love the dedication that comes with boxing. As a team game, football is very different. You can be having a nightmare, but your teammates can get you through it. In boxing, it's all down to you, and you've generally only got one shot. It's what you do in the few months leading up to the contest that counts, and I've always respected how hard the best boxers work. I've seen how people like Ricky Hatton train in those three or four months before a title bout − it's hell. It's a bit philosophical, maybe, but I reckon that boxing is a lot like life in general. There's no easy way in boxing, and if you put nothing in, you get nothing out. Talent counts for nothing if you don't have the determination, and no-one is going to be around to carry you. The mix of skill and willpower that the top fighters have is quite remarkable.

They were a great bunch at City. One memory that stands out is the time that we got a free box for an Oasis gig at Lancashire Country Cricket Ground − that was fantastic. It made me realise how lucky I was, particularly as a few of my mates from back home who'd have killed to be able to do something like that got to come along as well. It was a fantastic night. Occasions like that gave us real team spirit, and I made some good friends there.

We used to go out for meals with Steve Howey, and we still see Paul Dickov in Portugal when we go out there on holiday. Dicky always worked his nuts off, even though he loved a sly cigarette from time to time. He was a real honest pro, who'd run until his legs fell off in every game he played. He wouldn't give a defender a minute's peace, and he built a living on harassing them. As he got older, I think his quality started to shine through a little more; at Blackburn and Leicester he was a pretty reliable goalscorer and he started to get more of the credit he deserved. To run, run, run every game the way he did takes a lot of doing.

Towards the end of that season, when I wasn't getting many games at all, City started to bring even more players in. Signings like Steve McManaman and Robbie Fowler made it even more difficult for me to get games, and once again my confidence was hit. Fowler, of course, was a top player, but he'd lost something since he'd been at Liverpool. In his spell at Leeds, he'd struggled, and, while he could still prove his finishing ability in training, it was obvious that he wasn't as mobile as he had been.

In a way, it was the same with McManaman. He'd returned from a four-year spell at Real Madrid where he'd been playing alongside the likes of Zidane, Luis Figo, and Raul; he'd won two Champions League titles while he was out there. I remembered him from his time at Liverpool, where he'd been world class, but it was obvious that he was winding down by the time he came in at City. He made fewer than forty appearances in the league for them, which would suggest he was somewhat past his best during his spell in Manchester.

When you're getting towards your peak at twenty-seven or twenty-eight, that kind of thing is frustrating. Some people will tell you that football is like that, and that you just have to take it on the chin, but you can't ignore the fact that you're getting shunted out of the side in favour of players who, despite being world class, are clearly on the downward spiral. It really annoyed me that I didn't get an opportunity to play with Goats again, and the old frustration of being left out of the side was rearing its ugly head once more.

After the five minutes I got as substitute at the end of the FA Cup game against Liverpool in early January, I didn't play again until March, away at Watford for Forest. The loan switch to the City Ground was a bit out of the blue, but, as a Nottingham lad, it was near-enough perfect because it gave my family the chance to come and watch games.

It was, initially, only meant to last until the end of the season, but what I joined was an exceptional Division One outfit which, for a while, I'd have been happy to have pushed on with. The quality of the players there at that point was very, very high, and not far off – in my eyes – the standard of the City team I'd played in the previous year. Darren Ward was in goal, Matthieu Louis-

Jean at right-back, Michael Dawson and Des Walker at centre-half, and Jim Brennan at left-back – a solid defence. Paul Hart, the manager, played a diamond in midfield much like the one Paul Lambert's just used in getting Norwich promoted – Riccy Scimeca held, Gareth Williams and Andy Reid would be on the right and left respectively, and I'd play at the tip in a free role. In front of me were Marlon Harewood and David Johnson. All in all, it was an exceptional team for that level, and it had some real diamonds in it. Andy Reid has a beautiful left foot, and Dawson's obviously gone on to prove his quality with Spurs and England. He was brought through by Paul Hart, who was great at developing young ones. Gareth Williams had been given his chance by Hart too, and he was very tidy. Sadly, he had to give up playing early due to injury.

Elsewhere, Des Walker might have been coming to the end of his career but was still one hell of a player. He was fit, fast, and brave, and only misses out on my All-Stars side because I never played with him at his peak. In his first spell at Forest, before he went out to play for Sampdoria in Italy, there was no better defender in England, and some would say that he was the best in the world at that time.

Like Williams, Reid, and Dawson, Marlon Harewood had come up through the youth team and was a big, strong player who knew where the goal was. He's gone on to do well at other clubs but, for me, this was when he was at his most consistent. Alongside him, Johnson was scoring for fun. As I say, it was a really good team.

Once again, I enjoyed a perfect start, scoring a debut goal against Watford and then getting two in the next game on a Tuesday night, a four-one win at Gillingham. A couple of matches later, I scored against Derby in a three-nil win over Forest's local rivals at the City Ground, then added another in a four-nil home victory over Norwich. Basically, things were going perfectly. We went to Ipswich and beat them four-three, and I was stopping in a flat in Nottingham city centre. I was seeing my mates and my Mum and Dad regularly, making up for time lost in the years away from home, and I was banging in the goals. It was all agreed – if Forest went up, then I'd be joining them.

Then I pulled my hamstring against Leicester. It was awful luck, and I only got one game in the next month, a game in which we lost one-nil at Reading.

My final two games for Forest came against Sheffield United in the play-off semis. Once again, Neil Warnock stood between me and a major final. We drew one-one in the opening leg at the City Ground, travelled up to Bramall Lane for the second leg, and found ourselves two-nil up with about half an hour to go. I played a part in both goals; we appeared to be coasting, but then Marlon went off with a head injury, and it threw us completely.

Under Paul Hart, Forest played really good football, just as you'd expect of a side with the likes of Gareth Williams and Andy Reid in it. But for the second leg up in South Yorkshire, we changed it, deciding to go long and see how they would respond. I wouldn't say it was Route One, as such, but we hit it early into the channels and put it up to Marlon to let him knock people about a bit. We were cruising, but after losing our target man we crumbled. They pulled one back almost immediately after Reid had extended our lead – their free-kick took a horrible deflection to give them a really lucky goal – then levelled eight minutes later to take the game to extra time.

The second half of extra time was mad. Paul Peschisolido gave them the lead, then Des Walker, of all people, scored an own goal. We didn't let our heads drop, and my shot led to Robert Page putting through his own net to make it four-three with a couple of minutes to go, but we just ran out of time. By anyone's standards, it was an extraordinary game.

The run-up to it, though, had been difficult for me. In the previous month, I'd only played in the defeat at Reading, and to go straight into two Division One play-off games was incredibly tough. I was nowhere near my best; while I couldn't really feel the hamstring, I was lacking sharpness. No-one can miss the best part of a month's football and return at their peak. There was intense pressure on me to get fit to play Sheffield United, with work being done on the hamstring ever day. I had massage after massage on it, and the treatment was taking up four or five hours a day. It was a massive shame that I could give a better account of myself although, as I say, I played a role in all three goals we scored at Bramall Game. To be honest, I look back and see it as a game we really should have won.

It felt right being part of that Forest set-up, not least because it was a homecoming for me. If Sheffield United hadn't got the better of us, I'd have gone there, and I like to think it would have been happy days. Five goals in eleven games – from attacking midfield – is definitely a decent return, and I think I fitted into Paul Hart's side well. The scary thing was that almost immediately after the disappointment of the play-offs that team got broken up; Reid and Dawson went to Spurs, and Walker retired. Hart clung on to the job for a little while longer before being sacked. It was sad, given how close everyone had got there.

If we'd kept a regular line-up for the final league games of the season – which would have meant me not getting injured – then I'm sure we'd have got one more win and finished fifth instead of sixth. If we'd pulled that off, we wouldn't have had to play Sheffield United, who – back then – were the last side you wanted to encounter in a knock-out tie. Whatever people say about Neil Warnock, he knows what he's doing when it comes to motivating his teams for big games.

Of course, what ended up happening was that I went to Norwich and enjoyed the best spell of my career, but that time was a huge opportunity for Forest to get back into the Premier League. To this day, they haven't got that close. They've been relegated, returned to the second tier, and flirted a couple of times with the play-offs, but I'm convinced that my spell there was the best chance they've had of getting back to the big times.

The real shocking thing that took place that summer was the death of Marc Vivien-Foe. It was horrendous; as I've said, he was a big, strong guy who could run all day, and what happened was completely unexpected. He was playing for Cameroon against Colombia in the Confederations Cup in France, and we were watching the game while we were on holiday in Portugal. Everyone remembers it, I guess – he just dropped to the floor in the centre circle with no-one else near him. I remember ringing Shaun Wright-Phillips and trying to work out was going on. Apparently, he had an undetected heart condition.

It was so, so hard to comprehend. How can it be that someone so physically fit and strong can die like that? You just don't believe that it can happen. And it affects you hugely – footballers are very close to each other, because they're with each other every day for three quarters of the year. Especially at City, we were solid. After the match, we'd all go to the swimming pool together to warm down before heading out together in the evening. Obviously, it's dreadful when someone dies at any age, but it's a real tragedy to lose a twenty-eight year-old team-mate in those circumstances.

With Forest missing out on promotion, I was forced to cope with the insecurity of returning to Manchester City, where I couldn't be sure whether or not I was wanted. Being sent out on loan was a pretty sure sign that I wasn't – let's be honest, being shipped out on loan is very often a sign that the writing is on the wall.

Apparently, there had been a chance of a loan move up to Celtic the previous January; that was when Martin O'Neill was in charge there. While I'd have loved to work with him, because he's an exceptional manager who gets the best out of his players, I didn't want to leave my young family and go up to Scotland at that particular moment in time. I think on transfer deadline day Phil Smith left about fifty messages on my phone and in the end I just switched it off until after five o'clock so there was no temptation to listen to what I was being offered. Basically, the move wouldn't be fair on anyone else – we'd just had Ben, our second son, and Scotland was too far from home and family.

So, I was off back to Manchester City at the end of that summer unsure of what was going to happen or what I should do. As ever, I worked as hard as I could, and perhaps even harder because the insecurity made me want to be at the top of my game. I wasn't the only player who was staring at the door – Jon Macken, who'd signed from Preston the season before, was another – and new players, like Trevor Sinclair, had once again been brought in.

Effectively, things didn't fall for me. I didn't go back that summer looking to escape, but I wasn't stupid. When a manager sends a lad out on loan, as Kevin had done with me, then there's a very good chance that the player in question isn't in anyone's plans. City had brought in Sinclair, McManaman, and Fowler, three international forwards, and moving on was starting to look like an inevitability. Much as I loved playing for City and living in Manchester, I couldn't sit around getting paid for doing nothing.

Don't get me wrong. Competition is important in all areas of the team, but that competition has to be fair and judged on merit. If it's like that, then there's no problem. If, however, the players coming in aren't that effective, but are still getting picked ahead of you, then it's really hard to take.

The first time Norwich's name came up was when Phil Smith gave me a ring and told me that they wanted me on loan. My response was to say: 'Mmm…right. Let's see how far away it is.' I was thinking, just as I had been when Celtic bid for me in the January, that it was miles away from Manchester and that the

Mrs wasn't going to be happy. To go on loan to Forest, my hometown club, was very straightforward. I knew where to live, I knew where my friends were, and I could pop in to see my Mum and Dad. Norwich was a completely different kettle of fish, and a massive trek from Manchester. I think it would be fair to say that Lyndsey wasn't overly chuffed with the prospect, at least at first.

Presumably, there were other loan options that I could have taken at the time, but I've never been one to pull Phil aside and demand that he gets me a move to this or that club. But I knew nothing about Norwich, nothing about the place or the people. Why would I have done? When you come from Nottingham, and you spend the majority of your career in the north, there's no reason for you to have any idea about the ins and outs of Norwich or Norfolk. All I knew about came from going to Carrow Road to play matches; from staying one night in a hotel and then going home. You'd always look at that away game and think, 'Jeez, there's no easy way to get there'. It was famous for the long trek.

People seem to think that because you're a footballer and you're going here and there every week, that you get to know places. You don't, though, because you don't see anything. You get on a bus get to a hotel, get off the bus, go to your room. You get on the bus, drive to the stadium, play the game, get on the bus, drive home.

You see nothing – not the nice places to live, the picturesque streets, the shops, or the restaurants. Just hotels, and they generally all belong to the same chain, so all the rooms look exactly the same. Week in, week out, you see the same old stuff, and it's basically boring. So when people said, 'Oh, you're off to Norwich,' I'd have to say that I didn't know the first thing about the place. Unless you join a team from London or Manchester, you just don't know what you're going to get.

Until I discovered that you could fly down – which in those

days was actually cheaper than driving – it was a little bit of a hard sell. As soon as I got there I went and rented out a flat, fully furnished, so I knew that we'd be able to live like a proper family. I didn't want to be going mental in a hotel. Even with a flat, though, it was still a big upheaval to be going into a place where I knew almost no-one.

On your first day at a club, you're likely to meet twenty or thirty of the staff and, if you're lucky, stumble upon one or two familiar faces in the dressing room. Fortunately for me, I had one contact there in the shape of Marc Edworthy, who I'd played with at Coventry. It wasn't as if I'd been on the phone to him beforehand checking everything out, because in football you tend to drift apart from people you meet at a club when you move on. People tend to presume that you stay in touch with every team-mate you've ever had, which isn't the case. Maybe now there's Facebook, Twitter, and so on that's a bit more simple, but people weren't so closely connected back then. Still, it was good to have a familiar face to greet me.

On my first meeting with Nigel Worthington, it was a lovely sunny day and I was beginning to think that Norwich wouldn't be so bad after all. Big Peter Crouch was there too, as he was also coming in on loan. Nigel introduced us to each other and said: 'I just want you to come here and enjoy your football! Just do what you do…'

And that was it, really.

I know that every player says this when they first come to the training ground at Colney, but Norwich's facilities are of Premier League quality. They look even better when the sun's out and it's a nice day. Of course, it gets a bit cold when it's windy, but it is a great training ground. The pitches are fantastic, the gym is good, as is the indoor training dome. As a player coming in, you can't really ask for much more in terms of set-up. To tell the truth, I was pleasantly surprised. It's big and open, and there are probably at least half a dozen top-flight sides whose facilities aren't as good as those at Norwich.

I'd played against a lot of the lads before, so it wasn't like when I went to San Jose and knew no one. Norwich might have been far away from Manchester, but I wasn't arriving there as a foreigner in a new country. And Crouchy being there helped, too. Life is a bit easier if you're not the only newcomer. One look at him and I knew that he'd be winning ninety-five percent of his headers, which would obviously be interesting for anyone playing alongside him.

From a team point of view, there's a bit of a risk when two new forwards come in at the same time and they haven't played together before. It's very different to bringing one player into a well-established team; he drops in, does his thing, and mixes relatively easily with the rest of the lads. But it was a gamble by Nigel to bring in two new forwards who had played neither together or with anyone already at the club.

As they tend to be, the dressing room was nice and friendly. Initially, I kept myself to myself, even though I enjoyed being around the lads and getting involved in training for the game on Saturday. This was training with an end product, training with a purpose, and it was great fun.

As I've said, there's no rocket science to training sessions. You can go to all kinds of places and find the same things going on, or variations on a simple theme. At Norwich, it was no different. They were a hard-working bunch of lads; Doug Livermore, Nigel's Number Two was always at the manager's side. You got the feeling that they really trusted each other. The whole set-up felt exactly right.

My first game was on Saturday, September 13, 2003. We were at home to Burnley, and we won two-nil with goals from Crouchy and Iwan Roberts, who scored in the last minute. On the evidence of the first game, had we the makings of a decent front pair? The signs were good, but it was hard to be certain. I was still figuring out the strengths and weaknesses of the whole team.

We were lucky in as much as we had some really, really talented players. Paul McVeigh was exceptional. He wasn't really quick, and he was small, but his technical ability was frightening. Then there was Gary Holt, who sat in the midfield and did everyone's dirty work; he was a real unsung hero. I know it's been said before, but Holty would do the work of two people if you let him. The closest I'd seen to him before that was Lee Bowyer, another who could just run and run.

Where Lee's efforts were designed to get him on the end of things, Holty was all about covering everybody. When I was playing left-wing, Holty would cover me so I could take people on. If I lost the ball, he'd be right there to stop people attacking through the hole. He was selfless, a real example to everyone who always knew what he needed to do for the sake of the team.

Adam Drury was cut from similar cloth. While he liked to go forward, he was one of the best defensive left-backs I've ever played with. He didn't get the plaudits he deserved because people would see me taking two or three players on, but it was Adam's tackling and defensive awareness that allowed me to do that. And I'd leave him exposed a lot – defending wasn't my strong suit.

Marc Edworthy would be another example. I think Eddie has been promoted four or five times now, and he's another one of those unrecognised heroes that just does their job without receiving anything like the acclaim that forwards do. In between Adam and him, there were Malky Mackay and Craig Fleming, then there was Robert Green – a future England international – in goal. Greeny has gone on to become one of the most consistent keepers in the Premier League and, while West Ham have struggled since he joined them, his shots-to-saves ratio is staggering.

Off the pitch, of course, there was Delia Smith. I can't remember when I first met her – I guess it must have been on one of those occasions post-match – but she was a big star. I think my Mum and Lyndsey thought the most exciting thing about me joining Norwich was that there might be an opportunity to meet Delia. 'Can you get me a signed book?' they both asked, before I'd been at the club for five minutes.

Norwich is a great family club and, as I came to discover afterwards, everyone is looked after properly. They were great with the wives and kids; they laid on a great Christmas party for the players' children, and the girls got to go on nights out with Delia, the staff, and Sandra Worthington.

In the midweek after the Burnley game we travelled to Gillingham, where we won two-one, Crouchy bundling in Kevin Harper's cross. On the following Saturday, we went to Stoke, where we got a one-one draw in which I scored my first goal for Norwich. That took the weight off my shoulders, particularly given that Crouchy had already scored twice and I was being asked to play up front.

After that, we got on a run. We beat Palace at home two-one, then Reading came to Carrow Road and we won by the same margin. I scored in both games. From then on I knew that I wanted to play for Norwich – it's hard to explain, but somehow I just knew. I don't think I'd ever been at a place before where I'd get the ball and literally feel ten thousand people behind me stand up because they were expecting me to do something.

Not wanting me to do something, you understand, but expecting me to. And that stayed with me for virtually the whole period I spent at Norwich. It was there in every single game. Whether I had a good match or a bad one, the anticipation never went away. It sounds funny, but I have pictures of me getting the ball out wide and you can see the expressions on the supporters' faces, all waiting, watching, hoping, expecting.

As a player who is put in there to make things happen, there's no better feeling than that. To have so many people, every week, wanting you to be the difference between their side and the opposition. For me, the fact that they were giving me that level of support meant that I owed them something straight away. I just felt a connection with the fans, and it was a big reason that I wanted to stay at the club. No doubt about it.

The other big plus point was the city itself. I'm not someone who likes a lot of traffic; I don't like thousands and thousands of people hustling and bustling everywhere. I've had a few opportunities to join London clubs and been put off by that. Norwich struck me as a bit more laid-back. The people are really, really friendly and it was, basically, like a bigger Lincoln with higher expectations for its football club.

So, as I say, it only took three or four games for me to know that I wanted to stay. That didn't mean that it would definitely happen, but I knew that I wanted it to. It's a fantastic club and place to play, even if when I arrived late that summer the Jarrold Stand was still being built and the crowd were only on three sides of the ground. For those first three months, we could do no wrong; there were a couple of defeats, but we were full of confidence and always bounced back from them.

On top of that, that September was red hot. The skies were blue every day, and it seemed to me more like Marbella than Norfolk. 'It can't be like this all the time, can it?' I'd be thinking to myself.

Everything was right. Once again, I'd gone from not playing at one club to making people sit up and take notice of what I was doing for another. Belief was rising at Carrow Road; with Crouchy and I up front, people were quietly starting to murmur that there was a chance of promotion.

It was all building up.

Clearly, though, that expectation involved the question of

whether or not I would be able to stay on for the rest of that season. And, as everybody knows, that proved to be a whole different story...

9. WORTHY WINNERS

Match:	Norwich City vs Cardiff City
Venue:	Carrow Road
Competition:	Football League Championship
Date:	Saturday, December 13, 2003
Result:	Norwich City 4, Cardiff City 1
Attendance:	16,428

Norwich City: Green, Edworthy, Drury, Shackell, Fleming, Henderson, McVeigh (R Jarvis, 86 mins), Holt, Mulryne, Huckerby, Roberts (Brennan, 85 mins)

Subs (not used): Crichton, Francis, Rivers

Cardiff City: Alexander, Barker, Croft (Weston, 60 mins), Gabbidon, Vidmar, Campbell (Lee, 60 mins), Langley, Whalley, Boland, Earnshaw, Thorne

Subs (not used): Margetson, Prior, Bonner

Although I was really enthusiastic about the idea of switching to Norfolk full-time, feelings in the boardroom were less simple. While it was obvious that I'd added something to the team which had the potential to bring Premier League football back to Carrow Road, the general consensus – at least at first – was that I wasn't affordable. The directors felt that the transfer fee alone would be beyond them, and that was before my salary was taken into consideration.

Of course, Phil then came out and did his agent's piece, saying, amongst other things, that I was too good for Norwich. Predictably, this made for big headlines in the local press, and the result was that I had to get in touch with the papers and tell them that my future was down to me, not my agent. In short, it was all a bit of a ding-dong. All good fun in the end, though, and I've no doubt that the newsagents were a bit busier than usual that week.

In fairness to Phil, I think he just had me down as someone who should have been playing in the top flight – which I obviously wanted to be. But the Premier League isn't the be all and end all. A point comes where you recognise that finding stability in your home life, enjoying your football, and creating a legacy for yourself with a particular club is much more important than being a bit-part at a team where, a decade down the line, people won't remember you. That's the last thing I'd want. Ultimately, the reason you play football is to win things and leave a mark somewhere that's lasting.

There were other considerations. Although I was living in a flat on Riverside, I was getting to know the city and beginning to realise what a great place it would be to bring up the kids. I knew that there would be no problem finding a good school for them, and I thought that the pace of life was ideal for a young family. But that was all hanging in the balance – it was a long shot as to whether or not I'd be hanging around in East Anglia for very long.

The equation had several parts. Firstly, Manchester City were paying me good money, and they weren't going to let me go without a decent fee. My personal concern was that, while we were starting to make people sit up and acknowledge that Norwich were serious contenders for promotion, a failure to stretch our form out over the rest of the season would consign me to another year in Division One. For the supporters, meanwhile, there was almost certainly a slight uncertainty as to whether I'd be worth the outlay. It was all very well me deciding that I wanted to stick about, but I'd have to prove myself on the pitch. The last thing I wanted was to fail to meet the expectations people would have of a big-name signing.

Just to add to the complications, several other clubs were beginning to express an interest by the time Christmas rolled around. Sheffield United – Neil Warnock had obviously liked what he'd seen in the play-offs - and WBA were certainly in the frame. For me, though, there was no doubt, and I made it clear to everyone that I wouldn't be going elsewhere. There was no way I'd help Norwich get to the top of the table and then disappear off somewhere or other. The choice was simple – either I joined Norwich, or I sat the season out at Manchester City. It was going to be one or the other.

Out of courtesy, I did speak to Gary Megson at West Brom. We had a cordial enough conversation, but I had to tell him that I could never see myself playing for him, and that I wouldn't be going anywhere if the Norwich board decided they couldn't afford me. I could have shot myself in the foot badly there; if the whole move had turned sour then I'd have been stuck in the ressies at City for the foreseeable future.

In the middle of the loan spell, I had a dry patch in front of goal, which was as frustrating as they always are. This partially coincided with some dramatic events closer to home. About nine o'clock in the morning of the game against Crewe, right at the end of November, we were in the flat and Ben, our youngest, just keeled over. He couldn't walk or talk. Lyndsey was screaming – and neither of us had a clue what was going on. I rang up Iwan and said: 'Robbo, what do I do here? Where's the hospital? My lad's not responsive, he can't move his arms, his legs; he can't close his eyes, he's all over the place…'

Iwan gave me directions and we raced Ben up to the hospital; they immediately decided to keep him in for tests and observation. This at least reassured me that it wasn't going to get any worse. They said he was okay, and he started to come round a little bit.

It wasn't the greatest preparation for a game. It wasn't easy leaving Ben and Lyndsey, but I felt I had a job to do – yes, I was only on loan, but Norwich were really pushing on and I was aware of the part I had to play in that. I don't think I even told Nigel, in case he told me that I should go back to the hospital and miss the match. Realistically, there was nothing more that I could have done up there, and I felt that my son was in safe hands with the doctors and nurses. 'Right,' I thought. 'I might as well go and help the lads get three points!'

I scored the only goal of the game, thus ending my goal drought, and we won one-nil to take the three points. Ben was soon okay; he'd had a high temperature, and the doctors thought that he'd just had a little fit. It's never happened again, thankfully. I wonder what would have happened if I'd told Nigel and he'd sent me away – maybe the barren run would have continued. As it was, with Ben recovering nicely and me grabbing the winner, the day ended perfectly.

The game against Cardiff on December 13, which was the last of my initial three-month loan spell, was the one that was pivotal in earning me the move. To this day, I honestly believe that I wouldn't have signed for Norwich if that game had gone badly. There'd have been none of the 'Delia, Delia sign him up!' from the Barclay End – I can't be sure, but to my mind a defeat that afternoon would have put the transfer on the back burner. In the event, however, that game proved the perfect opportunity for me to show everyone what I could do; I could probably have scored four or five.

Clearly, you go into every single match wanting to win. On this occasion, though, I wanted to win the game convincingly. With Crouchy having gone back to Villa, the stage was set for me to leave a final, lasting impression, particularly if – as everyone suspected – it turned out to be my farewell to Norwich. I think that the fans knew how much their support had meant to me over the months I'd spent there, and I wanted to give them good memories.

Everything went right. Iwan got a great goal; I scored two – the second a deflection off Tony Vidmar – and could have had a third right at the death, but chose to pull it back for Paul McVeigh instead. Macca showed his gratitude by blazing it over. That aside, I think everyone remembers the first goal, which bore the hallmark of me at my best. I picked the ball up just inside the halfway line, beat a couple of defenders, put the ball past the last man on one side, cut past him on the other, and nicked it over the keeper. It was perfect – almost as if it was meant to be.

Given that I didn't think I'd be back, it was a great way to leave the club. I was convinced I wouldn't be signing; all the lads came out on the Saturday night for a farewell drink, and that was more or less it. While I knew that the fans would make noises demanding that I be kept on, it was always going to come down to the finances. Could Norwich afford to take the gamble? I think that, in his heart of hearts, Nigel believed he was seeing the back of me. We kept in constant contact, though. Even when it seemed dead in the water and I was back training with Manchester City at Carrington, he kept on trying.

Everyone knew that sacrifices would have to be made if it was going to happen. In the end I spoke to Kevin and told him that I wasn't going to go anywhere if I couldn't go to Norwich, a gesture which might have seemed to him as if I was cutting my nose off to spite my face. It was a big risk on my part, but he was as good as gold and Manchester City came round in the end.

I had to take a fifty percent pay cut to come to Norwich, but Manchester City helped out in the end to make the move viable. Knowing me, it probably would have happened in any case, but I knew that I had to look after my family and that there was only so much money that I could afford to lose. It was a gamble. If Norwich didn't go up, I'd have ended up leaving a Premier League outfit with wages to match to join a Division One side on half the money. Financially, I was putting a lot at stake. In the end, though, I knew in my heart that Norfolk was where I wanted to be; also, the fact that Nigel and the board were really pushing the boat out to make the signing happen proved to me that I was really wanted.

It turned out later on − quite a lot later on, in fact − that, in financial terms, the club weren't taking quite as big a hit as people thought they were. To guarantee that I stayed in East Anglia, a local businessman called Carl Moore had offered to pay my wages for the rest of the season. Now, putting your money forward to help the club you support afford a new player takes a lot of bottle; had I known what was going on behind the scenes, I'm not absolutely sure I could have made the move. Letting down a club is one thing, but letting down an individual prepared to lay down their money on you is quite another. I'd have really felt the pressure.

It was lucky, then, that I didn't find out. Since then, Carl and I have become good friends. He's a really generous guy, who's contributed in other ways to sport in Norfolk − he paid for Leroy Lita to come in on loan later on, and was involved for a while in backing local boxer Jon Thaxton. I was a guest at his wedding reception, where I presented him with one of the boots I wore in a game against Birmingham where I scored one of my best ever goals; on my first return to Norwich from San Jose he and I were invited onto the pitch as special guests before a game between City and Forest.

The fact that the move was taking place over the Christmas period added to the uncertainty. Most of the time, as a family, we didn't have a clue what was going on. One time it was on; the next time it was off. It was only really on Christmas Day itself that I spoke to Nigel and it became clear that it was all on for definite – he told me that terms had been agreed with Manchester City, and that everything had been done that needed to be. And that was it. I jumped into the car and found myself heading eastwards early on Boxing Day.

The deal was announced to the crowd before the one-nil win over Nottingham Forest that afternoon, but the Football League were unable to process the paperwork because of the holidays. I had to wait for New Year for their offices to reopen, which meant that I missed the four-nil win at Derby and the famous two-nil victory over Ipswich the week before.

There couldn't have been a better welcome to my new club. By then, people were really starting to think that the move could be the one that took Norwich into the Premier League; while there was over half the season left to play, that was genuinely the feeling people had. This idea was reinforced when Matty Svensson and Leon McKenzie came in ahead of the win at Portman Road – I'm not sure that Nigel would have signed both of them had he known that I was definitely coming back, but they were a useful pair of players.

As I see it, the club took a bit of a wager on me, but £750,000 wasn't a great deal of money in the Premier League scheme of things. To tell the truth, they got a bit of a bargain. They got me at twenty-seven, right at the beginning of what I consider to be the best period of my career. I knew the game so much better than I had done at, say, Coventry or Leeds; my decision-making had vastly improved. While I'd always caused havoc with my runs, I was getting much better at picking people out at the end of them.

I got a real buzz out of setting goals up. Everyone obviously enjoys scoring, but I was beginning to love making them. I put Iwan in for his first of the season on my debut, a move that was unselfish in a way I hadn't really been when I was younger. Back then, I didn't appreciate when people were in a better position to score than I was. Through my early twenties I always felt under pressure to get goals, but when I got a bit older I realised that it was really about what was best for the team. You realise that there's no point in you getting off the mark in every game if the side aren't winning.

Some might think that the welcome I got that Boxing Day confirmed that I'd made the right decision in coming to Norwich, but the truth is that my mind was made up after three or four loan games. The fact that it all fell into place in late December was, as far as I was concerned, just a Christmas bonus for the supporters. It took me hardly any time to settle into Nigel's team and, once I had, there was never anywhere else I wanted to play – I became completely focused on getting Norwich promoted, or at least into the play-offs. What's more, that feeling that I'd found the place I wanted to be never changed, even when – later on – we were relegated and other teams came in for me.

Watching the Forest and Derby games from the sidelines, it was apparent that we were on a real roll. As I said about the promotion season at Manchester City, you sometimes find that sheer momentum will keep driving a club on and on. I wonder sometimes if they would have gone up without me, and I reckon they might well have done. That said, even with Svensson and McKenzie in, most people assumed that the best chance of going up lay with me coming back.

Sod's law meant that my first game as a bona fide Norwich City player was a defeat, in the FA Cup against Everton, which was followed by a match in which Bradford nicked an unlikely win at Carrow Road. The doubting part of my mind, I can admit now, was asking, 'What have I done here?' But the quality of the team that Nigel had put together was high enough to set my mind at rest.

Greeny was shielded by the best defence in the league, who were in turn protected by Holty's tirelessness. That gave us the base on which everything else could be built. Damien Francis got up and down well, and had a Bowyer-like ability to turn up in the box just when you wanted him to. And we had more than our fair share of flair – Phil Mulryne could come in and spray the ball over the place, and Paul McVeigh was an extremely gifted forward. Up front, there was me, Matty Svensson, Leon, and Iwan, who picked his games well. In short, we had the ideal balance between sturdiness and creativity.

It certainly got to the point where I genuinely believed we could win every game we went into. No matter who was due to come to Carrow Road that week, I'd think 'This lot haven't got enough to stop us.' Our defence was so good that it was an achievement for teams to find the net against us; if they managed to do that, we'd make sure we scored two.

Leon McKenzie was someone I loved to play with. He came in and scored some really important goals. In fact, Leon is probably a favourite in terms of people I've played with. Why? Because I always knew where he was going to be, and he would run himself into the ground for you. Teams need people like him, individuals who will run all day, work the channels, and fight and scrap for everything. He did that. While he wasn't as clinical a finisher as Robert Earnshaw, and he didn't have the sheer class of a player like Dean Ashton, he really had a lot going for him. He was a proper team player, and everyone appreciated what he did.

Hopefully, Leon would tell you that I created a lot of his goals for him. That happened simply because I knew where his runs would take him to, and what positions he'd find for himself. He might not have scored all the time, but he gave a hell of a lot more than the stereotypical poacher.

Off the pitch, Matty Svensson was one of the nicest guys you could hope to meet. On it, I saw him be a bit naughty on more than one occasion. Even when we were training, he'd occasionally boot someone after the ball had gone. Well, sometimes you need that, don't you? You can't be Mr Nice Guy all the time, especially when half of your opponents want to kick lumps out of you or elbow you in the head when the ref isn't looking. Matty was neither the biggest nor the quickest, but he was left-footed and could finish, and he was clever in the ways he brought people into the game. We needed that at the time. With his first touch, he was the smooth to Leon's rough – while Leon would run through brick walls, Matty had class, and the two complemented each other well.

Towards the end of the season, when the team had really gelled, we just knew what we had to do in order to win games. Flem and Malkay were solid, having seen it and done it, and they loved the battle so much that we were never going to concede that many with them about. They wouldn't roll over for anybody, and they wouldn't let us do that either. Damien's engine became really important, too. Particularly later on, in the Premier League, the ball always seemed to fall to him at the right time. Trust me, that takes some doing in terms of covering ground.

Damien was lucky to have Holty beside him. If that hadn't been the case, he wouldn't have been able to bomb on in the way he did; likewise, I knew that I could afford to stay that little bit higher up the pitch thanks to the cover Holty guaranteed. The back four knew that, if the opposition broke on us, then Gary would be one of the first to get back. Every good team needs a player in that mould.

I think the game has been changing for a while now in terms of the sheer athleticism required to play the central midfield role and do it well. Gone are the days of the Le Tissiers and Mersons, playmakers who could amble around the middle of the park with their sleeves pulled over their hands while occasionally doing something extraordinary with the ball. Most Premier League midfielders now are the whole package – big, strong, quick, and capable of displaying a touch of magic from time to time. That you now have to have the lot is, for me, one of the biggest changes football at the top level has seen over the last decade or so.

Now and again you find a Lionel Messi type, a player whose attributes in one area are so outlandishly good that they don't have to hit all of the normal physical requirements. They're the exception that proves the rule, though. You see this all the time at Academy level. A big, strong, fast teenager will appeal to managers because they know that skills can be added to those physical characteristics. A kid who is small to begin with, on the other hand, is unlikely to experience a sudden growth spurt, and pace is also something that can't really be taught. Someone like Wes Hoolahan is lucky in that he's an exceptionally talented footballer, but it is very hard to get away from the fact that there's so little you can do to get away from an opponent who is giant and twice as quick as you.

One of the beauties of our team that season, and something that Nigel was arguably slightly fortunate with, was that the back four was absolutely set in stone – and none of them ever got injured. In turn, that meant that I knew I could get on with anything because I trusted the players around me. That's a big thing. The rest of us could rely on them to hold onto a clean sheet for us, and they often got us out of the mire. This was perhaps most true of Adam Drury; we used to joke that he did my defending while I did his attacking.

Perhaps I left him a little bit too exposed sometimes, but, for my part, I was really glad to have someone I trusted behind me. I'd like to think that Ads would say that I'm one of the best players he's ever had in front of him, and I'd certainly say that he's one of the best I've had behind me. He was a great runner, too, although it didn't take me too long to lose count of the number of overlapping runs he made only for me to fail to use him. 'Cheers, Ads – now get yourself back there!' I'd say as I cut inside and ignored him. In all seriousness, though, there was real respect and understanding between us, and he has gone on to become one of my best friends in football.

The dressing room was full of big characters. Although Craig Fleming would moan about everything under the sun, he was always up for a laugh and a joke. The Irish lads were all banter and craic, and Paul Crichton, our second-choice keeper, was always causing chaos. So they were good times, and we had a good bond – which was vital in sustaining the inner belief we held that we had the grit to go out and win games, even when we weren't at our best.

Unsurprisingly, a few of the lads liked a drink and a good night out, but not everyone was like that. There were all kinds of personalities in the squad. Holty, for example, kept himself to himself and was always one of the first to leave training. He was a real family man, but he had a great line in dry humour. His discipline and work ethic had been developed in the Armed Forces; he'd come to football late, having originally trained as a chef in the Army before making a name for himself at Kilmarnock. It wasn't then, as if everyone was into the same kind of stuff, which was fine with me. Everyone's different.

The other thing which made it easy to feel comfortable was the manager. Nigel and I got on from our first meeting to the moment he left. He really believed in my ability, and I was grateful for that. Even though he dropped me for a couple of games against Ipswich, I had a lot of time for him. It might not come across on TV, but he has a great sense of humour — and he's a good, honest man.

I felt that we could go all the way from pretty early on, but — looking back at that spring - I'd highlight the Wigan game at the start of April as a crucial one. It was live on Sky, they were third or fourth in the table going into it, and they had real quality in the shape of players like Jason Roberts and Geoff Horsfield. Greeny made a couple of decent saves in the first half, and the whole game was pretty tight until the break. Then, in the second half, we ran all over them — Matty Svensson smashed in a great opener, and I got the second to make it two-nil. Job done.

We did that to a lot of teams that season, and it was all down to our belief that the opposition really had to play well to beat us. And I mean really, really well. We knew that we had players that could hurt the opposition, and the opposition would turn up to play us fully aware that they could get hurt. They'd be on the back foot even before kick-off; everyone knew that we had pace, power, and that we could counter-attack effectively.

Teams who try the pass, pass, pass route to success risk being overloaded once the opposition get in amongst them and break up their play. If they have no outlet, they get stuck making patterns in midfield until they get frustrated and let a goal in. We had weapons, and a variety of them at that. When I started to play more on the left at the end of that season, we could use Iwan's aerial ability, which gave us something totally different to what Leon offered. Both of them were in turn different from Matty, and we had the extra option of dropping Paul McVeigh in behind a big man.

If we threw Iwan on for the last ten minutes, we could guarantee that he'd be brave, put his head in, and hold the ball up for us. Nigel had a great mixture at his disposal — if things weren't going right, he could always shake it up a little bit with the subs. That wasn't down to luck — he'd just been really, really astute in terms of who he brought in.

Of course, with the team flying the atmosphere at home games was unbelievable. As I said, the new Jarrold Stand was still being built when I arrived, but once it was completed every week was a 25,000 sell-out, some going in Division One. I'd say, though, that other teams who hit a run of form like we got on that season struggle to get a better atmosphere than the one we had at Norwich. If you look at the stats from that campaign, you notice that we won twenty-eight out of forty-six, and only conceded fifteen goals at home. It was a hell of an achievement, and we were near-on unbreakable at 'Fortress Carrow Road'.

We were unlucky in the couple of games we did lose. Watford were battered in the middle of November but nicked a two-one win, and the Bradford side that beat us in January were in a relegation place at the time. It's odd how often top loses to bottom – it's probably because the team who are, on paper, weaker come in thinking they have nothing to lose, while complacency may creep in on their opposition's side.

And, now and again, there are times when you're absolutely all over your opponents and you just don't get the rewards. Sunderland away was one of those. We really laid in to them for the first ten minutes, knowing that we needed only a point to clinch the title. Of course, we went in one-nil down at half-time. No-one could really put their finger on why exactly, but we were losing. In the dressing room, Malky and Leon were having a bit of a ding-dong about whether or not Leon was holding the ball up properly, then Nigel came in and started going mental. It was all kicking off.

At this point, I thought it would help if I chipped in. 'Oi, Gaffer,' I said to Nigel. 'You're telling them to calm down – but you need to calm down!'

In his anger, he booted one of the skips. It was full; Nigel all but broke his foot. There he was after that, hobbling around and all bruised up – one or two of the boys laughed out loud when he did it, but I think quite a few more were staring at the floor to stop themselves from cracking up. Eventually, it all calmed down. The point was, I guess, that we were already promoted and near-enough champions, but everybody still had that edge. Winning still meant so much to us.

We went back out for the second half, by which point West Brom were three-nil down at Stoke in a game that they needed to win to have even the slimmest chance of denying us the title. We were, to all extents and purposes, champions, and we were just waiting for the final whistle in the Potteries to confirm it. The ball went went out for a throw-in, just by the dug-outs, and I went to pick it up from next to where Nigel was standing. I took the opportunity to shake his hand and say: 'Congratulations, Nigel – we're champions, and you're a Premier League manager!' After a parting smile, I carried on.

That handshake, which only lasted a few seconds while the game was still in progress, is my lasting memory of that night.

There are plenty of players who just potter on throughout their careers without winning anything. I know plenty of them; they serve to remind us that there are almost certainly more downs than ups in football. What happened to us that season at Norwich isn't the kind of thing that happens all the time, which is part of why my Division One winner's medal means everything to me. Obviously, I'd won it before up in Manchester, and that was special in its own way, but the one I won with Norwich means more. At Manchester City we were expected, given the squad Kevin had put together, to win the title; with the greatest of respect, Nigel had a group of lesser players at his disposal, but they all came together to win the league. The boys who played in that team will all be friends for life.

No-one saw Norwich as contenders at the beginning of that season, so to finish with twenty-eight wins and ninety-four points was an enormous achievement. The risk I'd taken in coming to

Carrow Road had paid off for me, my team-mates, Nigel, and the supporters – I'd been thoroughly vindicated in choosing not to stay in Manchester. I'd wanted to come and achieve something special in East Anglia, something that would be remembered for a long, long time to come, and that had happened.

Parading the Division One trophy around the city on an open-topped bus and the civic reception that followed that ride were absolutely crazy experiences. The word in the press was that there were fifty thousand on the streets that day, but I swear there were more than that – I'd guess at seventy or eighty thousand. It was completely bonkers, and I've never seen anything like it. A lovely sunny day; a sea of green and yellow in every direction you looked. No-one can ever take moments like that away from you.

Norwich's support is amazing – thinking back to standing on the balcony at City Hall as Nigel, Delia, and the rest made their speeches, it's hard to imagine a group of fans as loyal and dedicated. Even in the recent grim patch, with the club dipping briefly into League One, there were still twenty-six thousand piling through the gates and creating that special atmosphere. They really are mind-blowing.

I personally celebrated promotion by getting a new tattoo – just above my wrist, and in Latin. It reads 'Per Ardua Ad Altiora', which translates, roughly, as 'Through Adversity to Great Heights', a motto which pretty much summed up how I felt about my career at that point. With it, I had the Roman numerals MMIV – 2004 – and MMII – 2002 – added, which acknowledged my promotions from Division One with Norwich and Man City respectively.

It should go without saying that there were one or two nights out after we'd won it; you won't be surprised to hear that a few drinks were put back. But we deserved it. It had been a long, hard season, near-on ten months of hard graft. In Division One, the pace of games is unrelenting, and you'll often have two matches in a week. Throw in cup-ties and training, and you're looking at a massive slog.

Nigel worked us hard up at Colney – his training sessions were tough, and you could come away from them feeling they'd been more difficult than a match. Matches can take care of themselves in an odd sort of a way, but in training everyone is still competitive. I've met very few footballers who can switch off their urge to win just because they're playing with their team-mates. Even in the little five-a-sides, nobody wants to be embarrassed, so they could be very full on. Occasionally, Nigel would join in, but his little white legs couldn't go like they used to.

We had one game to play that season after winning the title at Sunderland; we had to go up to Crewe for what was to be Iwan Roberts' final game for the club. By then, Robbo knew that he was being released, and he'd been given a big send-off before the final home game. I'd got pretty close to him, so I could see that it was tough for him, but Nigel was in a difficult position as well. With the benefit of hindsight, it seems that letting both Iwan and Malky go that summer was a mistake, but you have to take into account the budget – or lack of – that Nigel had available to him.

Was it feasible to pay a thirty-five year-old good money just to have him coming off the bench? In a world where money was no object, that wouldn't have been a problem – but we were very, very limited in terms of what we could pay in wages. It would soon begin to appear that we were trying to go into the Premier League without spending at all – but that, of course, is another story.

The final day of the season turned out to be pretty special for Robbo, who scored twice and might have had a hat-trick if I'd managed to win another penalty for him to take. 'Anytime anyone touches me in the box, I'm going down,' I told him – it was a really emotional day for him, and it would have been lovely if he'd been able to take the match-ball home. He didn't want to leave, and we all knew that he didn't want to leave. Leaving meant that his whole life was going to change.

I'm sure that it was the same for Malky. What Nigel was doing in letting him go was particularly risky, as it meant breaking up a defence that had been the best in its league. People will say that Malky and Flem would have lacked a yard of pace in the Premier League, but there are very few centre-halves that don't when you compare them to the likes of Thierry Henry. I don't think that the gamble we took there paid off, but it's tricky. A manager always has to raise the overall quality of the squad without losing the assets he already possesses – it's a real balancing act. There's a very thin line between adding class to a squad and harming the team spirit and camaraderie that already exist within it.

There were questions to be answered almost as soon as the celebrations had died down. If we were going to play 4-4-2 in the Premier League, then – realistically – we needed a right-winger and, with Robbo leaving, a centre-forward. Even if we'd kept Malky and not broken up the defence, we'd have been looking for another centre-half, although Jason Shackell was coming through impressively. Another thing we could have done with was a Gary Mac type, one of those hard-to-find midfield string-pullers; in the end, we brought in Youssef Safri who played in the same position as Holty, bringing about something of a selection headache for Nigel. David Bentley came in, but he was a young kid who didn't really know the game. Every match would see him trying a fifty-yard shot or some audacious, Le Tissier-style chip from a silly angle. In short, he was still learning.

We got Thomas Helveg, too. You couldn't argue with the CV of someone who'd played in Serie A for ten years – he'd been at Udinese, Milan, and Inter. But, at thirty-three or thirty-four, was he any more use to us than Marc Edworthy? It was debatable, especially when including him meant inflicting further damage on an established back four who knew each other's games inside out. Simon Charlton signed too; he was basically a left-back, or a left-sided centre-half, but he was tasked with replacing Malky. That was always going to be a tall order. Even Gary Doherty wasn't as imposing as Malky would have been, both in defensive terms and when it came to pushing up for corners. At the top level, winning games might come down to snatching something from a set-piece — and Flem was never the biggest. He was cute and smart, but never that imposing.

We went on a pre-season tour to Malaysia that summer, a trip which proved to be a nightmare for me as I pulled my groin the day before we flew. It was horrendous. I was thousands of miles away from home, unable to play, and unconvinced by the opposition. The trip had some logic; we were sponsored by Proton at the time and going out to Asia was potentially a money-spinner. It wasn't ideal preparation by any means, though.

Mattias Jonson arrived, and Nigel told me that he was a right-sided version of me. He was a lovely lad, but I don't think he was ever allowed to play in his proper position. To me he was a forward, not a right-winger — he didn't beat people, and he didn't cross the ball. On top of that, we lacked physical presence up front. From conversations I've had with him subsequently, I know that Nigel tried to sign Dean Ashton that summer, and that he offered a far lower sum than we ended up paying for him the following January.

There is absolutely no doubt in my mind that if Dean Ashton had come in at the start of that season rather than halfway through it, we'd have stayed up. I am absolutely convinced of that. The reason it didn't happen, I suspect, was because that signing a player of Dean's calibre was seen as too expensive, and the plan was to try and stay up on the cheap somehow.

The way I see it, you cannot stay in the Premier League if you're not willing to spend. Premier League players cost Premier

League money; 'Prudence with Ambition', as the club's saying went at the time, doesn't keep you up. We were about to prove that point.

10. PRUDENCE WITH NOT MUCH AMBITION

Match:	Fulham vs Norwich City
Venue:	Craven Cottage
Competition:	Barclays Premier League
Date:	Sunday, May 15, 2005
Result:	Fulham 6, Norwich City 0
Attendance:	21,927

Fulham:	Van der Sar, Volz, Knight, Goma, Bocanegra, Malbranque, Clark, Diop, Boa Morte (Cole, 87 mins), McBride, Radzinski
Subs (not used):	Crossley, Rehman, Pearce, Pembridge
Norwich City:	Green, Helveg (Jonson, 45 mins), Drury, Shackell, Fleming, Bentley (Svensson, 59 mins), Safri (Holt, 33 mins), Francis, Huckerby, Ashton, McKenzie
Subs (not used):	Ward, Charlton

People often say that the key to surviving in the Premier League is to get your season off to a flying start. In 2004–2005, we failed to win a game until the third week in November, when we got a two-one home win over Southampton. In all, we went thirteen games without a victory. We did, however, draw eight of them, and if we'd have been able to turn a few of those stalemates into wins who knows what would have happened? The maths says that we'd have stayed up with points to spare…

There were definitely games amongst the first, unlucky thirteen where we should have taken all three points. The one on the opening day of the season at home to Palace, for example, would have given us a perfect start, but we drew one-all. Villa and Blackburn at Carrow Road were also golden opportunities which we allowed to go begging. We really could have done it, too. It wasn't as if we were getting battered every week and just scraping the points we did get. We were holding our own, but we couldn't turn performances into the results we needed.

My pre-season woes certainly hadn't helped. The groin injury I'd suffered was a horrendous way to start a campaign. I didn't get on the pitch for a warm-up game until a week before the season started, so once the campaign proper was underway I felt tired and under-prepared. It's part and parcel of the game, I guess, and no player is going to feel one hundred percent all the time. Besides, I scored against Palace, just on the stroke of half-time, and that helped me to forget what the previous few weeks had been like.

Obviously, it was nice to get the club's first goal on its return to the top flight. What bothered me, though, was that we were playing without a recognised target man. For all of Leon McKenzie and Matty Svensson's qualities, their jobs were not about holding the ball up and relieving pressure. In the end, Gary Doherty played a few games up front, a fact which – looking back – is verging on the ridiculous. Doc had played there in years gone by, but he is simply not a centre-forward. To go into your big

Premier League season playing Gary Doherty up front was plain crazy, not to mention unfair on him.

We could have won when we travelled to Spurs in September. Given that we were the visitors, we were all over them. I should have scored – I knocked it round the keeper only for Ledley King to come from nowhere and make a ludicrous block right on the line. Maybe I could have hit it earlier; I was waiting for the ball to come down. Maybe it was just Ledley's brilliance. Their keeper also made a couple of brilliant saves that day, but no amount of excuse-making could disguise the fact that we were badly in need of a proper centre-forward.

That's where Iwan could have come in. He might not have started every game, but we could always have thrown him on for the last ten minutes to let him knock a few people about and maybe get onto the end of something. Otherwise, it seemed that we lacked the finances to get someone in that summer, which was extremely frustrating.

Winning a game in the opening weeks of the season takes the pressure off. When the sixth or seventh match comes around and you still haven't won, you become aware of everyone around you wondering when you're going to get off the mark. The thirteen game winless streak meant that we'd gone through over a quarter of the league season without notching three points; the fact that we weren't getting hammered five-nil every week, which proved that we weren't lacking in ability, somehow made it even worse.

I think that the Premier League has changed over the last couple of years in that the relegation fight now seems to suck in up to eight or nine teams. Back then, you'd usually be looking at three out of four going down. Certain games in the calendar you'd more or less forget about – the Manchester Uniteds and the Liverpools away, for example. You weren't going there for a good day out, and you'd put in your best shift, but you were always going to struggle if they played to their capabilities. That meant that you absolutely had to beat the teams around you; the games against the other teams scrapping at the bottom were absolutely massive. While it was great for the fans and players to go to Old Trafford for our second game – which we came away from having put in a respectable performance, keeping them down to two-one – the home games against sides like Palace and West Brom were the must-win ones.

The defenders in the Premier League are world-class and the teams often double-mark you, which surprised me – I didn't expect to have both a right-back and a right-sided midfielder for company. It was difficult enough, but I felt at times as if I was being over-relied upon slightly; if the opposition cut the supply line to me, it seemed as if the whole team was killed off. We didn't offer a comparable threat down the right, for one thing, but the most damaging thing was the lack of an outlet in the centre-forward position. We were crying out for someone who could hold the ball up when we got it forward to them; it wasn't an impossible task without that, but we'd made life very hard for ourselves by neglecting to replace Iwan. It was crazy.

The finishing touches could have been added to that team without doing too much. Youssef Safri had made a difference since he'd come in. Yes, he could leave his foot in when he wanted to, but his range of passing was superb. Technically, he was very good, and I always had a lot of respect for his ability. Off the pitch, he was quiet, and it was always tricky for him come Ramadan because he could only eat during the hours of darkness. Not being able to refuel between training sessions or eat before games is hard for a footballer. Meanwhile, Simon Charlton was doing the best he could to overcome the fact that he wasn't really a centre-half. We were holding our own on the pitch, but we were just short of a target man who could help take the pressure off and turn draws into wins.

We got beaten at Chelsea and at Liverpool, but most people did. On the day we lost three-nil at Anfield, Xabi Alonso put on a display of passing the likes of which I've never seen again in my life. It was unbelievable. The ball was coming to him and he was hitting it first time with both feet, over fifty or so yards, to either side of the pitch. Afterwards, the lads were all saying he had been brilliant. Alonso was just smacking it, as hard as he could, to feet; he was finding all kinds of space down both flanks. On days like that, you can't do much other than hold your hands up and say, 'Look, that's as good as it gets!'

If you're playing against the best players in the world and they have a good day, there really is very little that you can do. That's particularly true when they're at home and things are falling for them, as they were for Alonso that afternoon. You can't afford to dwell on experiences like that; you know you've another tough test coming up five or six days later and, mentally, you've got to be ready to go all over again. You can't beat yourself up because you couldn't get near an Alonso or Henry. Yes, it's a massive cliché, but in that league every game is a cup final for clubs of Norwich's size – you're scrapping for every single point, and there are no easy games. Get on a decent run in the Premier League, and you've a good chance of surviving. Get on a poor one, and there's a risk that you might cave in under the pressure. There's no way you can look down the line and start marking out games you expect to win.

It went on and on and on. We should, I think, have won when we lost three-two to Everton in October, having been by far the better team on the day. In the event, Duncan Ferguson snatched the winner right near the end. It was that season in a nutshell, basically.

Perhaps another difficulty was the changeover of players in midfield that summer. Safs was really good, but we'd had to fiddle around with the line-up to accommodate him – Gary Holt was no longer guaranteed his place in the side, and the chest

Top Left: On the pitch with Delia Smith after agreeing a permanent deal to sign for Norwich. [26/12/03]

Top middle: Iwan Roberts – top player, great mate. [24/04/04]

Top Right: After scoring against Cardiff in my last game on loan. [13/12/03]

Middle Left: With Craig Fleming after beating Ipswich 3-1 at Carrow Road. [07/03/04]

Middle Right: Celebrating our promotion to the Premier League at Crewe. [24/04/04]

Left: Celebrating with the Barclay after Scoring against Wigan. [09/04/04]

Above: Getting the crap off McVeigh's Aston Martin after I parked it on the training pitch. [2005]

Right: Celebrating winning the league on an open top bus parade around the City and on the balcony at City Hall during the civic reception. [13/05/04]

Below: Scoring Norwich's first goal back in the Premier League. [14/08/04]

bove: Helping up Manchester United legend, Roy Keane. [21/08/04]

Above: An emotional hug with Dion Dublin in his last game before retirement. It also turned out to be my last ever game for Norwich. [04/05/08]

Above: Seeing red against Ipswich Town in my first game under Glenn Roeder. [04/11/07]

Top Left: Celebrating with Crofty after scoring a wonder goal against Birmingham. [3/03/07]

Top Right: Bye Bye Carrow Road. [04/05/08]

Right: Me and my good friend, Adam Drury, with our kids. [04/05/08]

Above: Celebrating with the San Jose fans – different country, same passion for the game.

Above: Scoring for San Jose.

Top Left: Coming home to cheer on the Canaries during the MLS break.

Middle Left: Walking on to the Carrow Road pitch with Carl Moore. [28/12/08]

Left: Going for a run. [2009]

Below: Alongside Beckham, against L.A Galaxy. [2008]

Top: Lining up with Norwich City legends at the 'Greatest Ever' event. [18/05/2008]

Middle Left: With lifelong City fan during a hospital visit. [2010]

Middle Right: Some of my former team mates giving their support at the launch of The Darren Huckerby Trust. [09/08/10]

Bottom Right: Watching Thomas play for the Norwich City Youth Team. [2010]

injury he received in mid-season didn't do much to help that. It did get to the stage where it felt as if the team was changing all the time; we'd been built around settled partnerships in Division One – Flem and Malky at the back, Holty and Damien in midfield – but we'd become less stable since promotion. Everything changed, and there was no real sense of cohesion until Dean Ashton finally arrived in January.

Ash was the man who was going to hold the ball up and bring other players into the game. He was going to give the opposition centre-halves something to worry about. He was going to take the pressure off me a bit, and hopefully pull defenders about so I'd have space to run into. The problem was that he wasn't the fittest lad in the world when he joined. Dave Carolan, our fitness coach, had devised a really intense warm-up routine for us, which we did before Dean's debut at Villa. Ash was absolutely shattered before the game began – he could hardly breathe, something which might have contributed to him deflecting Liam Ridgewell's header into his own net within nine or so minutes of kick-off.

He wasn't ready for the rigours of Premier League football. If we played on the Saturday, he'd be unable to train on the Monday, and he'd only just make the Tuesday session. He told us that Dario Gradi used to let him have Mondays and Tuesdays off when he was at Crewe, which was barely believable given that he was only twenty-one. Basically, it took him a while to find his feet. He wasn't carrying much excess timber, but he was extremely concerned about his hamstrings; he was a very stiff bloke. He had a stretching routine which would last for an hour and a half before training.

Even so, there was almost an audible sigh of relief when he walked through the door in January. We knew that he was a good enough player to give us a fighting chance; although he'd only played in the lower leagues, he had genuine class. He had a great first touch, he was clever, and he brought people in. He could finish with both feet, and he was good in the air. To my mind, if we'd signed him in the summer – and if he'd got a full pre-season under his belt – he'd have gone on to score fourteen or fifteen Premier League goals.

Once he was fit, he was a real handful. The volleyed lob he scored with the outside of the foot against Manchester City was sheer class, and he'd show time and time again in training that he could hit the ball devastatingly hard with both feet. In that, he reminded me of what I'd seen of Alan Shearer in training at Newcastle; he was frightening in that respect. In fact, his only downside was that he didn't have the pace that Shearer had had when he was younger – Dean wasn't overly quick.

What I liked most about him was that, as a front man, he made other people better. He made Leon a better player; he made me a better player. You could trust that you could smack the ball into him and he'd not only hold it up but give it back to you and then get on into the box. That's an art, believe me, which few are capable of. Earnie, for example, was one of the best goalscorers I've seen, but he didn't make the team better. Ash did. There was a touch of Dion to him, even.

Dion was more aggressive than Ash in the air, but Ash was the better finisher. Don't get me wrong – Dion could finish. But Ash was an absolute natural – he could hit volleys, bend it, score tap-ins and headers. He was the real thing, and he improved our prospects no end. I remember his home debut, the extraordinary four-all draw with Middlesborough at the end of January when we were four-one down with eight minutes on the clock. He pulled one back, which led the way for Leon to get another and Ads to level from a corner in the dying seconds. I ended the game with four assists; getting Ads a goal is almost a miracle!

If you don't have a player who can take chances and score goals at that level, you are screwed. Look at what Kevin Davies has done for Bolton – he's been a player they've been able to rely on for nine or ten goals a season. And Dean transmitted a bit of confidence through the team. Once he arrived, Leon started to bang them in, and between them they became a bit of a handful. With me on the left bombing on, we were starting to cause teams real problems towards the end of that season.

Our best performance that year was the two-nil win over Manchester United at Carrow Road, a result which I expect Norwich's supporters will have fond memories of. Ash was instrumental in the outcome of that match, putting in a showing which hinted at what the season might have been like if Nigel had secured his signature in the summer.

It was during one of United's transitional spells; Cristiano Ronaldo was just beginning to prove that he had it in him to become world-class. Oddly enough, he ended as one of my markers, tracking back to help Gary Neville deal with me, and there was one moment when I did him for pace and he had to resort to fouling me. As you can probably tell, we were really fired up for that match – and everything fell into place for us. We kept it tight in the first half, frustrating them and breaking up their play, then took the game to them in the second period even though they brought Wayne Rooney off the bench at half-time. A beautiful ball from David Bentley allowed Ash to score with a great header and make it one-nil, then Dean and I combined to set up Leon to double our lead with a close-range volley.

That result gave us a real fighting chance, and showed what we were capable of when we had a proper centre-forward in the team to get on the end of moves. It was also one of Bents' better days in a yellow shirt – he'd won his way back into the team, but he'd had a fairly difficult season up to that point.

Bents was a proper Cockney lad, lively and a bit brash. He couldn't always be relied upon to take things seriously, which wasn't always a problem – during tough times you need those lighter moments – but he occasionally rubbed Nigel up the wrong way. He was never disruptive, but he could take things a bit far sometimes, and this was most in evidence with his 'Ave it!' moment in training. We were playing a match, and Bents just picked up the ball and lumped it. We all found it pretty funny, but he probably overstepped the mark. It was disrespectful to Nigel, and he had to be reprimanded.

While Bents was inconsistent, Damien Francis was having a great season in the middle of the park. I think he really came to the fore and showed people what he could do, getting on the end of things constantly by making well-timed forward runs. He was a real goal threat. People seem to think that he didn't mix with the other lads, but to me he just came across as a bit quiet. While he was never one to be cracking jokes all the time, he was still had a part to play in our good team spirit. I often wonder if he'd have gone on to become a big Premier League star if he hadn't had his knee injury – he wasn't overly aggressive, and he wasn't an Alonso-style ball player, but he played to his principal strength, namely getting into the box at just the right moment. He did that very well.

The belief really came back towards the end of that season. A lot of that was to do with having Dean, but we felt even more upbeat having beaten Manchester United. If you can do that, you shouldn't feel that anything is beyond you, and we acquired renewed self-belief after that game. Our run-in was pretty good – we took six points from back-to-back home matches against Newcastle and Charlton, and another three when Birmingham came to town. The make-or-break moment, and what settled the matter in the end, was the visit to Selhurst Park to play Crystal Palace.

Prior to that, of course, came an encounter with Manchester City at Carrow Road which will stay in the memory for reasons not entirely to do with football. I actually missed that game, having picked up a slight knock, but we played pretty well. Ash scored a wonderful goal and I thought we might hang on, but we were done in the last few minutes.

I was in one of the boxes as events started to unfold at half-time. In fairness, 'Let's be 'avin you!' has become something of a catchphrase for the club now and all Delia was ever really doing was showing her passion. At the time, though, I think it caught everyone sideways, and it will go down as one of those moments in Premier League history just as Kevin's outburst against Manchester United and Alex Ferguson did. For me, you can't fault such passion. Delia and her husband Michael Wynn Jones have taken a bit of stick over the last few years – particularly during the slump into League One – but they're brave, brave people for having put so much of their wealth into a football club.

You're unlikely to find many people who would say: 'Here, have half my money – good luck with it!' Delia is, unquestionably, a wealthy woman, but she's not that wealthy – certainly not compared to some of the multi-billionaires you get in the Premier League these days. And does anyone really believe that they're going to get all of their money back? I doubt it.

At the same time, I can understand why the supporters get frustrated. If you take, say, two kids to a top-level game and buy a programme and a few drinks, you're probably £100 lighter come five o'clock than you were at lunchtime. Throw in travel and perhaps food and it could well come to even more than that. Going to watch football, even in the lower leagues, isn't cheap, and you want both entertainment and success. If you're splashing out a good portion of your monthly wage on following a side, the likelihood is that you're going to want to see similar commitment on the part of the club's board.

The problem with that is that, at least in the Premier League, the playing field isn't level. If you support a side like Norwich, your hope for the season is always going to be survival. Even once-massive teams like Villa don't really offer much more to their supporters than a battle for a Europa League spot – there are only four or five clubs who can realistically expect to challenge for the title. That means that, as a supporter, a substantial amount of the games you attend are going to end in disappointment, and that you're unlikely to be watching your captain lifting a trophy at the end of the season.

At that level, it's always going to be difficult. The majority of a side coming up from the Championship may be solid, several players may be above that standard, and one or two might be excellent – but you're still going to have to cope with playing teams that can put out eight or nine world-class players. It is extremely hard. That means that you simply have to win in the crunch games against sides of similar ability – games like the one at Palace in the final weeks of our Premier League season.

I wouldn't say we were cruising, but we were easily on top and had created a lot of chances. Ash scored twice, Leon added a third, and we were three-one up with twenty minutes to go. We hadn't won away all season, a fact which had become a monkey on our back, and we'd put ourselves in a great position to put that record to bed while beating a rival in the relegation dogfight. Palace, however, had other ideas and, in Andy Johnson, a striker who'd scored plenty that season and who knew how to suck defenders in and win penalties. He'd scored the equaliser at Carrow Road on the opening day of the season, and we were fully aware of the threat he posed.

Johnson set up Michael Hughes to pull one back with seventy-four minutes gone and then, well...Jason Shackell is a good player, but I think that he was slightly naïve that afternoon. You simply have to know who you're playing against and what they're likely to do. If you're playing against Andy Johnson, you have to be aware that his game is all about getting into positions where, if you make a lot of contact with him, he'll go over. He'd gone over three or four times already in that game, which meant that we really should have known the ref would give a penalty. Sometimes you've just got to stand there and force people to try and beat you

– going in for the challenge is exactly what they want you to do.

I'm quite close to Shacks, and I thought, in general, that he did a tremendous job when he came in that season. He was very young, and the Premier League was a very steep learning curve for him. Perhaps Jason's problem is that he doesn't always see how good he is – he's six-two, left-footed, fast, and brave. You don't need more than that as a centre-half. But it doesn't matter how much faith you have in someone's ability, they have to be confident in themselves.

I think it would have been nice if he'd been able to come in and learn off somebody with real presence. Gary Doherty did a really good job when he came in, but Malky would have been the ideal partner for someone just starting out in the first team. Shacks needed a leader around, someone who could pick him up and reassure him when he made a mistake. There it was again – the lack of finances having a real impact on the team. If we'd been able to have Iwan and Malky, even if they were only being used occasionally, we'd have had players capable of bringing in a bit of level-headedness when it was needed. That kind of experience can be priceless when you're trying to blood younger players.

As I say, you could see that penalty coming. Every time Johnson found himself in the box with the ball, there was that danger. He's got a low centre of gravity, and he goes sprawling the minute anybody makes a silly challenge. It would have been better to let him shoot. If someone shoots and the ball flies into the top corner, and you've got as close as you can, then fair play. Going in for the tackle isn't always the cleverest thing to do.

It would be wrong, though, to point the finger at Shacks alone. As a team, we should have closed the game out at three-one with twenty minutes to go. We should have put the match to bed. For me, it was our inability to do that at Selhurst Park which got us relegated. Even if some of the things that happened at Fulham on the final day of the season weren't acceptable, I still look to the Crystal Palace fixture as the one which killed us.

What was it down to? A lack of quality? A lack of experience? I'd say it was a little bit of both of those, combined with the pressure of not having won on the road all season. It was hard not to look back and think about how close we'd been on a couple of occasions, particularly when Ledley King cleared my shot off the line at Spurs. If we'd won away from home early doors then that burden wouldn't have been there.

As it was, we carried that weight into the very final game of the season. The game at Craven Cottage on Sunday, May 15 2005 is undoubtedly one of the darkest days in Norwich City's history, and rumours and myths abound about it. Word has it that there were fights on the team bus even before we got to the game, an idea which has no truth to it whatsoever. We went in there believing we were going to win, whatever anyone says about it. The previous Saturday we'd beaten Birmingham at home to lift us into seventeenth and out of the relegation zone; we were one point ahead of Palace and Southampton, and two above bottom club WBA. With one game to play, we were sure we could do it.

I'd picked up a slight water infection and spent the night after the Birmingham game throwing up, but I'd recovered for Fulham and everything felt good, in terms of preparation, throughout the team. On the day, however, people just didn't turn up.

I believe that the heads of some people had been turned a little bit. There were a few loan players, and I feel that, maybe, Damien thought he was away anyway. I'm not saying that he didn't turn up for Fulham, but I think that his head was maybe elsewhere for a few months prior to that match. It happens – people can whisper things in your ear, promise you this and that.

It had happened to me that season. Two agents called me, both saying they represented Liverpool. Apparently, they were interested in me. I just told them both to speak to Phil, who would deal with it – and that it wouldn't be happening anyway. I knew where I wanted to be. I've never known how true any of that was, but the fact that two agents contacted me suggests that maybe there was something in it.

If I knew that my future lay in Norwich regardless of what happened, the same couldn't be said for everyone. Matty Svensson's had a knee problem, so he was probably going to be finished anyway. Bents was going back to Arsenal; you wondered if Helveg and Jonson maybe wanted away. And who really knew where Damien was? It struck me that he was in a difficult position, but we could have done without the uncertainty. If you have four or five players with question marks over their futures, you're in trouble.

We didn't start the game too badly, creating a couple of chances and having an appeal for a penalty turned down. After that, it was a catastrophe. Every time they had a chance they scored; we were pushing more men on to try and score, and exposing ourselves in the process. The midfield were reduced to chasing shadows. Everything was going wrong. Safs picked up a knock after half an hour; even before the game started, our first-team coach Steve Foley had been taken ill. He was a lovely guy whose bubbly character kept things ticking over; to see him whipped off to hospital wasn't exactly ideal.

No excuses, though. We just didn't turn up – and by 'we' I mean all of us, not just the lads who wanted away. However hard we tried, it wasn't good enough. The fans had travelled down in their masses to create a carnival atmosphere, but we just couldn't do it for them – I felt for them so much. Given all the work we'd put in over the second half of the season to give ourselves a lifeline, it was horrible – we blew it, pure and simple. It's up there as one of the most painful games of my entire career.

The collapse at Fulham was live on TV, which made it doubly embarrassing. What has to be remembered, though, was that it was what we'd done – or failed to do – over the course of the season that got us relegated, not that one result. We should have got an away win; we should have pushed or held on for wins early in the campaign; we should have seen out the game at Selhurst Park rather than letting Palace back in. There's a whole list of little things that didn't happen, and all of them contributed to us going to Fulham with so many doubts in so many heads.

I know for a fact that Ads, Flem, Shacks, Leon, Ash, Holty, and Greeny gave it their all that day. We've talked about it. I can't speak on the behalf of the others; I can't say what they were feeling as we walked out onto the pitch that afternoon. Maybe some of them couldn't face the thought of dropping down a league.

When the final whistle eventually blew at Craven Cottage, I looked at the supporters and thought how much we'd let them down. It was horrendous for them – they truly, truly believed that we could do it and we hadn't repaid their faith in us. It wasn't like we'd been dead and buried for ages, like when Derby and Sunderland went down. We'd gone into the final game of the season with an opportunity to stay up which we hadn't managed to take. A few of the lads disappeared pretty quickly into the dressing room, but I stayed out there for a while. Everyone deals with such events in different ways, but I think you have to show your appreciation for the fact that the supporters do spend a lot of money following their team around the country.

When I did go in, I heard Nigel saying, 'Well done, lads! It's been a good season...'

I couldn't agree with that. 'It's not been a good season!' I said. 'We've just been embarrassed in front of millions of people when we had a chance to stay in this league – and some haven't even turned up!'

And that came out in front of everybody.

The one person who really, really deserved a move at the end of that season was Robert Green. He'd been there at Norwich, having come through the youth team, and was just on the verge of playing for England. He'd been superb, and had earned his chance to stay in the Premier League.

As for the others? Well, Damien had had a great season. He scored a lot of important goals, even after the accidental elbow he took in the face from Leon in training during the opening months – the press, again, made that into something that it wasn't. There were rumours that Charlton were looking at him, which might have turned his head given that he was a South London boy. I expected more from Helveg, I guess, but maybe that was unfair. He wasn't going to turn in the level of performance that he had when he'd been in his mid-twenties playing in Serie A. There would have been a strong case for us sticking with Marc Edworthy, who knew English football properly, in the first place.

There was no huge post-mortem on the Monday morning. There would have been no point. The Premier League had gone, and we had to look forward to next season in what was now called the Championship. We had our testing before we disappeared for the summer, we were given our fitness programme, and we had a debrief with the manager. After that, we were away.

I felt sorry not only for Nigel, but for the football club. It deserves Premier League football. It can't be stressed enough that the problem lay in our lack of resources – we just didn't spend the right kind of money until January, when Ash came in. You can't, by any stretch of the imagination, really compete in the Premier League if you spend as little as we did that season on transfer fees and wages.

The speculation started straight away. Ash had made a name for himself in the short time he'd spent with us, so I always wondered if he'd be on his way. Greeny, too, was always going to generate interest, and he was at a point where his career needed to be progressed. Damien, meanwhile, went on strike when he came back. He refused to play in a pre-season friendly at Colchester –

I can't think of anything worse you could do as a professional, but I'm not really sure what kind of pressure he was under.

Anything could have happened behind the scenes, I guess, and I wouldn't have put it past his agent to advise him against playing in that game. That said, once you get in the position where you're unwilling to play for your club then there's only one thing that's likely to happen. After that, I don't think that Norwich had the power to do anything except sell him and hope they got good money. What was odd was that, for all the talk of him going to Charlton or another London club, he wound up going in the opposite direction and signing for Wigan. He got a few goals there, but I don't think he ever recreated the form he showed for us in the Premier League season.

I thought the way Damien went about it was all wrong. Only Greeny really had to right to walk away at the end of that season and say: 'Look, I've given everything for this club since I was a kid, and now I deserve another crack at the Premier League.' Even then, he stayed at the club for the whole of the following season in the Championship.

I didn't want to move on, either, and I actually ended up falling out with Strachs because he wanted me to come and join him at Celtic and I refused. We were in a taxi on holiday in the Bahamas when he called and said: 'You've got to come! We've got Champions League football...What are you staying for? You've been relegated...'

I told him that I wasn't going to leave, no matter what he said to try and persuade me. I didn't want to fall out with him, but I wasn't going to let him try and change my mind. He didn't talk to me for six months or so after that. There was no way I was going to go, though. I didn't care who came in; it could have been Real Madrid and I wouldn't have left. It was the whole package that was keeping me – the club, the city, the fans. I had nothing to gain from leaving only to become a bit-part player once more. By this stage of my career, I wanted to be somewhere

where I could give my all week in, week out, and be remembered for doing things the right way. I didn't want to chase the money.

One strange one that summer was Marc Edworthy, who didn't sign a new contract. He's a good mate of mine, but I always see that as being the result of pig-headedness on both his and Nigel's parts. Eddy was probably underpaid for his time at Norwich – he came in, won the league, and played more than half of our Premier League games. On the back of that, he felt that he was worth more than the club were willing to offer. That left him at loggerheads with the manager and, at the end of the day, they decided to part company. If you ask me, both sides lost out there.

I think that, after that, he went on to get two more promotions. He was a good, experienced player who knew that league, and I think letting him go was a massive mistake. With Flem not getting any younger, you would have been looking at Eddy, Gary Doherty, Shacks, and Ads as the back four for 2005-2006; they would have done a job. With Safri in front of them, Ash and Leon's goal threat up front, and me on the left, we'd have had a real chance.

As it stood, we weren't that many players away from getting the squad right. As we all now know, however, life was never going to be that simple.

11. CALM BEFORE THE STORM

Match: Norwich City vs Burnley
Venue: Carrow Road
Competition: Football League Championship
Date: Sunday, October 1, 2006
Result: Norwich City 1, Burnley 4
Attendance: 24,717

Norwich City: Gallacher, Colin,
Boyle (Shackell, 62 mins), Fleming,
Doherty, Croft (Hughes, 71 mins),
Robinson, Safri, Huckerby,
Dublin (Thorne, 63 mins), Earnshaw
Subs (not used): Camp, Ryan Jarvis

Burnley: Jensen, Harley, McGreal, Sinclair,
Duff, O'Connor, Jones, Gray,
Elliott (Mahon, 75 mins), Hyde,
Noel-Williams
Subs (not used): O'Connor, McCann, Lafferty, Foster

CALM BEFORE THE STORM

From the very first game of the 2005-2006 season, life started to get difficult for all concerned. We were due to play Coventry away on the opening day, but, because they hadn't quite finished building the Ricoh Arena, it got switched. We had, therefore, to play them at home, a game which was followed by visits to Carrow Road from Crewe on the Tuesday and Crystal Palace the next Saturday. We drew all three games one-all and, immediately, the pressure was on. Even if we'd won one, lost one, and drawn one, we would have been better off than we were with those three draws. People were expecting us to make an immediate return to the top flight with the players that we had, but it was a disappointing start.

Inevitably, there were also stirrings of speculation concerning Ash's future. Was he going to leave? If so, where was he going to go? I think it began to unsettle him a little bit. It was a tough call for Nigel. On the one hand, you don't want to begrudge any young player the chance to play at the highest level, but you also don't want to let one of your most talented assets go. Did we have even the slightest chance of replacing him with someone as good? Now that we were in the Championship, that was highly unlikely.

All manner of stuff was being said. Throughout that autumn, there were stories that Ash was feigning injury and this and that – all of it was absolute rubbish. He might not have been one hundred percent because his head had been turned, but he'd never fake his way out of anything. That's not Ash's way. I remember he got concussion in one of our games and was forced to wear this daft mask for the next few fixtures; if he'd wanted to sit those games out he'd only have needed to tell the physio he had a headache and he couldn't play. It all ended up with Nigel having to tell the press he had a scan to prove that Ash was injured when they were asking questions. Everything got completely out of proportion.

The club probably did want to sell him. In all fairness, £7 million is a lot of money for a player who'd only cost £3 million a year before. Even now, though, I don't believe it should have happened without a like-for-like replacement being lined up. We didn't have one. We went from having the best target man in the league in Ash to having, in Robert Earnshaw, one of the best finishers, but we needed someone who could hold the ball up. Accommodating Earnie meant changing the way the whole team played. It might sound daft, but we'd have been smart to do a deal with West Ham whereby Ash joined them at the end of the season. That would have given us three months with Ash and Earnie playing alongside each other. With those two, Leon, and myself, we'd have been able to have a decent crack at the play-offs.

Our transfer policy wasn't quite working. Not only was Earnie dissimilar to Ash, he was the same type of striker as Leon. It seemed that we couldn't identify exactly what it was we needed. Midfield was also a problem. Obviously, Damien had to go – there was no way back for him with the fans – and yet he wasn't replaced until Dickson Etuhu arrived. We made it too easy for people to leave, a reluctance to stand in the way of want-away players that was to continue when Earnie, Youssef Safri, and Dickson went.

As I've said, Greeny deserved the move he ultimately made to West Ham. He was one of the hardest-working players we had – I was always one of the first in and last out, but Greeny would leave after me more often than not. He did loads of weights and was always working on his game with the other keepers and the goalkeeping coach. He was a little different to the rest of lads, a polite guy who preferred the company of his own mates. Nothing wrong with that, of course. If he wanted a drink with the lads, he would; if he didn't, he wouldn't.

As I've already said, keepers aren't typical of football players in general – the reason you've heard that said so often is because it's true. The only one I've ever known who was just one of the lads was Darren Ward. At Norwich, the funniest keeper would have been Paul Crichton, who rivalled Schmeichel in the crazy stakes. He terrorised the physios, and indeed everyone else. You'd find he'd put boot polish on the phones in the office, or fixed your locker so everything would fall out as soon as you touched it. Legend has it that he stole a whole set of Nigel's hub-caps; he'd replace one every now and again, then change another one.

All sorts goes on when you have such a big group of lads together. I've had my moments. One that stood out was when Paul McVeigh bought an old Aston Martin, a genuine classic car. He tried to keep quiet about the fact that he'd got it, but I spoke to the groundsman and got him to open the gate where the tractors access the pitches at Colney. Just before our post-training meal, I drove it round and parked it on the pitch nearest the canteen so everyone could see it. Little did I know that the keepers were still out doing a session and Greeny put stones, mud, and all sorts all over the roof, leaving scratches everywhere. I did feel a bit bad about it; there's a picture of me cleaning the roof with a pair of Marigolds on. Flem was always conjuring something up, too. All sorts would go on in that dressing room – to all extents and purposes, we were a load of big kids messing around.

For a club struggling with a Premier League hangover, we needed those moments to keep spirits up. Ash went in the January, and it was a well-known fact that Greeny would be flying the nest as well; it started to look as if we weren't giving it a proper go. It felt as if the club were only viewing players in terms of their financial worth, an attitude which, for me, killed the season. We wound up finishing in ninth, thirteen points of the play-offs. It fitted the message we'd sent out in January by selling Dean – letting our best player go at the half-way stage seemed akin to waving a white flag and admitting our campaign was over. Dean might not have been overjoyed if we'd kept him until the summer because he went on to play in one of the great FA Cup finals at the end of that season – the three-all draw between West Ham and Liverpool – but I think we'd have got just as much, if not more, for him if we'd been able to hang on. All in all, his exit finished us that year.

Dean left with nine days of the transfer window left, yet we were still hunting for a replacement as it closed. At the eleventh hour, we got Earnie, whose ability as a finisher failed to mask the fact that we didn't have anybody to do Ash's job. My feeling is that it was a last-minute decision made to placate the fans, who would have gone mental if nobody had arrived. I'm sure Nigel didn't just want a finisher; he must have known he needed a target man. I think he went for Steve Howard at Luton that summer, but he ended up going to Derby for £1 million, and they ended up going up via the play-offs. It just shows you how valuable it is for a team to have that kind of outlet in the Championship.

Earnie needed to play off someone, and we didn't have a man to do that. Peter Thorne came in, but he struggled with injuries. With no presence up front, the dynamic of the team disappeared – we had the finisher, but no-one to make opportunities by bringing players into the game. Earnie doesn't hold the ball up, and he doesn't even work the channels like Leon can; his whole style revolves around playing off the defender's shoulder and looking for through balls. That's not a bad thing at all, but we weren't set up for him. It may well have been a case of right player, wrong team.

You can imagine what Leon was thinking. He'd had a good time playing alongside Dean in the Premier League, and he'd got quite a few goals. All of a sudden, he found that he was being asked to get flick-ons in for Earnie to chase, but they were just too similar. Moreover, he was getting unsettled, having just split up with his wife. He felt that it was getting to be time to move on. He eventually went to Coventry, but I'm not sure it was the right move for him; he never recaptured the form he showed at Carrow Road.

It was a similar story in midfield, where nothing was quite gelling. Safs was still there, but Damien and Holty had left; Dean Marney came in from Spurs but did his Achilles. Andy Hughes – a top guy who's still a good mate – came in, but he wasn't a like-for-like substitute for Damien. He had a good engine, but he wasn't going to have Damo's goal-rate. It just felt like we were stuck on a massive downer after the Premier League, and that there was a malaise which would affect anyone who came through the door.

Given the increasingly obvious shortage of money, the emphasis had to be on youth development. Greeny and Shacks aside, not many had come through at Norwich for quite a while, and an exciting young prospect making waves in the first team would have been a shot in the arm for the fans at that time. There were four interesting ones, namely Ian Henderson, Danny Crow, and the Jarvis brothers, Ryan and Rossi. Ian and Danny had good little spells but didn't quite cut it at Norwich; Hendo first broke into the team when we won Division One, and worked really hard, but has only really turned his career around recently with some really good performances for Colchester. I'm really pleased for him. Ryan Jarvis was the really interesting one. He had real ability, yet we couldn't quite find a place for him. He wasn't tall or aggressive enough to be a target man, and he wasn't blessed with a lot of natural pace. Really he wanted to be playing off a front man in the hole, a position you really have to be exceptional to play.

The things is, though, that the Championship is a tough league, and bringing in a kid with talent in spades, but no single outstanding attribute, to play as a creative second striker is a massive risk. It's full-on, and bedding people in is hard. You have to be the whole package, because you're coming in to play with battle-hardened men. If you're going to do it, you have to be ready to acclimatise very, very quickly to the huge step up from the youth team. These days, there appears to be no in-between stage – you seem to go straight from the youth team into the first team, and reserve football is no longer taken very seriously. As a result, there's a bit of a void in which promising players in their late teens can get lost. What should they do? They're too old for the youth team, but aren't quite ready to be part of the squad for the Saturday. My own days playing ressie football were very frustrating, but any time on the pitch is better than none.

The other issue is that teams are looking for proper athletes these days. I watch my son Tom play for Norwich City Academy and the London teams that he plays are full of big, strong boys, even at ten and eleven. Looking at the catchment area Norwich recruit from, it's going to be tough for them to adapt to how the game is changing. As I've said, the youngsters we had at our disposal that season all had ability, but they weren't physically ready to be thrown in immediately. There's a massive difference between men who know how to play football and kids who are learning; experience goes a long way, and it's often worth more than raw talent.

With no young players really pushing on, I guess we suffered from a lack of competition for places. The back four generally looked after itself, and we didn't have an abundance of players elsewhere in the team. Ian, Danny, Ryan, and Rossi were just bulking up the numbers. We were stagnating where we'd been expected, at least by the bookies, to sail back into the Premier League with relative ease. In that, we weren't alone. Southampton finished three places below us in twelfth, while Palace sneaked into the play-offs courtesy of seventeen goals from Andy Johnson, who they'd persuaded to hang about for a season. That was testament to what might have happened if we'd kept our best player. That might sound like a cop-out, but facts are facts. Dean would have made a huge difference.

It was also hard for me through the middle months of that season. I went to the sports scientist and told him that I'd been feeling shattered at the end of every game; I felt I'd lost my normal spark.

We didn't think much of it until we did the third set of tests for that season and saw my stats were a little bit off. I was sent for a blood test and the doctors informed me that I'd had glandular fever for half the season and not known anything about it. I'd been contributing in games, but I just didn't feel right. It was weird.

We never really put a decent run together, or at least not when it mattered. It became a season of rebuilding. Towards the end, Dickson Etuhu came in on loan from Preston, one sign that we were beginning to take positive steps for the future. I knew Dickson from his early days at Manchester City; he'd come in for seven or eight games at the end of the season where we won Division One and done really well. He'd fallen out with Kevin over a contract, which earned him a more or less instant transfer to Preston.

I don't think Norwich fans ever really saw the best of Dickson, and probably regarded him as a bit hit and miss. He'd play well some games and then go missing for a few. I always had great belief in his ability. From watching him in training as well as in matches, it was obvious that he had everything – he was a big man, really strong and brave, but he matched that with technique and a knack for getting forward. I think his biggest weakness was similar to Jason Shackell's, in that he didn't really believe in himself all the time. I'm still one of his biggest fans and I believe that, even now, he has it in him to go on and play for a team at the top end of the Premier League.

Dickson is one of the strongest men I have ever seen, and it's all natural. He doesn't do any weights. I once saw him and Shacks messing around and he just lifted Jason up – he was only joking, but he had him pinned up against a wall. Shacks is six-three and weighs fifteen stone, and Etuhu lifted him as if he wasn't there. When he tackled you in training, you always knew about it.

As I say, his shortcomings lay with confidence issues. He needed to be loved by the fans, and I don't think the Norwich supporters ever took to him as they could have done. That said,

I know for a fact that he enjoyed his time in East Anglia and he still comes back quite regularly. He would have stayed, as well. He would have taken the release clause out of his contract but the money the club offered him as an incentive to do so came to an embarrassing amount. He got on well with Nigel; I remember we were warming down away somewhere and Nigel volleyed the ball right at Dickson, who properly went on the warpath chasing Nigel full speed. Dickson was in his socks and, right at the last minute, Nigel dived out of the way causing him to go over right in front of everyone. We were laughing our heads off and telling him that even the manager could beat him in a race.

We needed all sorts, though. A right-back was required, because I'm not sure Nigel really fancied Jurgen Colin, the Dutch lad we'd got in, and a keeper was obviously about to become a priority. Paul Gallacher signed and did okay, but he never had Greeny's presence between the sticks. I wasn't sure he was ready to play first choice at that level, and it felt as if were trying to do it on the cheap once again. There was still a pressing need for a target man, too, and that continued right into the following, fateful autumn when Dion arrived. Even then, he couldn't offer what he had when he was in his late twenties. He still had bags of ability and presence, and you don't get a bigger character in the dressing room, but I'd still like to have seen us invest in a younger version.

We weren't dipping very deep into our pockets. We were playing Gary Doherty up front again, which was a strange move. Doc's brave and he gives it his all, and he's deceptively fast. He might not look like an athlete, but testing showed him to be the second quickest in the team. No-one gave him much credit for that. His problem was that he never stamped himself on the game as much as Malky when he played in defence, and that he was under pressure to deliver in a position that wasn't his when he got stuck up front. He was also having to cope with being relied upon in a team that was obviously on the decline.

By the start of the second Championship season, however, we'd found a new formation which gave Dickson a role and encouraged himself to have a bit more self-belief. Earnie was always going to get us goals, too, even though we couldn't build a team around him. Other changes were being made. On the coaching front, Steve Foley left and Martin Hunter came in from the FA. He was excellent, and I was very impressed with him. His organisation was spot on, and he knew his stuff tactically – after several meetings, we were told that we would switch to a 4-3-3 similar to what most teams on the continent play now. The right-sided player we'd brought in to make this possible was Lee Croft.

I knew Crofty a bit from Manchester City, but, back then, he'd only been another kid emerging into the senior squad. At Norwich, his character began to shine through a lot more clearly. Without a shadow of a doubt, he's one of the funniest people I've ever encountered in football. You laugh with him, and you laugh at him – although the emphasis is on the latter. Not only is he not the most natural-looking footballer, he's not the most natural-looking anything – he's got a big arse and an enormous head. On top of that, he talks absolute drivel all the time.

He'd been living in Manchester where his Mum and Dad did everything for him. Immediately upon his arrival in Norwich, he bought a house that was miles and miles away; he then tried to tell me that it was only fifteen minutes from the city. I said: 'Crofty, it's not fifteen minutes away in a helicopter.' It was nowhere near anywhere, right out in the sticks. Later on, he bought a dog which ripped up his house and he had to pay someone to take it off his hands. That was Crofty all over – he was completely impractical.

He was one of my most frequent victims. I'd always be doing something, whether it was cutting his laces or setting fire to his trainers. In my defence, he was continually nicking my stuff and wearing it. He had the locker next to mine and he'd keep putting my shoes on. I'd warn him, but he'd never listen. In the end, I made a little funeral pyre for his trainers, got some lighter fluid, and set a little trail ablaze so when he came out of the showers he could see flames heading towards all his stuff.

He pestered me for weeks to borrow my car, saying he wanted to take a girl out in it. Eventually, I told him that he could, but he had to let me know where he was planning to go. Daftly, he told me the name of the restaurant he was going to, and I kindly booked a table for him. Flem and I had conjured up a plan – I was going to 'nick' the car as soon as they sat down to have their meal, and I was going to film his reaction when he came out and realised it was gone. Of course, the resulting footage would then be made available to the rest of the lads.

The table was booked for half seven. Flem had got hold of a little Corsa so Crofty wouldn't know that we were following him; however, as we arrived in the car park, Crofty was driving out. What had he treated her to, a packet of Monster Munch? It was annoying – we'd been super-prepared, and even brought some broken glass to make it look as if one of the windows had been smashed. Undeterred, we decided to follow him and pull off the fake theft wherever he chose to stop for meal. But he kept driving and driving, heading for Great Yarmouth, of all places. He got to the Acle straight, which is a long road that leads towards Yarmouth and put his foot down, hard. Crofty was in my car, weaving in and out of oncoming traffic like an absolute idiot. We tried to catch him, but the little Corsa just couldn't compete. He must have been doing 120 mph.

We lost him; the next day, Flem and I pulled him over in the canteen. 'So, how did the date go?'

'Good,' he said. 'We just went for a quiet meal in Norwich.'

'You're a lying git – you were in Yarmouth! And how fast were you going in my car?'

'I never went over seventy-five, eighty…honest, Hucks,' he said, and told us that he'd seen a car behind him overtaking people.

He was like that all the time, and he was absolutely great to have around the place even if, for the first three months, he used my stuff all the time. He brought nothing with him. No wash bag, no spare kit, nothing. In the end, Lyndsey and I took him shopping like he was a little kid and dragged him round John Lewis to get a wash-bag, deodorant, aftershave, and hair-gel. It seemed right to take him under our wing; as I was No. 6 and he was No.7, we sat next to each other in the changing room.

Oh, the stories that I would have to listen to there. Lee, of course, has now shared most of these with the world thanks to his slot on Soccer AM, but I got a sneak preview. Amongst the highlights was a tale he told about seeing a horse crammed into the back of a Range Rover, something he absolutely insisted was true no matter how much you questioned him. Then there were the monkeys. Apparently, there's a thriving population of them in Wigan, where he comes from. They live in the trees. If that wasn't weird enough, he also claimed to have seen a wasp that was as big as his fist.

Lee was a breath of fresh air that summer, and he was a good player when he was on his game. He needed to work on his crossing, but he was really good at getting at players and putting them on the back foot, skills which really worked in the new formation. However, his game relied heavily on work-rate, so I would have liked to have seen him fitter.

The three in midfield were Dickson, Youssef Safri, and Carl Robinson. Robbo was another that the fans never particularly took to, but he had over sixty caps for Wales, had played for some good clubs, and knew the game well. He was a good footballer, but he was the type more appreciated by other players than by supporters. The likes of him don't spend a lot of time in the limelight, but they always do a good job.

Robbo wasn't exceptional in anything that he did, but he did everything competently. Players like that — the ones that make you tick — are vital. Norwich have one of them at the moment in David Fox; Paul Telfer played that role for Coventry. With Robinson in, I think it was fair to say that you weren't going to find a stronger midfield in the Championship that season than those three.

Up front, there was me on the left, Crofty on the right, and Earnie through the middle. You could tell it was going to work well before the season even started. We played a few games against the reserves in preparation and we were looking at five or six-nil every time; we were pummelling them. We were all confident that we knew what we were doing, that we had a good formation, and that we were generally pretty dangerous. Strong at the back, threatening on both flanks, and absolutely solid in midfield — everyone in the team really believed we had a chance.

Sure enough, we played very well on the opening day of the season at Leeds, even though we lost the game one-nil, Crofty conceding a penalty on his debut. Overall, though, the performance was very good, and we felt strong as a group. Switching formations is never easy, but I felt that the new set-up was perfect for me. It got me off the hook as far as defensive responsibilities went, and gave me the license to stay high and push onto the full-back. I was ninety percent certain that Adam could deal with their right-winger behind me and one hundred percent convinced that I could take care of their right-back in a one-on-one. It also meant that a lot of teams wouldn't push their full-back on if they knew I'd be standing there, because they knew that a break from us would put them in a world of trouble. If Crofty could do the same on the other side, and if Earnie could continue to provide a goal threat, then I felt we had a genuine chance.

As long as the three in midfield can play, 4-3-3 works well, a point proven by the fact that nearly all the big teams use it now.

It's adaptable too, as you can pull the wide forward back into midfield away from home, leaving one up front in a 4-5-1, and switch it back instantly if you're chasing a goal. At heart, Nigel was a traditional 4-4-2 man, but Martin Hunter's arrival encouraged him to experiment.

It worked for a while. After the Leeds game, we beat Preston and Luton at home, drew at Derby, and smashed five past Barnsley. Going into a fortnight's break for internationals, we were second in the league, and we'd scored ten goals in out first three home games. However, I picked up an injury against Barnsley and, on my return, Nigel got sacked. And that's exactly how the story went.

You couldn't get away from the fact that, despite our ninth place finish the season before, Nigel was very much on borrowed time. We'd felt it the season before a little – the booing had started, but we'd halted it by winning five on the spin over Christmas with Nigel collecting December's Manager of the Month and Paul McVeigh having a great spell. That probably saved him that year, but, come next autumn, his position had basically become untenable. By then, he'd have had to pull off impossible feats to win the fans round again. Everyone saw us as being on the decline, and every player who came in was perceived to be inferior to their predecessor.

In many ways, that was true. Andy Hughes, for example, had a fantastic attitude, but he didn't have Youssef Safri's outright ability. That meant that he probably tried to work too hard, which is how most players respond when they want the fans to like them. He'd work his balls off all the time, but then he'd try and play a fifty yard diagonal pass with his left foot. He wanted so much to prove that he could play, something that got in the way of the fact that things are best kept simple when the chips are down.

His versatility was also a setback for him. It was tempting for the manager to stick him in at any position whenever someone got injured. He'd get thrown in at right-back, left-back, or midfield, but he saw his best position as playing just off a front man and making diagonal runs into the box. He got quite a few goals doing just that job for Reading; things got difficult once he found himself classed as a so-called 'utility man'.

I picked up the injury in the five-one win over Barnsley at the end of August. My groin stiffened up; I told the physios at half-time, thinking I'd be okay if I cracked on and played through it. I stayed on, set up Crofty for the third, scored one in the bottom corner for the fourth, and won Man of the Match. We went second, and everything felt great. Because we had two weeks off, Nigel gave the lads the weekend off and I planned to take the Mrs to Marbella for a few days just to chill out. But my groin was weird; it wasn't the usual stiffness you can feel after a game. The pain was lingering.

I persevered with my idea that a drop of sunshine would sort it out. It got towards the end of the week, my Mum and Dad were coming down to look after the kids, and Dad came to watch training on the Thursday. By then, it really wasn't starting to feel right, so I decided to knock the trip on the head. By the Monday, as we were starting to prepare for the visit to Coventry on the Saturday, I'd got round to thinking that it would be okay and I'd be able to ride it out. I was wrong. Within five minutes of the game starting, I knew something was up. Sure enough, a scan revealed a little tear in my abductor muscle. I was out.

In hindsight, I shouldn't have played that game at Coventry. Hindsight's a great thing, though. As any professional will tell you, you're always feeling little discomforts in your body, and you tend to put it down to the sheer number of matches you get through in a season. And you're desperate to play – I didn't feel pressured to by the management, but I wanted to be on the park for my own sake. Everything was going well, and I wanted to be a part of it. On top of that, I knew that there had been countless occasions in my career when I'd gone into a game doubting my ability to get through it and, thanks to the magic of anti-inflammatories, been around for the final whistle.

Not on this occasion. I went off, we lost three-nil, and everything fell apart. We should have won at Southampton the following Tuesday, but we drew three-three; we lost successive games at home to Palace and away at Plymouth. We'd started off so well, but we were getting dangerously close to one of those deadly spirals where you can't buy a win. Even now, I can't really put my finger on it. The tension built up until, in the run-up to the Burnley game, Nigel was being forced to take ridiculous levels of personal abuse. What he went through was not at all justified by the team's lack of form.

In the end, he had to go, but his record speaks for itself. He turned up when Norwich were Division One strugglers, took them to a play-off final, rebuilt, then won them the league. He'd also nearly pulled off survival in the Premier League, and a respectable ninth-place finish in the gloom of the following season. When he left, we were thirteenth. Ninety percent of managers would have taken Nigel's record over a four or five-year spell.

The buck always stops with the manager. But Nigel was seriously underfunded towards the end, and he often got caned for the signings he did pull off. He brought Dion in just before his exit and got hammered for that, and Dion went on to win Player of the Season. It was a shrewd move – I'm not sure even Dion expected to have the impact that he did, which was fair enough for a guy in his late thirties having to face Mother Nature's harsh realities.

It wasn't everyone, but things like the 'Worthington Out!' bumper stickers were clearly orchestrated. It was never clear who the instigator was, but a section of the fans had turned against Nigel, and there would have been very few ways for him to turn that situation around. Every single dodgy patch we hit would have meant that the question got raised again, and that kind of scrutiny can cause problems.

Players do read what is written in newspapers, and some take more notice of it than people would think. I know a lot of pros who take a real interest in the mark they're given out of ten in the papers on a Sunday or Monday – for a few, it can become a bit of an obsession. I know even now that Jason Shackell will be picking up the Sun on a Monday to see how his performance has been rated; he always used to take it to heart. He'd make one mistake and worry about it for weeks; he'd come round to ours and fret about it, even though I'd tell him that he had to let it go and focus on the next game. It's really important that you know in yourself how you've done, and don't get affected by the judgements of others.

I look at the press, and I generally feel that, when people have a bit of a pop, it's within reason. Local journalists, at least, never go out of their way to belittle you. I guess one of the biggest problems with football, though, is that everyone thinks that they can play, and the fact that virtually everyone has some experience of kicking a ball means that they believe they understand the ins and outs of being a professional. The fact is that there are worlds between being a reasonable non-league player and being a Championship-stroke-Premier League player. It's an enormous, enormous difference.

Too many Sunday footballers reckon that it's only misfortune that has prevented them from doing it for real, but that's simply untrue. Scouts are not stupid. Chuck someone who thinks they can play into an environment where everyone is a professional, and it would be horrible. The level required is so much higher than it's generally perceived to be. Like all professions, playing football at the top level requires years and years of work. It's the whole package – the skill level, the fitness, the know-how.

You have to have the mental strength to match the physical strength; you have to be able to take the pressure. It's a huge ask. It's so hard explaining that to those who watch the game on TV and think that it's dead easy.

The game against Burnley was being screened live, so it was available for exactly that group of people. All of us, and particularly Nigel, were going to be right in the public eye. I felt I owed it vto him to play, even though I wasn't physically ready; the statement made by the board following the Plymouth defeat made me want to do everything I could to help save his job. If we lost, he was gone.

Given that the game was broadcast, it's hard to think of it as anything but a public execution. He deserved so much more than that, being an unbelievably nice bloke a decent, honest fella. Take the football out of consideration for a moment and there's no way he deserved some of the stuff that went on that autumn. His kids were getting abused as school, and his family were being yelled at in the street. It was disgusting, and it's not often I say that.

We were short on confidence; there was nothing left. It was horrible, but the writing on the wall could be seen by everyone. Even before that game, we'd been able to hear the protests outside the ground. While we were in the showers after the game, we were thinking, 'Where do we go from here?' They were sad, sad times, and I think everybody – not just Nigel – lost out. We could have won three or four on the bounce, but the doubts would have remained and there would still have been people saying we needed a new manager. I'd counter that and say that I'm one hundred percent sure that the club would never have been relegated had they kept Nigel – not in a million years.

After the game, we all knew what was coming. We'd played poorly and been turned over by a Burnley team who were average at best. There was no way back. He knew it.

When the moment came, it was difficult for me. We'd gone through an awful lot together in a relatively short space of time –

the whole saga of me signing, the story of Ash coming and going. We'd been part of the best thing that had happened at the club for years. I continue to believe that we would have stayed in the Premier League if money had been invested correctly, and I don't think anyone had a clue about how much worse it would get with Nigel off the scene. With the benefit of hindsight, I think most people would have been happy with thirteenth place.

Once a manager is out of the door, no-one knows what's going to happen. Who's coming in? Will they like you? You haven't a clue about their thoughts and beliefs about the game, the budget he's going to be given, or the players he'll try and bring in with it. On top of that, you get squad members who have been out of the team and expect that the grass will be greener given a change of boss.

Of course, that's not always the case. Things can very easily go from bad to worse...

12. FORCED EXIT?

Match: Sheffield Wednesday vs Norwich City
Venue: Hillsborough
Competition: Football League Championship
Date: Sunday, May 4, 2008
Result: Sheffield Wednesday 4, Norwich City 1
Attendance: 36,208

Sheffield Wednesday: Grant, Burton, Beevers, Wood,
Watson (Kavanagh, 54 mins),
Johnson, Bolder, Spurr,
Sahar, (Clarke, 82 mins),
Songo'o, (McAllister, 54 mins),
Slusarski
Subs (not used): Burch, Esajas

Norwich City: Marshall, Otsemobor
(Pearce, 72 mins), Bertrand, Shackell,
Doherty, Fotheringham, Russell,
Pattison (Croft, 58 mins), Huckerby,
Dublin (Cureton, 66 mins), Evans
Subs (not used): Rudd, Chadwick

Given the circumstances of Nigel's exit, it was going to be hard for Peter Grant from the very beginning. The side he was taking over was low on confidence, and City's supporters were, for want of a better word, in disarray. You couldn't find a pub in the city which would deliver a unanimous verdict on the sacking. Half of the fans still liked Nigel, and half had wanted him to go. It was a mess, and Peter was brave to take it on in the first place. The saving grace, if there was one, was that he was inheriting a few very good players.

Perhaps that moment in time demanded a more experienced manager. It was a hard call to make on that front, because Peter is an excellent coach. Both before and after his time at Norwich, he has coached good teams. The question would be whether he was really cut out for the management side of things – arguably, he could never quite lose his coach's attitude. I'd come in on a Sunday to do my own warm-down after a game and Granty would be there, up at Colney, sorting the kit out. He wanted everything to be so right and perfect that he'd try and do it all hands-on, which you can't really afford to do. The board were paying him to manage, but he wanted to do well so much that he tried to shoulder all manner of duties that other people were being employed to do.

I had a lot of time for Peter. Like Nigel, he's an honest, decent man, and he has proper integrity in everything he does. He sticks to his beliefs, and has enormous conviction in what he's doing at any given moment in time. The trouble came when he proved to be incapable of stepping back from things; the difference between great coaches and great managers is that the latter don't let themselves get overly affected by certain things.

The goalkeeping situation had come to be a bit of a farce as a new loanee would appear every other week – Tony Warner, Jamie Ashdown, and Lee Camp all turned out for us. You can't go on like that. If there's a position where you need to have stability, that's it. We hadn't filled the gap between the sticks since Greeny left, and being able to do that would have been a real blessing for

Peter. There are a lot of times when having a good goalkeeper gets you out of the crap – you can have the best game in the world, but if the opposition take their one chance you're back to square one. A decent keeper is so important, and Granty was always desperate to find one.

Nor was his cause helped by an injury to Earnie midway through that season, which left us without his goals for a large part of it. Young Chrissy Martin came into the team and started to do really well, which softened that blow, but we were missing some key ingredients. While we obviously wanted to push on for the play-offs, we probably knew deep down that it wasn't ever likely to be a reality that season.

I was pleased with our midfield, where Dickson and Safs were doing a great job. Shacks was coming on again and looking good, and Ads was the same as ever. Crofty was a bit in and out; however, we had Dion back around the place. That was fantastic. As a kid at Coventry, I tended to take his presence for granted, treating it as part of the big joyride my career was at that moment in time. Ten years or so down the line, I'd started to appreciate him as a bloke a lot more. He'd become a real mate, and I valued sharing a dressing room with him. He's a great leader, but he's got it in him to give a good bollocking out. He's not all talk; when he says something, he means it.

What people didn't ever realise at that time was the toll playing was taking on Dion. They'd see him on the pitch for seventy or so minutes on a Saturday, then he'd spend the following three days barely able to move. He wouldn't train on a Monday or a Tuesday; he'd spend that time having massages and ice baths. I think he was lucky in the sense that he played in a position where he wasn't being asked to get up and down a lot – there are very few who can fulfil that role when they're thirty-seven and be as effective as they've been in the past.

Chris Brown arrived from Sunderland to play up front, but he never did quite as well as he had the potential to. I like him as a player; however, he's one of those who are arguably too unselfish for their own good. He doesn't get as many goals as a striker should because half the time he's running the channels, chasing and harassing. As I've said before, there's the team players and there's the goalscorers, and it's not often that you get both. Ash was one of the few, and I think Norwich now have another in the shape of Grant Holt, who works hard and scores goals. Browny and Earnie would be on opposite ends of the spectrum. Browny would do all the donkey work, but wouldn't hit the net on a regular basis. Likewise, Earnie would never track back, and didn't really run the channels, because he was all about the goals.

Come the second half of that season, I was really starting to enjoy my football. Kicking off with the FA Cup game at Tamworth where Dion and I both scored, I went on a run of six goals in six games, and I got another four before the close of the campaign. We won one-nil against Birmingham and Stoke, and I scored the winner in both games. Against Birmingham, I got one of the best strikes of my career, picking the ball up just outside our own box and charging down the left before cutting infield past several defenders and driving home from twenty yards. I was feeling very strong. My training regime was good, my work-rate was good, and I was getting on the scoresheet. I began to believe that, with a few more players, we could think seriously about the play-offs the following season.

I won Player of the Season that year. Dion came second, and got another short-term deal, which made sense. As long as he wanted to play and felt that his body was up to it, having him around the place was a really good idea. Beyond what he offered on the pitch, younger players had a lot to learn from him – Chrissy Martin up front, and Shacks and Gary Doc in defence, had a great tutor in the form of Dion.

FORCED EXIT?

Winning Player of the Season means everything to me. We didn't do a Player's Player back then – that might have meant even more – but it's picked by the fans and I was lucky enough to win it twice. I was gutted not to win it a third time, because no-one has ever done that before. In my first season I won Division One Player of the Year, but not the Norwich one. Flem won it that year, and I was delighted for him; he's a good mate and he truly deserved it, having played in every game and contributed so much to keeping a tight ship. From my point of view, though, three Player of the Season awards would have been amazing. I guess you can't have everything.

We clearly needed to sign a keeper that summer – in came Celtic's David Marshall. We also needed a right-back, in order to fill a position that had been a problem since Marc Edworthy left. On that front, we required someone consistent who could deliver week in, week out. And then there was the old question of a target man, because Browny was still learning the trade.

David Strihavka arrived, but the Championship is a really physical league. People have an edge to them that they don't necessarily have in the Premier League, and every game is a ninety-minute battle. Every single team, without exception, has to be willing and able to mix it, and I'm not sure Strihavka was the man to help us do that. It didn't help that he couldn't speak any English, or that we were in a situation where we were scrapping for our lives. We didn't have six or seven games spare to bed him in.

Foreign signings proved to be a bit of a sticking point around that time. Who can forget Julien Brellier? He was known as The Judge, for some reason; word got round that he was a proper enforcer, but I never saw anything of that from him. I remember one game in particular. Around an hour in, he had the ball in midfield, and I was open on the left about twenty-five yards away. He had about three opportunities to put me in, but didn't. I went over to him.

'Julien, what's up?' I asked him.

'I can't kick it over there,' he said. 'I can't kick it that far…'

It really made me think back to the beginning of Granty's first summer in charge, when we still had Safs and his ability to ping a forty-five yard ball to within millimetres of your toes. Safs could do that any time I asked him to. The problem was that he was no longer with us, and he wasn't the only one.

At the beginning of pre-season, the team was shaping up in a way that suggested we wouldn't be far off. Having reverted more or less to a 4-4-2, we had me on the left, Crofty on the right, and Dickson and Safs in the centre. I'd have taken that midfield against anyone else's in the league, and, bar a right-back, the back four was pretty strong. I was full of optimism.

Then I hurt my hip. Physically, I'd been feeling great for the second half of the previous season; this was a new problem. We were doing box-work up at Colney the week before we were meant to go to Holland on the pre-season tour when it went. Initially, I though it was just a pull; after all, you put your body through some ridiculous stuff in those first three or four weeks. There it was, though, just in front of my groin.

I went to Holland, tried to play in one of the practice matches, and felt it again. I left the rest of the lads and flew home early for treatment; all I could really do was hope that it settled down. Meanwhile, poor Jimmy Smith arrived on loan from Chelsea and did his ankle in the first twenty minutes of the first tour game. Granty was never really blessed with luck during his time at Carrow Road.

It was while I was injured that the club decided to sell a few players. I was sat in the dressing rooms, waiting to do a photo-shoot for a sponsored bus, and I heard that Dickson might be off to Sunderland. And that Earnie was already on his way to Derby. Oh, and that Safs could be on his way as well. I heard all of this in the space of about twenty minutes. 'Right,' I thought. 'That's this season done, then!'

I felt that all the work we'd put in over pre-season had been cancelled out in less than half an hour. It had taken me a couple of conversations to realise that the season had basically gone before it had begun. I then did something a little out of character. I came out and said to the press, 'You want to hear this…' and went off on one; I didn't feel right holding my tongue. A few fans had a pop at me, saying that I shouldn't be rocking the boat, but what was I supposed to do? Just take it on the chin? We'd lost three of our better players in what seemed like a week and a half.

Dickson would have stayed, as he's told me on a number of occasions. For that to have happened, all they'd have had to do was take out his release clause and offer him an improved contract. When the offer did come, it was a joke. It seemed that we were making it easy for players to leave, and that really annoyed me. Anytime that anyone came in for one of players, we were just rolling over and letting them go.

I was fuming; absolutely livid. I was also feeling for Granty. How must he have felt to lose three of his star men a fortnight or so before the beginning of the new season? Don't get me wrong – I know that a football club is a business, so they're always going to need to balance the books. But it felt to me as if there was, on some level, a failure to think in the long-term. For example, we brought in Jamie Cureton, who had got goals the previous season at Colchester, but he was no Earnie. He didn't offer the same threat.

Darel Russell came in, and he would have been a fantastic addition to our existing squad. Imagine adding Darel to Dickson and Safs – we'd have had power, strength, engine, and ability. Even now, I can't get my head round why we'd want to let players of the calibre we let go leave. If a player has a three-year contract and you don't want him to go, keep him.

It seemed to me that the remaining players, along with Peter, had been dumped on. It seemed that we got nothing out of it; we got the raw end of the deal every time. Some adequate players came in, but I wouldn't have swapped Dickson and Safs for anyone else in that league. I knew how vital they were to the team. I look back at the FA Cup tie at Chelsea the previous February, a game which we eventually lost four-nil but had allowed Dickson to show that he wasn't out of place at that level.

Coming on top of the injury, it was a hammer blow. My heart didn't go out of it, but I felt cheated. I actually said that we'd be in danger of getting relegated if we carried on the way we were. I genuinely saw that as being the risk we were facing. I hurt for Granty, I really did. It was his first job in management, and not only did he lose three key players on the eve of his first full season, he had to contend with me being injured, a situation which lasted for the majority of the time until his sacking. I don't like to sound full of myself, but I definitely feel we'd have got more points than we did had I been fully fit.

The injury was to prove pretty serious. Whatever I did, it wouldn't go away fully, and that went on for more or less the next three and a half years. I had a near-constant nagging pain in the right side of my hip. There were ways to numb the pain from time to time, but to go from complete fitness to being continually aware of an injury was incredibly hard.

Mark Fotheringham, Simon Lappin, and a few others came in, but you could see the writing on the wall. Granty was being forced to replace very good players with cheaper alternatives, and some of them just weren't up to it. To be fair, Lapps was a superb signing for £60,000 and has been a great servant for the club, and Fozzy was a decent enough player, but Safs was absolutely class. When he played, he dictated the pace of the game and, when you've got that kind of control, you've got a chance. I never knew the ins and outs of Safs leaving, but it was a massive, massive loss.

It was a losing battle from thereon in. My first game came away at Rochdale in the Carling Cup at the end of August, but my hip was still killing me. It really was. In the end, however, I didn't really try and sort it out until after Peter was sacked.

What Nigel went through, and what Peter was subsequently to endure, you wouldn't wish on anybody. It can't be right when people's kids start to get abuse at school. I guess that's the nature of football, and it'll happen again. It seems to some that you're fair game because you're in the public eye. What the public don't necessarily see is the human face of it all, and both of the managers in question were good, honest men who deserved better. When Peter did walk, he did it with his head held high, and I don't think he took a payment from the club. I still speak to him now to get advice about my coaching badges, and I know that he's a fantastic family man.

I'm sure he'll work in football for ever because people are aware of what he brings to the table. In the end, it was possibly his passion and commitment to doing well that clouded his judgement; near the end, we would be training, absolutely full on, for an hour or so on the day of games. You can't do that. He was trying everything he knew to make us win, and it just wasn't happening.

I went down to London with Pete Shaw, the No. 2 physio at the club back then, and saw the top man in the UK – a Mr Villa. Having looked at the scans, he said there appeared to be a tear in my labrum, the tissue that goes round the hip joint. Eventually, he told me, I was going to have to have something done about it. Unlike every other injury I'd had, this one wasn't going to go away. Basically, it felt like having really bad toothache in the front of my hip all the time, from the moment I woke up to the moment I went to sleep. For the time being, there was little I could do other than carry on. The problem wasn't so much the pain, which I could more or less handle, than the fact that I was getting less and less movement in my right hip joint. You can't help injuries; they happen. As with Nigel, though, I felt funnily as if I'd let Granty down. I really did.

John Hartson was another odd one. He was signed by Jim Duffy, who was caretaker in the period following Granty's dismissal. In his day, Hartson had been an absolutely fantastic player – when he was younger and lighter, he'd been a proper handful. I remember playing against him at Coventry, and he'd been an animal. I think, however, that he'd be the first to admit that he didn't really look after himself at all by the time he pitched up in Norfolk. He was carrying masses of weight which, while not stopping him from holding the ball up, meant that he couldn't run. It wasn't great. He was doing his best, but us signing him seemed to show how desperate we were to stay up.

The day Glenn Roeder's appointment was announced we were all sitting around in the canteen, waiting to hear that Martin 'Mad Dog' Allen was the new manager. That's what we'd all heard. Then, from nowhere, it turned out to be Glenn. We'd heard a few crazy stories about Allen – how he wouldn't let some players get changed in the changing room, and all sorts like that – so, in a way, the appointment was a relief. However, you don't really know what you're going to get with a new manager until you started working with them.

We were struggling, no question about that; we'd lost our way and it was going to take a lot to turn our season around. But we were sure that, given the players and the characters that we had in the dressing room, we had more than enough to stay up. My injury, though, was going to be a thorn in our side. The day that Granty left, I'd had an injection, which had taken some of the edge away without making it one hundred percent right. The lack of movement ultimately prompted me getting surgery – I had forty-five percent less flexibility in one side than the other. I was starting to second-guess what I was going to do.

FORCED EXIT?

It definitely didn't help that I managed to get myself sent off in Glenn's very first game in charge, a match which just so happened to be the derby clash with Ipswich. When I went, it was the 90th minute, and the score was level at two–two. For once, I hadn't talked my way into trouble; for the first time in my career – more or less – I kicked out at someone. The ball was bouncing between me and Jon Walters and I genuinely thought he was going to do me, but he pulled out at the last minute. I guess he expected me to do the same, but I didn't. It was a bad tackle, but it probably looked worse than it was, and half the Ipswich bench jumping onto the pitch probably didn't help either. I'm not a dirty player; I've probably only made a couple of bad tackles in my entire career. As the saying goes, it was a forward's tackle, and I didn't mean to kick him. In the end, though, I deserved to be sent off.

Martin 'Tiny' Taylor scored the first for us that day, although we were already two-nil down when that happened. He was an excellent loan signing. He knew the game well, had played at a decent level, and had real presence. Glenn was making an immediate impact, bringing good players in and changing things around to make us more solid. Ryan Bertrand was a good, solid left-back who covered us in that position because Ads had a bad injury; Matty Pattison was a workhorse who put his foot in. There was also Ched Evans, who came from Manchester City with a big reputation and – no two ways about it – delivered the goods.

Ched scored the Goal of the Season in the away game at Cardiff. I'd started on the bench; when I came on, I was in acres of space and busy bollocking him as he lined up the shot. Then it flew into the top corner from thirty-five yards out, leaving us all gobsmacked. Alongside Ash and Shearer, he had one of the hardest shots I've ever seen. His technique was fantastic and he could just leather it off both feet. He was a talent and, to be honest, it's surprised me a lot to see how he's struggled at Sheffield United.

There's nothing like putting a few wins together to build confidence and boost team morale, and we put in some good results during the early days of Glenn's tenure. However, I wasn't playing as much as I'd have liked to, a fact which was down both to the hip and the way that Glenn was shaping up his team. He wanted to do his own thing and, maybe, I wasn't as sharp as I should have been. Clearly, though, things were going to come to a head at some point.

That took place at Bury in an FA Cup third round replay in the middle of January. I've known people who were there, including other players, to tell me that it was the worst they'd ever seen me play, and they're right to say that. I was horrendous. I couldn't do anything right, and everything I tried went wrong. In the dressing room afterwards, Glenn was saying some stuff to the tune of me being finished, a has-been. I didn't answer. It was the lowest I have ever been. At the time, I took it on the chin, because I felt I couldn't answer back given the way I had performed.

Something was going on there; I knew I'd put in a terrible shift, but I felt that I was being singled out. I can honestly say that I've never heard a manager come out with anything like that in the dressing room after a game – this was much more severe than the usual dressing-down you can expect to get after a poor showing. As Glenn said his piece, I'd been looking around the room, and I could see how surprised all of my team-mates looked. I might be wrong, but I don't think he would have said anything like that to Dion, he'd probably have sparked him out.

Straight after the game I headed back to Nottingham as it was my Grandmother's funeral the next day. When I got there, I went round to Tosh's house for a couple of beers and said, 'I can't go on like this…' I was really, really down, and talking about packing it in. I'd played poorly, been hung out to dry in front of all my team-mates, and, on top of that, there was the injury.

It was getting too much – the pain in my hip was constant. So I got back and went to see the manager to say that I was going to go and see someone to get it sorted out. At the very least, I wanted another injection. However, it seemed as if he doubted whether or not I was telling the truth, something I found very, very strange. I told him that I'd seen the surgeon, who'd said that I was going to have to get something done eventually. In the end, Pete Shaw came in and backed me up on that, so I was able to go and have it attended to. This time, they knocked me out, put me in traction, and did it that way; that way, I got much more relief from the pain.

I was struggling, and it's the manager's job to do what is best for the team. I didn't feel as I was being singled out, particularly. He was the same with everybody. I just never really got going once I had that injury; I couldn't hit the level I'd been for season after season before. Once I'd had that second injection, though, I felt better almost immediately, or at least pain-free, which was a big relief after four months where it had been constant. It was almost a new lease of life, a sense that everything was going to be okay again. Good stuff was happening on the coaching front, too, with Lee Clark and Paul Stephenson coming in. I knew Clarkie from Newcastle and it was clear he'd be going on to bigger and better things. He wasn't a natural No. 2 and I think he was seeking out a bit of experience before trying his own thing.

Then it happened. It would have been just before the January transfer window shut that Glenn pulled me in and said: 'I think it might be best if you and the club part ways.'

He said that Neil Warnock wanted me; I told him that I wasn't remotely interested.

'I think it might be best for you and the club...'

'Nah,' I said. 'I'll just stay and fight my way back into the team. And I can guarantee you that before the end of the season I'll be back and starting.'

'But we think it'll be best if you go...'

I said that it was never going to happen; that he was never going to get me to walk away from Carrow Road. And that was that. I said 'You happy with that?' and, in fairness, he said that he was.

I'm not sure that he was that happy, but I was certain that I would get back into the team if I was pain-free. And I did get back in. However, Glenn was playing me on the right, where both he and I knew that I didn't like to play. I'd been drifting off to the left for the last twelve years; I wasn't comfortable on the other side. It was difficult, but I didn't want to go saying anything because I wanted to play. At the back of my mind, I was wondering if he didn't want me to play my natural game.

He tried Kieran Gibbs out there, and James Henry who came in on loan from Reading. But, as I've said, the Championship is a real man-against-man league, for ninety minutes and forty-six games. Gibbs and Henry were kids, being asked to come into a relegation battle – it was always going to be tough for them.

I didn't go knocking on Glenn's door to find out about the following season. I didn't think it was my place to do that. I had no idea which way it was going to go; I was back in the team, feeling strong again, contributing and scoring goals. But I didn't want to rock the boat. Clearly, I was one of the highest earners, so there was always a chance that I was going to be asked to take a pay cut. I'd have said yes to that, no doubt about it – I'd taken one every year I'd been there. There was, however, never even a conversation about money.

Coming closer and closer to the end of the season, it wasn't just me the uncertainty was affecting, but the wife and kids as well. Norwich had become our home; we'd settled and made friends here. The last thing we wanted was to be unexpectedly uprooted and have to start all over again somewhere else. I spoke to Neil Doncaster, City's chief executive, about two weeks before the end of the season and said that, whatever happened, we should be prepared and have something organised by which both the club and myself would come out looking okay. Basically, he said that it would be down to the manager; Glenn would decide how everything would be handled.

Coming up to thirty-two, I knew that my game had changed. When I was twenty-seven, I could − literally − take on three or four men and work my way through a defence to make something happen; causing havoc had been my speciality. But I'd worked hard to adapt so that I'd be able to do something else once I'd lost some of my pace, and I still had more than enough in my locker to beat one man − or to beat one man and score a goal. Whatever Glenn had said up at Bury in the January, I wasn't a has-been.

I remember the end well. We were doing fitness testing, and Pete Shaw, the No. 2 physio that had accompanied me to see the surgeon in London, was called in for a meeting before me − and got the boot. Some people might see it differently, but − honestly − I believe that he got the sack for standing up for me and my hip. He was a damn good physio, so I can't see the reason being anything to do with the work he was doing. Then it was my turn.

I waited in the weights room to go in and see Glenn. I was called in, and the message was simple. 'We're not offering you anything. Thanks for your time here. Good luck in the future.' That was it − literally. Five years, two Player of the Years, a league championship; they were all gone in twenty seconds.

I came out, and went back to the dressing room to tell the lads. I spoke to them for five or so minutes, went back into the weights room to finish off my gym session, and there − within fifteen minutes of seeing Glenn − the story was on Sky Sports News. 'Nine players have been released by Norwich City, including Darren Huckerby,' it said. That's how Lyndsey found out about it; she'd heard by the time I called her, which she wasn't too happy about. To tell the truth, I didn't want to ring her because we had such a good set-up in Norfolk. It seemed to me as if they'd pushed a button the minute I left the room which got the news out to the press.

Before I walked into Glenn's office, I still didn't know which way it was going to go. I genuinely believed I had a chance; I had played my way back into the team, and I was contributing. The other lads were all telling me that there would be no problem, that I'd be kept on without a shadow of a doubt. When I walked in, though, that was blown away immediately. And it was the start of a cull. Out went the assistant physio, the Academy physio, the kit man. All of those people had been at the club for a long time. Glenn wanted to make changes, which happens — but you have to be careful that you don't do too much too soon.

Dion, of course, knew that Sheffield Wednesday away would be his final game in professional football, but I couldn't tell. On the day, I scored a good goal, and — although this sounds stupid given the eventual result — we could have been three or four up by half-time. Just before the break, they got a penalty, and we crumbled. Afterwards, I didn't know what to do. I wanted to go out and say goodbye to the fans, but, equally, I didn't want to take Dion's big moment away from him. He's had a marvellous career, and he deserved that moment. In the end, I stayed behind, and I think I made the right decision.

I'm not dead sentimental, but they could have told me a week before. We'd made ourselves safe from relegation the week before, so nothing was at stake for us at Hillsborough that afternoon. However, it just seemed that Glenn wanted to do things his way. Fair enough, but you can understand why twenty-five thousand fans weren't happy about it. It didn't need to be the way it was. We could have had a joint press release, stating that the club and I had decided to move in a different direction, or something like that.

It would have been easy for me to come out afterwards and have a go, but it would just have looked like sour grapes, and I didn't want to affect the future progress of the club. I actually thought that Glenn was a decent manager; training was very good with him. It was just that his man-management wasn't great. The way he spoke to people sometimes had a kind of arrogance about it. Even if you know more than other people – or you think you do – you've got to show a bit of respect when you talk to them. That's true in every walk of life. It doesn't matter how clever you are, you have to be careful in how you put your points across.

There was no great fall-out between us. I didn't kick off when he told me I wouldn't be offered a new contract – it wasn't at all like that. It was fair enough, I said, and I could see that he wanted to do something different. Because my deal wasn't up until the end of June, I continued to train at Colney, and he came up to me and said that I could still come down whenever I wanted to use the facilities and keep myself fit before I went on somewhere.

Later that summer, I was in Toronto, I had to talk to the club there before I went to San Jose. Phil Smith also represented Dejan Stefanovic at the time, and he told me that Dejan wanted to ring me to talk about Norwich, the city, and the manager. I said: 'Phil, I cannot talk to him about Glenn Roeder, because he might not sign for the club. I don't think Glenn's a very nice man. And the club is a great club. I don't want to say something and, in doing so, jeopardise the move.' That was that; I didn't think any more of it.

Then, when I came back to Norwich after my first season in the MLS, I popped up to Colney. They'd just lost another game; the lads were in a meeting, getting a bollocking. I was thinking that I couldn't have picked a worse time to go up and ask to train. I went in and Glenn said: 'I hear you told Dejan that I wasn't a very nice man.'

'No, I didn't say anything to Dejan. I spoke to my agent and said that I wouldn't.'

'What did you say to your agent, then?' he asked.

'I told him that I didn't want to speak to Dejan because I didn't want to jeopardise anything, and I said to him that I don't think you're a very nice man.'

Glenn then told me that I couldn't use the grass at Colney, and that I could only use the gym at certain times, but that he wanted us to be men about it and not let the press hear about our conversation. Of course, I never mentioned it to the papers.

That was that. I haven't spoken to him again. As I've said, he knew his stuff tactically, but he wouldn't be in my close circle of friends. It certainly wasn't the ideal way for it all to end. After all that happened, I bumped into Dejan who said I'd been right about Glenn, and that he wished that I'd spoken to him in the first place.

Because Glenn had done so well in his first period in charge, I honestly think that Neil, Delia, and everyone had told him that he could do what he wanted, and, in fairness, I think that his performance had earned him the opportunity to have things his own way for a bit. But you only need to look at what happened afterwards to see where that got everyone.

I would never have left the club by my own free will. Also, I was given opportunities to stay in England after I went. I spoke to two managers of Championship clubs that went up into the Premier League, so I definitely know they wanted me. Neil Warnock, too, was always up for me to join him; he was at Palace at the time. I could never do it, though. People might think I'm mad, but I could never, ever play against Norwich. I'd rather have just packed up, which is what I'd have done if the America thing hadn't come off. Phil Smith thought I was nuts when I told him that it was the MLS or nothing.

The club had been, in a way, my home for over eleven months of every year. I was in literally every day, and I knew how much I'd miss the people I'd tended to take for granted at times. There are people you see on a daily basis – in the laundry, the offices, the canteen and so on – who you just think will always be there. If you're honest with yourself, you know it's going to end sometime, but you can't anticipate what it will be like. Wherever you go, that happens, but it's far more difficult when you have a special bond with the place.

It was hard clearing out the No. 6 locker for the last time. Shirt numbers influence who you're friends with, which is why I ended up close to Flem (No.5), Crofty (No. 7), Shacks (No. 4) and Ads (No.3). The only reason I ended up with a 6 on my back was that I didn't want to be No. 24, which was what was on offer when I walked through the door with Crouchy. I'd always prefer to be either a No. 7 or a No. 11, the old-fashioned wingers' numbers.

Funnily enough, after Phil Mulryne left they asked if I wanted the No. 7 jersey, which would have meant that more people might have to buy that number shirt with my name on it. I'd been No. 7 at both Manchester City and Coventry, but I didn't think it was fair on all those supporters who had bought No. 6 Huckerby shirts, so I kept it the same. Bizarrely, when I went on to San Jose, they'd just got rid of their No. 6 so I ended up with that shirt again – it was weird how it followed me.

I abused Jason Shackell's locker before I left, drawing a big No. 6 shirt in it. I wrote 'Huckerby' across the top, so he'd remember me every time he looked in it – which he would have done until Glenn sold him to Wolves. Then I wrote 'Who's Yer Daddy?' underneath.

I've made some lifelong friends from my time at Norwich. Adam Drury is probably my best friend in football – I'd do anything for him. Iwan Roberts. Craig Fleming. Paul McVeigh. People who've gone away and come back again – they'll be mates forever.

And I wouldn't ever want to move away from Norwich now. I love it here. I have no ill feeling towards Glenn Roeder, but my wife? Well, that's a different story.

13. SHOW ME THE WAY TO SAN JOSE

Match:	DC United vs San Jose Earthquake
Venue:	Buck Shaw Stadium
Competition:	MLS Western Conference
Date:	Saturday, September 6, 2008
Result:	DC United 1, San Jose Earthquake 2
Attendance:	10,021

DC United: Crayton, Martinez, Burch, McTavish, Zaher (Cordeiro, 64 mins), Quaranta, Dyachenko, Simms, Guerrero, Doe (Thompson, 39 mins), Gallardo (Carroll, 75 mins)

Subs (not used): Kirk, Thorpe

San Jose Earthquake: Cannon, Hernandez, Riley, Garcia, Denton, O'Brien, Grabavoy (Johnson, 58 mins), Lima, Huckerby, Alvarez (Kirovski, 68 mins), Sealy (Gray, 81 mins)

Subs (not used): Cochrane, Salinas

There were a few options on the table in the summer of 2008. Neil Warnock's Crystal Palace, Burnley, and Hull all expressed an interest; someone at Ipswich contacted me too, although that was never going to happen, obviously. I was also given the chance to go and play in Qatar, but that would only ever have been a money thing, which meant it wasn't for me. All in all, there were a fair few avenues I had to explore, and those had opened up without me having to tout my name around.

However, I had thought about trying the MLS – the Major League Soccer set-up in the States – from quite an early point in my career. Since I'd become settled at Norwich, I'd put it to the back of my mind; I thought I'd finish my career in Norfolk. Then everything had unfolded in an unexpected way, which was how I found myself speaking to Frank Yallop, the manager of San Jose Earthquakes, the club I presumed I was going to end up at.

In the States, though, the rules regarding player transfers are completely different. It's not easy to buy players for money, as usually happens in Europe, but I was supposedly okay as I was available on a free transfer. However, they also have a 'discovery rule', which is really strange. It basically means that a club can put a 'discovery' clause on you, which means that you have to speak to them first even if you have no intention of going there. It's crazy – a club can get first refusal on you even if you're not remotely interested. And that's what Toronto did with me, even before I had contacted anyone at the club. Apparently, this happens every season – clubs will put six or seven 'discovery' notices on players who might be coming in from the European leagues.

It was really strange. I don't know whether it was down to my former team-mates Carl Robinson and Jim Brennan, both of whom were at Toronto, or if it was because I'd said I didn't want to play for another English club after Norwich alerted everyone to my availability. Perhaps it was the latter, and Toronto decided to take a chance on bringing me to Canada. To this day, I don't know the full story.

Neither did I have much idea about the standard of the football on offer on the other side of the Atlantic. Robbo had gone out there, and David Beckham was already at LA Galaxy, but it was all completely new to me. There was very little coverage of the MLS in England, so the best I could really do was fly out and see what it was all about.

From the first time I spoke to Frank Yallop on the phone, we got on; he seemed like a really nice guy, very laid-back. As I say, though, I had to go to Toronto to speak to them before I could hook up with Frank at San Jose, even though I never had any real intention of playing in Canada. A big reason for not wanting to go to Toronto was that they played and trained on Astroturf, which would have been crazy for me with my hip not being one hundred percent. On top of that, there was definitely a bit of me that was California dreamin'. I'd lived in England all my life, and while the stadium and facilities in Toronto were great, I saw the moment I arrived in San Jose that the lifestyle out there was the best you could ever ask for.

It wasn't LA, but the weather was just as good. The biggest problem, obviously, was working out what we could do as a family. First off, Lyndsey and I looked at taking the boys out of school for a year, but we realised that, financially, that wasn't an option. Also, they were getting on well at school in Norwich, so it wasn't a great idea to remove them. The solution came when I looked at the MLS schedule. In the States, you play through the summer and have a break in the winter, which meant that the kids could come out in the holidays, have eight weeks in California, and that I could come back to Norfolk in mid-November and stay until halfway through February. That way, there would be lengthy spells away from the kids, but it would never mean anything as bad as being away for six or seven months in one stretch.

San Jose played their home games in the college 'football' stadium, and they would probably get eleven or twelve thousand through the gates, which more or less filled all the seats. Clearly, it wasn't the same as playing in front of twenty-five thousand at Carrow Road every other week, but I didn't see it as a bad thing – just different.

The fact that the Beckham roadshow was already in LA made no difference to me; by then, the choice was simple. It was Qatar and a financial windfall, or the MLS, which – to my mind – wasn't going to be that different to playing in England. Everyone speaks the same language, and the food is pretty similar. If I'm being honest, I also felt that the kids would be safer in the States than in the Middle East. One thing I hadn't considered, though, were the hoops I had to jump through to get to San Jose. They were crazy. For one thing, the Earthquakes had to negotiate with Toronto for my rights due to the Canadians having marked me down as their 'discovery'. I think that, in the end, they had to pay $100,000 for my rights, which was a lot for a club that originally thought I'd be arriving on a free transfer.

All of that threatened to be a big stumbling block. Over there, people don't pay transfer fees as such, because the league – rather than the individual clubs – owns the players. All contract discussions go through the MLS, who decide what your value is. It was incredibly different to what I was used to. Having to deal with Toronto was an unexpected complication; as I say, the facilities were good, and I knew a few of the lads there, but I've never been one to do something just for the sake of it. If it had been Toronto or nothing, I would have come home and that would have been that.

At that stage, the hip was fine. Since the second injection, it had virtually returned to normal. However, I knew that it would only be so long before it flared up again. That summer, I felt great – I'd kept myself fit and I was raring to go. At the back of my mind, though, there was the knowledge that it would only be a matter of time before I had to have the surgery. The problem was what would happen after I'd had that; until that point, I'd just have to keep going. That's me all over; keep pushing until it's literally impossible to go any longer. One mercy was that there were fewer games in the MLS – the regular season had thirty matches in it, and I was going over there at the halfway stage. Also, I knew that, while I'd be training every day, it would take place in the heat, which would help. Those factors influenced my decision in the end.

When I walked into the Quake's dressing room for the first time, I didn't know anyone at all. That in itself was really strange. Usually when you go to a new club, you'll recognise people from having played against them in the past even if you don't know them as such. Even if that isn't the case, someone will have played with someone that you've played with at some stage. In the States, though, no-one knew who I was – they didn't have a clue. Perhaps they'd seen a clip of some goals on Youtube, but that was about it. They didn't know who I was or how I played.

It was all very odd. The American lads all speak English and watch the same kind of TV, but the banter is completely different to what you find over here. They are more educated, for a start. Nearly all of them have got some form of higher education behind them – there are very few US players who come straight into the MLS without playing college soccer first, and getting a degree in the process. They're all pretty bright lads, so they must have been wondering who this clown from England going round playing tricks on everyone was. Fortunately, they all seemed to take to me straight away.

The first game was Toronto away – would you believe it? To get ourselves used to playing on the Astroturf, we spent the first three or four days training on the stuff. 'Oh, God!' I was thinking. 'This is the last thing I want to be doing, what with the hip...'

The other problem was that I still hadn't managed to get a work permit by then. When I flew from Toronto to San Jose, I had to tell them I was going on business; I then had to go back to Canada for the game. After that, I had to try and get a work permit to get back into the US. It turned out that me and this Brazilian lad, who didn't speak any English, got stuck in Toronto for a week trying to get the paperwork sorted. Don't get me wrong, Toronto is a lovely city, but it wasn't the best to be stuck there all alone trying to sort out the work permit and worrying about what would happen if I couldn't. It turned out to be a full-on week. I walked into the American Embassy with a cup of Starbucks coffee in my hand and there were security guys with guns everywhere. 'Put the coffee down – now!' Honest to God, I thought they were going to shoot me. It was an eye opener.

As for the game itself, we drew one-one, and both Carl Robinson and Jim Brennan were playing. I got thrown in up front; I did okay, but it was quick and, obviously, Astroturf is difficult to play on if you're not that used to it. Afterwards, I told the manager that I didn't really want to play up front; I said that I'd rather play in my normal position on the left wing.

The standard was much better than I expected, and they were a great bunch of lads. Joe Cannon, the goalkeeper, and I got on straight away – he was one of the older ones like me. All of the Quake players, though, were good athletes. I don't think people appreciate that American lads are all strong, quick, physical athletes who can run all day, and that they are probably fitter than a lot of the players you find in league one and two. The Americans could definitely compete at that level; if anything, the drawback for them would be a slight lack of know-how. A twenty-four year-old fresh out of college and coming into the MLS doesn't have the same footballing education that a player in England would have when they're starting at sixteen. Getting that knowledge takes time.

I don't want it to sound as if I'm doing down the standard in the MLS, because there are some very good players out there, but I also think that it would take American players time to get used to playing the amount of games we have here, particularly in the Championship. They play thirty matches a season, which amounts to one game a week at most. There's no Tuesday – Saturday, Tuesday – Saturday thing going on; there's a huge difference between a warm evening in California and a rain-soaked midweek night at Rochdale in January. They'd struggle with that, I think.

I liked the way that they had a whole points system for individual players; they'd put together all your stats for assists and game-time, as well as goals. It's done on merit. If you set up twenty goals in England, no-one really cares, but it's all about the stats over there. While they don't always tell the full story, they're helpful for attacking players; knowing how many chances you've put on the plate helps you assess your contribution to the team.

Out there, games are an event, just as they are in the NFL and the NBA. Supporters arrive early and have barbeques in the parking lot, which took a lot of getting used to. It was a long way from England, where the fans' pre-match routine seems to involve a few pints and then a rush to the ground at twenty to three. That said, there was hardly anything in the local papers about the 'soccer' – to come from here where you're got the Sun and its twenty-page pull-out to a place where the game basically isn't reported was crazy. It was nice in one way – Shacks would have loved it – but it also made you think that the lads weren't getting the credit they deserved. They're professional sportsmen, yet football is so far down the pecking order there that it's frightening. Amongst women and kids aged six to sixteen, it's probably one of the biggest sports in the country. But the really gifted athletes will always find themselves drifting into American football, baseball, or basketball just because that's where the real money is.

To a certain extent, footballers are the same the world over. However, the American sense of humour is slightly different and, while they might occasionally like a beer in the States, the rules regarding drinking there are different. Everywhere in California shuts at two in the morning, and after that there's no alcohol allowed on the tables. We played most of our games in the evening; by the time they had finished, it would be eleven o'clock, so we'd only have three hours to go out in.

In terms of where I lived, I have to thank Norwich's then-chief executive Neil Doncaster. He rang up before I went out there to say that one of the associate directors lived near San Jose, and that I should ring them up if I needed any help. As I didn't have anywhere to live, I did that and, sure enough, it turned out that I'd found some Norwich fans; as soon as I got there, they took me round, and they basically proved to be my surrogate Mum and Dad. Sue and Andrew Cailes had three kids, JP, Rachel, and Louise, who were all City fans – they showed me round San Jose, helped me find an apartment and get furniture, and took me on some great nights out while I was there. It was nice to find people like that to help me settle in; if that hadn't happened, I'd probably have been stuck on my own quite a lot. You end up spending a lot of time alone when you're abroad without your family.

With Sue and Andrew's help, I found a really nice, three-bed apartment with its own communal swimming pool just across from a big supermarket. To drive, I found myself a nippy little VW Golf. On the very first day I got it, I drove it to the supermarket next door, and found myself getting pulled over by a traffic cop. When you first get a car over there, it has no registration plate, only a sticker in the window.

'Can I see your driver's licence, insurance, your documents?' he asked.

And I didn't have anything – literally nothing. I was still in the middle of applying for my US driver's licence, and doing all the tests you need to do to get that.

'Look, mate — I haven't got anything,' I said. I'm not even going to try and blag it with you... I've got insurance, but no documents. No licence and nothing to say that the car is even mine...'

Fortunately, he was good as gold as I explained that I'd only just arrived. But that was a big lesson learned; you always have to have your documents in your car.

'So what do you?' he asked.

'I'm a professional soccer player,' I said.

'Who do you play for?'

'The Earthquakes...'

He didn't even know that San Jose had a soccer team. That's how it is out there. There will always be a few who care passionately, but the vast majority in San Jose didn't know — and probably didn't care — that the city had a soccer team. That said, the eleven thousand who filled the stadium out were probably just as passionate as any other set of supporters out there, and possibly more so.

It's hard to compare the levels of passion among supporters in the US to those in England as people don't really travel to away games. How could you expect them to when, to name one example, San Jose to Toronto is a seven-hour flight? Even our closest game, the 'derby' against LA Galaxy, was forty-five minutes away by air. All of that meant that you had to make the most of your home advantage. For the long away trips, we would always fly on the Thursday beforehand, be there for all of the Friday, play on the Saturday, stay over and fly back on the Sunday morning.

That meant that we always got a night out together after the game, which helped us bond as a team. Whatever anyone says, everyone is different after a couple of drinks, and Frank was one of those managers who liked to let the players do their own thing on a Thursday and Friday. The MLS would give you a little bit of money to spend on meals out, so if you were in New York or Toronto or wherever, you could visit a nice restaurant before a game. That was something I found a bit hard to comprehend. The first few times we went away, I didn't know what was going on – we'd get to the hotel and all the lads would disappear to get changed because they were going out.

At first I was confused, this was alien to me, I'd been used to the strict rules of english clubs when staying at hotels. I have to say that it was a good idea because it meant that you actually got to see the places you were playing rather than being holed up in your hotel, bored. You could go and have lunch at the beach or something like that – that was just the way Frank let us take care of ourselves, and I enjoyed it from day one. On top of that, the football was going well. When I first arrived, Earthquake were properly struggling, but we managed to turn it around with a few new additions, myself included.

Inevitably, I felt the pressure at first to get that all-important first goal, but the thing was that none of my team-mates knew what my game was or what I was likely to bring to the table. In a way, that was good for me, because I didn't feel as if I was expected to conjure up particular things because people had seen me doing them before. It was almost like having a blank slate. There was, however, pressure for a financial reason. In America, everyone knows how much money you're on; In England, everyone thinks they know what you earn, but in the States there's no question about it – they definitely do. Everything is documented. And if you're going into a club and getting $200,000 more than everyone else – some players in the team were on $12,000, and you try living in California on that – then you're going to need to prove you're worth it. I had to show them all I was worth the money I was being paid.

Even though I wasn't getting paid anywhere near what I had been in England, I still needed to earn respect amongst my new team-mates in terms of what I was going to bring to the side. I think that within those first nine or ten games, they could see that I wasn't just there for the ride. It would have been easy for them to assume that people like me are just coming over for one final pay-day, even though that pay-day didn't amount to half as much as it would have done in England. That's why it was so important to show what I could do, and that I was a decent player; I didn't want anyone to think I was only interested in a pay-cheque.

My first goal came against New York; it was a one-yard tap-in. It was good to get on the scoresheet there, because the kids had come out to see me that weekend. For TV reasons, I suppose, the game kicked off at 1pm California Time, and towards the end it must have been ninety-five degrees out there; I was thinking how tough it was. Usually we'd play at night, but this was absolutely baking. Anyway, I got through the game, and the goal took the pressure off; after that, I hit the ground running.

The internet played its part in the American story. Before I'd even played a game for the Quakes, I did an interview with the local TV station; it was live and, while I could hear the interviewer's voice, I couldn't see what he was watching. And the interviewer knew absolutely nothing about football. Nothing whatsoever. I think he thought that I was Ryan Giggs or someone – he introduced me as 'A football legend…a football superstar'. I was trying to calm him down a bit, but it went downhill from there. The goal he was watching on his monitor was against Birmingham, but he'd somehow got it in his head that it was against Manchester United. I think, in the end, that the Youtube clip of that interview got 200,000 hits or something daft, but it was all good publicity in the end.

That was before I was on Twitter; that only really came about relatively recently when I got my own website and I needed to find a way of people seeing it. To be honest, it wasn't something that I thought I'd get into. Yes, I'm opinionated, but I normally keep quiet. I keep myself to myself and don't tend to be in peoples' faces. I've found, however, that Twitter is a really great way of getting your thoughts across. It's an extension of an attitude I've held throughout my career, namely that I've always been up for a conversation with the punters. It's not always easy, because sometimes people want more than you can give them. I will stop and talk to anybody, but if you've got thirty or forty wanting to talk to you at the same time it's virtually impossible, especially if you're out with your kids for a meal or something. I've never knowingly turned down an autograph, but sometimes people expect a bit more than you're equipped to provide. It's all part and parcel of the game, though. You're – hopefully –recognised because of the little bit of pleasure you've given them when they've been watching you down the years. Giving an autograph is the least you can do.

The American fans, of course, had never seen me play – although I didn't take that as an excuse to change my style of play. I still looked to get the ball and rip the defender to bits; they didn't seem to know what was going on. Out there, it tends to be much more about possession – keep ball, keep ball. But when I got it, I was just myself. The defenders didn't know how to cope. Because of that, I think the fans took to me straight away. Supporters anywhere in the world appreciate players who try something a bit different.

The standard MLS right-back was athletic, quick, and a generally good player. However, I came in confident in my ability, and I wasn't doubled-up on as I had been in England for the previous four or five years. That made it easy for me to score some classic 'Huckerby' goals, cutting in from the left. I also managed to score a header, something that's incredibly rare for me! In fairness, it was a bit of a tap-in as far as headers go.

Everything went really well. Frank Yallop proved to be great – in fact, he's probably one of the nicest guys I've ever met. We still get on really well and he rings me up about players from time to time to see if they're worth a look or not. He was a fantastic bloke, even if he did used to play for Ipswich. In fact, the whole coaching staff were great. I got on particularly well with Bruce Morgan, the physio, especially once I'd finally had the operation on the hip; Bruce and I spent a lot of time together while I was rehabilitating. Bruce was the fittest physio in world football.

So they were great times. I won MLS Newcomer of the Year for 2008 which was a great honour, not least because David Beckham didn't get it. It's the players who vote for that award, so it was really nice; I also won San Jose's Player of the Year, for which I was chosen by my team-mates. That was great, although I felt it was a bit wrong, to be honest, as I only arrived halfway through the season. Even so, being voted Player of the Year by your team-mates is one of the greatest accolades you can get.

However great life at San Jose was, I still missed my family and Norwich. And then, the following February, the hip started to become sore again. Bruce would check it out; my mobility was starting to decrease again. I had another injection to take a little bit of the pain away, but I worried both about the number of games that were being played on the college pitch and about the fact we were starting to do a lot of our training on Astroturf. I could feel the hip grinding away every time we went out on the plastic.

I wanted to train – I've always trained hard, every day, throughout my career. But I could feel it getting worse and worse, and I'd be thinking constantly about what the pitch was doing to me. I didn't miss games; rather, I got to the point where I felt that I was cheating the people at the club. To his credit, Frank was as good as gold, and between him, Bruce, and me, we came to the decision that we couldn't carry on as it was – I was to have an operation.

Fortunately, I was going to be in the hands of Marc Phillipon, one of the best surgeons in the world, when I travelled to the Steadman Clinic in Colorado for the operation. They said I would be able to play on afterwards, but at thirty-three going on thirty-four I knew that I'd only have so much to offer, given that my game was built around pace. I remember the last few games before I had the op, because I was knocking it past defenders I'd usually have gone straight past – even though they were big and strong – and realising that they were still there.

It wasn't fair on either me or the team if I just went through the motions, so I travelled to Colorado. By the time I got there, I think the damage was worse than they expected it to be. The surgeon said that I'd probably played too much football when I'd been a kid, which meant that bone spurs had been growing on my hip and shredding away at the joint for the seventeen years that I'd been a professional. When I first saw the specialist in London with Pete Shaw, he said that he suspected there would be a small tear in the joint; when they actually went in, there was a seven-centimetre tear and there was nothing left. It was completely shredded. In the end, they took tissue from my leg to help reconstruct the labrum in my hip which – hopefully – means that I won't have to have a full hip replacement. I was told, however, that the left hip was probably on its way out as well.

I've been lucky, really, that it's only been my hip. I've had my cartilage done on my knee, but apart from that I've been pretty good. I strapped my ankles up for ten years, so they haven't suffered too much wear and tear.

I could have played on – I know that I could have played on. I could go and play lower league football now. But I made the decision three or four years ago that I wasn't going back down the leagues. I've been there and I've done it, and I wouldn't want some kid in League One or Two taking pot-shots at me when – at his age – I'd have ripped him to bits. I just felt that I'd had my time. Strachs came out to see me in San Francisco just before I had the operation done and said: 'As soon as you think you can't dictate a game or have an influence on a game, then don't play.' That was coming from a man that I've always listened to and who played on himself until he was nearly forty.

HUCKS

I think it was in a game against Columbus Crew where I knocked it past somebody, and I just didn't go anywhere. I came in and shook my head at Bruce, who tested the hip and found that my movement was forty percent less down my right-hand side. That was what provoked me finally to get the operation done. It wasn't as if it had been hurting me for a two or three weeks, it had been doing so over a period of more than two and a half years.

Life without football was always going to be strange. However, you've always got to be ready to go and do something different.

14. BACK IN THE REAL WORLD

Match: Norwich City vs Coventry City
Venue: Carrow Road
Competition: English Championship
Date: Saturday, May 7, 2011
Result: Norwich City 2, Coventry City 2
Attendance: 26, 268

Norwich City: Ruddy; Russell Martin, Ward, Whitbread, Tierney (Drury, 72); Fox; Crofts, Surman (Lansbury, 60); Hoolahan; Jackson, Holt (Pacheco, 57)
Subs (not used): Rudd, Lappin, McNamee, Chris Martin

Coventry City: Quirke; Clarke (Wood, 81), Keogh, Cranie, Hussey; Clingan; Gunnarsson, Baker (Deegan, 77); Bell; King (Eastwood, 90), Jutkiewicz
Subs (not used): Burge, O'Halloran, Cameron, Bigirimana

As a youngster with hopes of making a career out of football, I was generally too busy playing to attend matches as a spectator. Even with the City Ground and Meadow Lane within spitting distance of Clifton, I tended to be restricted to midweek games at Forest and County; it was unlikely that I'd be in action on Tuesday or Wednesday nights. That's probably the case for a lot of professional footballers. They've never really had the typical supporter's experience of following a team all over the country, and they tend to consider the game from a pitch-eye view. Growing up, I wasn't a massive fan of a particular club, and I could never really get involved in rivalries and things like that. The short spell I had at my hometown club was nice, but it wasn't as if I was going back to a club I'd been completely mad about as a kid.

When you finish playing, you get an opportunity to have a different perspective on the game. The chances are that you've settled down somewhere, often wherever your last club happened to be. Perhaps you've got kids and they want to go and watch; perhaps you miss the atmosphere on a match day. Maybe you've retained connections at the club, or you're doing some work for it. Whatever the reason, there's a good chance of you finding yourself in the stands, getting used to the idea of being a follower.

I'm not saying that that's the case for everybody, but it certainly has been for me. Norwich are my club now, without a doubt – I've become a proper fan. As the majority of the people reading this book will probably know, much has changed at Carrow Road since my departure, and the team have had a rollercoaster couple of years to say the least. Being on that ride as a supporter rather than as a player has been weird; it's often been accompanied by a desperation to put my boots on and get out on the pitch. Still, I'm learning – slowly – how to let the current crop of players get on with it.

When I look back at the Division One title triumphs I enjoyed in my playing career – first with Manchester City under Kevin and then with Nigel at Norwich – I take pride in how comfortably my team won the title on both occasions. That Manchester City outfit were far, far superior to anything else the league had to offer that season, and we swept aside opponent after opponent playing open, attacking football. Nigel's Norwich, meanwhile, were a fantastic unit in which solidity was balanced with invention; we went up that year because we knew our system well and could really rely on each other. For different reasons, both of those titles represented huge achievements.

What's happened at Norwich over the last two years, though, has to be one of the biggest accomplishments I've ever seen during my time in football. Two years ago, they were getting smashed seven-one at home to Colchester in the opening game of their season in the third tier; right now, they're competing in the Premier League. Paul Lambert's securing of back-to-back promotions, given the state of complete disarray he found upon his arrival, is nothing short of staggering.

I was in America for the real downturn and the end of the Glenn Roeder era, but I could tell that Carrow Road wasn't a fantastic place to be. That season just went from bad to worse, and its climax – relegation at Charlton – was a terrible, terrible day for the fans. My heart went out to Bryan Gunn, who was in the dugout by then, but I don't think he should have been in the job. He shouldn't have been offered the position, and he shouldn't have taken it. Gunny is an exceptional bloke who has never wanted anything but the best for the club, but Roeder should have been succeeded by a safe pair of hands. Bryan obviously has a great relationship with the supporters, but it was unfair for him to have been put in the situation he ended up in.

The club went into League One with a solid base of players. Grant Holt, who'd signed from Shrewsbury, was a proven goalscorer at that level, and Chrissy Martin was always going to be a threat. Wes Hoolahan was obviously far superior to anything in the third tier, and Ads had been there, done it, and worn the t-shirt. Even so, after starting with a performance so bad that a couple of supporters ripped up their season tickets, it was absolutely startling for the boys to take the title in the way that they did. That they then managed to take second place in a very competitive Championship beggars belief.

It's hard to single individuals out from the current team. Wes Hoolahan and Grant Holt have often taken the plaudits, but the true foundation of Norwich's recent success has been a fantastic team ethic. Nigel's promotion side were a great unit, but there was still a reliance on individuals – such as myself – performing. Paul's is a real team – whichever XI he has out there, he can be guaranteed that they'll run through walls for one another. While he's spent a few quid, it's been nothing compared to the outlay QPR have made in order to get the Taarabts and the Routledges in. What he's managed is to build a formation around Wes Hoolahan which really allows him to play; some have struggled to get the best out of Wes, but the decision to play him at the pinnacle of midfield diamond has really come off.

You've also got to look at Norwich's fitness levels, which have been consistently superior to their opponents. Too many people will say that scoring lots of goals in the closing minutes of games is down to luck, an idea which, admittedly, has a tiny element of truth to it in as much as it often happens because the opposition lose concentration right at the end. Mostly, though, it happens because one team is physically capable of keeping the pressure on right to the end while the other isn't. It's not rocket science. The fitter you are, the more pressure you can put on; the more pressure you put on your opponent, the more likely they are to make mistakes; the more mistakes they make, the greater your chance of scoring becomes. It astonishes me that people think that it's random; that it's all about good fortune. It should be absolutely clear that the best teams are those that can go the longest and work the hardest – for all the superb players Barcelona have in their team, they close the ball down as well as any team. You make your own luck, as the saying goes.

When you add the confidence that comes when a side gets on a run to Norwich's fitness and togetherness, you're definitely onto a good thing. There was sometimes a slight sense of stagnation around the club over the last few years of my stay, but the opposite seems to be true now. The mood is vibrant and confident, and the fans are once again approaching games expecting to win them.

Over the course of the season that's recently finished, I've been writing reports of the games for my website. Each match review has a section for positives and a section for negatives, and, looking back, sometimes it seems as if I've struggled to find any weaknesses at all. The run City got on in the second half of the season was remarkable, and they often looked as if they just weren't going to be beaten. With QPR looking dead certs to go up as champions, the race for the second promotion slot became a battle of wills which saw a lot of teams fold. Forest couldn't last the pace, Leeds dropped off, and Cardiff couldn't quite hold it together despite holding second spot with four games to go. Norwich had the mental toughness teams need to prosper in the Championship, and a skill for turning draws into victories right at the death.

A few games from the closing weeks of the season stand out for me. Towards the end of April, City travelled down to Portman Road to face Ipswich in the East Anglian derby, a game which was beamed back live to a huge audience at Carrow Road. Not only did Norwich take the points, they did so in style, hammering home five to Town's one. It was a real team performance, with four Canaries players getting on the scoresheet – and the fifth was an own goal. In my match review, the 'Bad Points' section simply says 'The goalkeeper and the back four deserved a clean sheet.' The second half in particular featured some breathtaking counter-attacking, with the full-backs pushing on in a way which really demonstrated the strengths of Paul's diamond formation. Most importantly, perhaps, the number of goals scored was a huge statement of intent in a situation where it looked as if goal difference might come into play.

I watched the game on the beam-back, and found myself in a bar in the city afterwards. The atmosphere was absolutely fantastic; you could tell just how much it meant to the supporters, who had not only seen their team overcome the disaster of relegation but return to the Championship as a force comparable to the team I'd played in under Nigel. Just as the party mood threatened to die down a little, the supporters who'd actually gone down to Ipswich on the trains arrived to liven things up again. You sometimes see footage of fans in Spain and Italy celebrating as if their team means more than life or death to them – after the Ipswich game, the Prince of Wales Road in Norwich felt a bit like that, and it was brilliant to be involved in it.

Immediately after that came the game with Derby at Carrow Road, a match which City really needed to win to gain advantage over their rivals. Simeon Jackson scored twice but, both times, Derby pulled themselves back onto level terms. The visitors may well have deserved to take something away from the match; however, in the last minute, we won a corner. Wes Hoolahan flicked it on, and it went across the box to Chrissy Martin, whose shot was deflected onto Jackson and into the net.

Promotion was confirmed at Portsmouth. Cardiff had surprised everyone by losing three-nil at home to Middlesborough that afternoon, meaning that we'd go up if we won. City really rose to the occasion, overcoming the pressure to control the first half and take the game to their opponents in the second. The goal that won the game was an absolute beauty, David Fox – who I think has been a real unsung hero this year – lofting in an inch-perfect pass for Jackson to score with a diving header. You'd have thought City might end up hanging on, but they created several other chances to score as the clock ticked down. It was a classy, professional performance and it just about summed the season up. I was absolutely ecstatic.

That left one game to go, at home to my old club Coventry, and all that was left to do was celebrate. The match itself ended in a two-all draw, but it was really all about the party. We stuck around in the Gunn Club at Carrow Road for a while after the game, then headed over to the Riverside where the bars were overflowing with fans. I got talking to a crowd of them in Wetherspoons, which was so packed we couldn't get to the bar, then we headed over to Prince of Wales Road where the festivities continued until three or four in the morning. When it came to the parade a few days later, I watched from the streets with my boys as the players took an open-top bus ride just as we had in 2004.

I was delighted for everyone concerned. Grant Holt has played a massive, massive part in the club's successes over the previous two seasons – to have got over fifty goals since joining is a real achievement. Wes Hoolahan's been fantastic, too, and you can be certain he won't be out of place in the Premier League. David Fox has kept things ticking over nicely in midfield without anybody making a big fuss over him, and Russell Martin has provided an attacking threat from right-back. I'm especially pleased for Ads, though. He's seen the highs and the lows since he came in, and he's just such a good, honest professional. Few players these days spend ten years with one club, and, with his testimonial year coming up, he deserves all the recognition he gets.

Off the pitch, some big changes have been made since I left. If they hadn't, the club could well have gone under altogether, which would have been an absolute disaster. Certainly, you suspect that they'd have been in real trouble if they'd been forced to spend more than a year in League One. I'm delighted for Delia Smith and Michael Wynn Jones, who've been right through it, taking more than their fair share of stick in the process. Their persistence and patience has allowed them to turn it around and get the right people in – they've deserve huge credit for sticking by the club in the dark days, because they could have lost all of their money. If we'd gone into administration, how much of their £12 million would they have been able to get back? Not much, I reckon. The game has changed, too – it's not enough just to be a millionaire any more. Look at all the owners who've got £500 million or some other daft sum. Delia and Michael, however, have done it their own way, and they've made some brilliant decisions in recent years. Bringing in David McNally as Chief Executive was a very smart move, particularly as McNally was the force behind Paul Lambert's arrival.

The next challenge, obviously, will be staying in the Premier League. As I know from experience, that's always difficult, and there's a massive difference between turning Scunthorpe over six-nil and having to try and shut out the likes of Rooney and Torres. That said, I think there's a massive difference between now and the season I played for Norwich in the Premier League. Back then, as I've said, there was a scrap at the bottom between four clubs, of whom three were going to go down. When I look at what happened in the top flight last year, the relegation battle was really open, and as many as eight or nine teams were in danger with a month or so to go. String a couple of wins together in April, and you might find you've leapt up towards mid-table. The situation as it is now makes things more interesting for all concerned, which is a good thing, and it means that teams aren't going to let their heads drop as easily. Still, you need your better players to stay fit, your new signings to bed in straight away, and to get off to a good start. Even if you come out of the blocks well, though, it's not always enough, as Blackpool have just discovered.

I'll be at all the home games, playing host at The Darren Huckerby Matchday Club. In my head, I'll still be kicking a ball but, given all that's gone right over the last two years, I'm not sure that they'll be needing any help from me. To win back-to-back promotions doesn't happen that often in professional football, so it's not as if confidence and team spirit are in short supply at Carrow Road at the minute.

So, Norwich are unquestionably my club now. It's funny, but even on Twitter, I find myself saying 'we' whenever I talk about City. I'm Tweeting to over twenty-three thousand or so people who might know me from my time at Coventry, Leeds, or Manchester City, but 'we' always means Norwich. The city is my home now, and that isn't going to change. Wherever the future takes me – perhaps I'll be going into coaching or even management – I'll never be too far away. I've even got the in-laws moving down, so I won't be off anywhere in a hurry!

Coming out of the game is hard. On my website, I've interviewed former pros like Darren Eadie and Dean Ashton, and a question that always comes up is how you're supposed to fill your time when you don't have training to go to every day and a match to prepare for once or twice a week. Darren talked about how many footballers suffer from depression once their career is over, something which seems to be caused in part because they come to rely on the energy and banter that comes with being around a bunch of lads every single day. When that's not happening, there's a risk that you end up sitting around doing nothing. As a player, you become very used to having other people structure your time for you; from the age of sixteen, you spend all of your time being told where to go and what to do, and you often have very little say in it. When all that ends, it can be difficult to know what to do with your freedom.

Bearing that in mind, I've been finding as many ways to keep myself busy as possible. One big part of my life in Norfolk at the moment is The Darren Huckerby Trust, which came about after I'd been asked to play in a charity match. When I realised how much of the money raised went in administration fees and the likes, I decided to try and do something quite direct which would ensure that a little bit was given back to people in the community, whether that be money or time. With some charities, it can be hard to see where the money goes , and who benefits from your contribution to events – with the Trust, I can use my profile to bring in money from all over and make sure it goes to the right causes. We've had benefactors from close to home – Carl Moore has been one of those – and as far away as the United States, which is brilliant. No money goes out of Norfolk – it all stays locally. So far, it's gone really well.

The aim, I guess, is to try and help the little man. What we're doing isn't like the Big C or the RSPCA or anything like that; I see it more as a way of supporting smaller charities. We've worked with The Hedgehog Society, sent a lady to the Transplant Games, and assisted a woman who couldn't afford the headstone for her husband's grave. There are lots of things that we're looking at and doing; it's diverse and not set up for one specific thing. Likewise, we've done our best to set it up so there are no administration costs. If you give a pound, a pound goes back out to a cause in Norfolk. It takes a little bit of time a fair bit of organisation, but we hope that it can look after itself and build year after year. If we make ten thousand pounds or fifty thousand pounds in a year, then we can give it all back.

That's my hope, now – being able to give something back. There's no guarantee that I will get a job back in football; while I've got my coaching badges now, there are lot of lads doing them and only so many jobs to go into. You often find that a manager will take their own team around with them, bringing a set of coaches and scouts from club to club, so there aren't necessarily that many openings.

One of the things I'd really like to do is to work with young players who are in that void between youth team football and the first team. Now that reserve teams are taken less seriously by clubs, that's a dangerous area – boys are coming through, but they're not always getting enough opportunities to develop their talents. Some don't even go out on loan, and stay at a club for a number of years without really getting a lot of match experience under their belt. The risk is that these kids start to behave like they think footballers are supposed to, but don't learn to play the game as well as they should do. It's a delicate age to be at, and I think players in their late teens need a helping hand. When I think back to how Gordon was with me at Coventry, I really appreciate the fact that he cared about more than what I could give to the team straight away – he was genuinely bothered about making me into a better player.

That's how I'd hope to be as a coach. Obviously, everyone has a different style, and I'm not sure I would do everything in the same way that Gordon did, but I know that I'd always aim to help a young player build on their natural attributes. When I came to Coventry, I was very raw – I had pace, could go past people and cause chaos, but my decision-making wasn't always great and I could frustrate the supporters with my inconsistency. Strachs took the good bits of my game and encouraged me to channel them; he helped me see how to really play for the team. If I do find myself coaching, showing kids how to bring their game on would be my main objective.

My son Tom is now part of Norwich's Academy set-up, so I can be found on the touchline, often being pretty vocal. As I said early on, I always like to have my say, even if Lyndsey doesn't always like it. It's just that, after you finish playing, you still see the game as a footballer, and notice things that aren't right. Would I want a career in the game for him? It depends. The players in the top league make a very good career out of it, the players in the lower leagues don't. It's a tough call – there's no better life than being a footballer, but having to retrain at thirty-five when you're up against kids of sixteen or seventeen who are looking to get into the same thing can be very difficult.

I like to think that I've come out of football with my eyes open, which is something that too many players don't do. Few see the end coming; when it does, it hits them before they know what's going on. The adjustment you have to make is huge, and, very often, you don't have any other skills to fall back on. The press will go on and on about how much footballers earn, but they're really only talking about those at the very top of the game. Below that elite, everyone who comes out of football has to find a way of earning money for the rest of their lives. You might have enough to keep you going for a bit, but it doesn't last for ever and you have to find a way of supporting yourself and your family. The thing that you've been trained for is suddenly useless, and the majority of people aren't going to want to go to retrain or go to university at thirty-five or thirty-six.

To get on properly in football, you have to dedicate yourself to it completely from a very young age – there's not a lot of time to concentrate on other things. At least when I was young, clubs didn't really encourage their youth players to develop other skills or put much time into their school work, and you can kind of see why that was. You need a certain skill level, and that level – as I've said – is higher than some people seem to think it is. It isn't as simple as just turning up and kicking a ball around with your mates, and it won't take you very long at all to get found out if you're not good enough. These days, there are enough scouts watching youth football to mean that players with the right ability and attitude get spotted. That thing you hear all the time – 'Oh, I could have made it, but then I got an injury…it just didn't happen' – is wishful thinking. It doesn't happen for a reason. If you apply yourself properly and you have the ability, there's no reason why you shouldn't get spotted.

Training has always been a huge thing for me. I'm awful at doing nothing, which is why I train every day even in the summer. I went ten years without having a day off, and that includes my wedding day. It's how I get my frustrations out – it doesn't have to mean having a ball at my feet, just doing some form of work. I see it as a job that I have to do before I can enjoy the rest of my day. Even now, I'm the same. When I go away on holiday, even if I've got the family with me, wherever I stay has to have a gym. It's one of the first things I look for. Lyndsey knows that; she knows that between this time and that time, it's time to work.

I just have to be prepared. If people say you're not good enough and you've done everything right beforehand, that just means you're not good enough. But if you haven't done the right preparation and they tell you you're crap, it means that you've let yourself down. It goes back to Winners, to being in that gym when I was a teenager. I've probably taken it to extremes at points, but I've been lucky – or clever – in always knowing how to structure training. It's never as if I went in and ran twenty-six miles for the sake of it; I knew what I had to do, and did it.

I suppose my inability to have a day off is a bit addictive – training is a like a drug to me. My thing, especially in summer, was testing. I'd always aim to be the best in testing whenever I got back after a break. I'd get back from the holidays and feel incredibly driven going into those tests, even at Norwich, where I was supposedly the best player. I wanted to prove to everyone that, even if I'm not the fittest, I'm one of them...'

So, you've got no excuse. If I can do it, anyone can. It's funny. Some have an idea that there are players who are so naturally talented that they don't really need to train, but that's very rarely the case. Look at David Ginola, for example. He was such a born footballer that he gave the impression that he wasn't one for the runs, the weights, and everything, but that wasn't the case. He was proper ripped, a unit. There's no way you could get in the sort of shape he was in without looking after yourself. He played like a million dollars, and he looked like it too.

So, you have to be good enough, and you have to work incredibly hard to go on improving. On the other hand, you're very privileged – you go in and breakfast is ready for you, then you train, after which lunch is laid out for you. You don't have to do much apart from the football but. It's certainly not like my Dad working ten hours a day plastering walls; footballers couldn't do that. When that privilege ends at thirty-four, thirty-five, or whatever, trouble can begin.

I'd say that eighty percent of players haven't earned enough in their careers to allow them to hang around doing nothing. There are ninety-two clubs in the Premier League and Football League, in addition to a handful of full-time outfits in the non-league game. Bearing in mind that only twenty of them are in the Premier League at any given moment in time, you're not looking at that many clubs who can afford to give players the money to live the footballer lifestyle that the papers seem to want people to think is the story for everyone who pulls on a pair of boots for a living. The problem is lots of players who can't afford to will try and live in that way. The Professional Footballers Association generally does a good job, but every month they send out a magazine which is full of advertisements for £200,000 speed boats and £3 million houses. How can it be responsible to wave such luxuries in front of League Two players who aren't anywhere near to being able to afford them? But players in the lower leagues will end up chasing the dream, even though they can't afford it. I find that pretty sad.

Dion Dublin is one of my closest friends, and he's got his head screwed on when it comes to this kind of thing. He waited until he was forty to buy a Bentley, which made it a reward for all he'd achieved in his career. I've seen players of twenty-two or twenty-three, who've probably earned a fortieth of what Dion has, try and do the same thing. It's mad. On top of that, the pension rules have changed, so you don't get that until you're fifty-five. What you make over the course of your playing days has to last you, unless you manage to find something else to do.

BACK IN THE REAL WORLD

You have to be realistic. Down in the bottom divisions, some players earn between three and four hundred pounds a week, which isn't a hell of a lot. I think of Dick, who is still one of my closest friends, and how his path differed from mine. He got a really bad injury just as I was starting to push on into the Premier League, dropped into non-league and became a plumber. Lincoln wanted to take him back, but he realised that he was earning more money plumbing and making a bit extra by playing part-time. Financially, it made no sense for him to go back into the professional game. Everyone thinks how brilliant it would be to be a professional footballer, earn lots of money, and have their new house or car on TV or in Hello! Magazine, but they don't realise that it's only a select few who have that. The great majority are grafting hard, every day of every week, to make ends meet. That's the reality for most professional footballers.

EPILOGUE

Darren Huckerby's All-Star XI: Schmeichel, Nilsson, Woodgate, Dunne, Drury, Wright-Phillips, McAllister, Benarbia, Huckerby, Dublin, Ashton
Subs (from): Martyn, Berkovic, Kewell, Whelan, Shaw, Fleming, Goater

Greatest Opponents XI: Given, Neville, Ferdinand, Stam, Ashley Cole, Keane, Scholes, Gerrard, Cristiano Ronaldo, Shearer, Henry
Subs (from): Giggs, Vieira, Adams, Le Tissier, Lampard, Pearce, Fowler

EPILOGUE

Writing this book was never an activity that I had planned on doing. In reality, it was just something that came around, and perhaps nobody will want to read it. Let's hope that's not the case and that, if you've come this far, you've enjoyed what I've had to say for myself. In looking back, I like to think that I've had some interesting stories to tell and points to make – I've been around big clubs at big times, but I've also seen the other side of the coin on plenty of occasions. With any luck, I've been able to give some insights into the things that not everyone knows about the world of professional football.

I know that I've been fortunate. One of my claims to fame, as I said earlier on, is that I have scored in every competition a professional footballer can be involved in at club level in England. I've got goals in all four divisions, in what is now the Europa League, the Champions League, the FA Cup, the Carling Cup, and, indeed, the Johnstone's Paint Trophy. My guess is that this makes me unique, but I've yet to hear the question come up in the pub quiz. What it definitely means is that I've had experiences at every level of the full-time game and, nowadays, there aren't that many who can claim to have started right at the bottom and played themselves all the way up to the top.

I'm proud of that story, and of the fact that I've come out of it all with my morals intact. I never chased the money, and I always, always tried to make the right decision when it came to both leaving and joining clubs. I never went anywhere just for the money, which a lot of people do; even when one of my most lucrative moves came through – to Leeds – I was reluctant to leave Coventry.

Throughout this story, I've mentioned many great players I've had the pleasure to take to the field with. Perhaps now is the time to nail them down into a team – to pin up the teamsheet for Darren Huckerby's All-Star XI. The only rule is that I have to have played alongside them during the course of my career.

Peter Schmeichel's in goal, even at the age he was when I

teamed up with him in Manchester. In Schmeichel and Steve Ogrizovic – who was unbelievably good – I've played with two absolutely legendary keepers, but Peter edges it. He had an aura, a presence which was phenomenal, and he was unbeatable on some days.

Roland Nilsson would be my right-back. One hundred and thirty caps for Sweden probably says enough on its own, but he was a really classy player, and a lovely bloke who always had time to give advice.

Who'd be the centre-halves? Jonathan Woodgate's a definite; without his injuries there's no doubt that he would have played for England loads and loads of times. The biggest compliment I could pay him is that, in my opinion, he was a better defender when I played with him than Rio Ferdinand, who is also one of the best I've seen. Alongside Woodgate I'd have Richard Dunne, who really turned his career around in spectacular fashion during his time at Manchester City. As I've said, he was perhaps a bit too relaxed when I first played alongside him, but he went on to win four Player of the Season awards for City, which was a fantastic achievement.

Left-back is difficult, and probably comes down to a choice between Ian Harte and Adam Drury. Harty was a cracking attacking left-back, but I have to go with Ads, who is definitely the better defender.

I'm setting this team up in a relatively traditional 4-4-2. Shaun Wright-Phillips would be on the right; he's an exceptional player whose lack of size is made up for by his being as brave as a lion. I'd play on the left, getting up and down, nice and steady. In the centre, Gary McAllister would be a definite. He had so much – great technique, a fantastic engine, and superb shooting ability. He was also a superb leader. Steven Gerrard had much the same to say about him, and he should know. Alongside him, I'd have the little genius, Ali Benarbia, who came to Manchester City and tore it to bits, basically. He had exceptional ability; he knew what to do before the ball came to him, every time. It's just a pity he was getting on a bit by the time he turned up at City.

Up front would be Dion and Dean Ashton. Dion was a great leader who scored great goals, and I couldn't have asked to play alongside a better target man over the course of my career. Alongside him, Ash potentially had it all – he matched ability with vision, and could score with both feet or with his head. It was a huge shame that, due to his injuries, the Premier League never got to see his full potential.

When it comes to the bench, Nigel Martyn would be as good a back-up to Schmeichel as you could ask for. Richard Shaw was a great man-marker, and Craig Fleming would be a great addition for both his ability and his manner around the dressing room. Eyal Berkovic only narrowly misses out to Benarbia, and Noel Whelan had everything. Shaun Goater would be my substitute striker.

Who would this team play? Well, a side made up of the greatest players who I've lined up against would have Shay Given in goal; he hasn't quite got the recognition he deserves for having consistently been one of the best keepers in the Premier League over the last twelve or thirteen years. Consistency again influences my choice of right-back – I'd have Gary Neville in there. Alex Ferguson always knew exactly what he was going to get from him, and he did a great job for Man United over the years.

In the centre, I'd have Rio Ferdinand, who I think has a good claim to be the best English centre-back of all time. He started off as a midfielder, moved backwards, and has been absolutely class ever since. Next to him, I'd play Jaap Stam, who, for a big bloke, could really shift. At left-back, Ashley Cole is surely the best player in that position of his generation, so he'd have to go in.

I'd go for a different formation for this team, a kind of 4-3-3 with a holding midfielder. Roy Keane would play that role; for me, he epitomised everything that made Manchester United the most successful team during the course of my career, namely strength, power, and a phenomenal will to win. In front of Keane,

Paul Scholes is probably the best English passer since Glenn Hoddle, and I admire him all the more for the fact he wasn't interested in being in the papers and just got on with the game. I'd pair him up with Steven Gerrard, one of the most complete midfielders I've seen – he can play anywhere in the middle, and could probably do a similar job at the back.

Up front? Well, Cristiano Ronaldo would be on the right – that needs no explanation, as he's possibly one of the best attacking players we've seen in the last thirty years. Alan Shearer would lead the line; his goal record speaks for itself. His game changed over the course of his career and, although he only won one league title, he even managed to score goals in a weakened Newcastle team as he approached retirement. On the left flank, I'd have Thierry Henry, who changed the way Arsenal played with his drifting in and fantastic goals.

It seems a bit unfair to leave Ryan Giggs on the bench; if this side reverted to 4-4-2, he'd come back in. Alongside him, there'd be Patrick Vieira, an absolute man-mountain, and Tony Adams, who excelled for several different Arsenal teams during the course of a long career. Then there'd be Matt Le Tissier, who just had unbelievable ability on the ball, was a wonderful player to watch, and deserves credit for staying at Southampton even when the big boys came calling. He'd not be the only goalscoring midfield player amongst the subs – Frank Lampard gets in too, for the fantastic job he's done for Chelsea over the last decade. The last two spots would go to Stuart Pearce, an immense figure, and Robbie Fowler, for the great goals he scored for Liverpool.

Reading the line-ups, I'm not sure I'd like to imagine the match report on this one...

ACKNOWLEDGEMENTS

I'm sure that there are many more that I should've included on this 'thank you' list. You know who you are, I'm sure – let it be known that your omission from the list means the debt of gratitude I owe you special individuals is just too great to put into words (or something like that).

Now, for the others…

Firstly, I'd like to thank Wensum Publishing for bringing the whole project together and making this book a reality. I'd also like to give a shout out to my friends Stuart Shaw and Michael Byrne over at CBS Media, for their general help and support.

Then there are the 'creative types' that have helped to realise my vision for the book – Mr Rick Waghorn, for putting all the endless interviews with me into a readable format, and my editor, Mr C J Kennedy, for giving structure and breathing a bit of life into my story.

Many thanks to James Miles and his team at 'Flip Creative Media', including Adam Knights, Carl Prettyman, Richard James, Thomas Watson and Stephen French, for their design and layout work on the book.

Thanks also to Carl West and his team at Kiss Marketing, for the helpful advice they've provided on all marketing- and website-related issues.

Finally, and most importantly, I'd like to say a huge thank you to all the fans – at every stage in my career – who have supported me over the years. However, my special thanks goes out to the people of Norfolk. From the moment I arrived on loan in 2003, the fans at Norwich treated me as one of their own, and have really stuck by me ever since. I'm still amazed by the warmth shown to me by these fans, along with their support of my charitable organisation, the Darren Huckerby Trust.

Today, I am very proud to be a Norwich supporter.